SUPERNATURAL MISSIONS

The Impact of the Supernatural on World Missions

Compiled By

RANDY CLARK

"One of the greatest privileges of my life has been to see what God is doing around the world in missions. It is stunning. What we see right now was but a dream not many years ago. Wherever the supernatural power of the gospel is displayed, there is eternal fruit for the King and His Kingdom. It's not that the enemy rolls over and gives up. It's that we get to see the effect of Scripture: "No weapon formed against you shall stand!" Randy Clark and this wonderful team of authors write from their rich experiences gained from the front lines of this battle for the nations. I believe this book will have tremendous impact on how we do missions - on how we do life. *Supernatural Missions* is a must-read."

- Bill Johnson, Senior Pastor of Bethel Church in Redding, CA, author of When Heaven Invades Earth and Face to Face with God

"*Supernatural Missions* is a provocative, practical text book exploring the biblical, historical, strategic and supernatural dimensions of world missions. A billion-soul harvest is waiting for a supernatural army of world-changers that have made His last command their first priority. You are holding in your hands a manual that will make sure that people from every tribe and tongue and nation will gather around the throne of God to honor the Lamb of God. Supernatural Missions will release God's purpose with God's power for God's glory."

- Leif Hetland, President of Global Mission Awareness, author of Seeing Through Heaven's Eyes

"While the academic field of missions has come to appreciate the normative restoration of New Testament signs and wonders among Pentecostal and charismatic movements in the expansion of the church worldwide, scholarship has failed to provide a useful "how to" manual to train those who would participate in this biblical missions process. This lack is filled admirably by *Supernatural Missions*, a collection of articles compiled by Randy Clark. This book not only supplies the essential content of those New Testament processes, but does so in the most effective way to facilitate learning supernatural ministry, that is, by generous use of case studies which "carry a prophetic invitation to enter into the same kind of experience with God." Accordingly, this book should be a required text for any beginning missions course."

- Dr. Jon Ruthven, author, What's Wrong with Protestant Theology and On the Cessation of the Charismata

"When Randy Clark writes a book on missions you have to take notice. His new book is backed up with a lifetime of ministering with signs and wonders in America and other parts of the world. This book will be valuable reading as a textbook in seminaries and Bible Schools all over the world."

- Dr. Vinson Synan, Dean Emeritus, Regent University School of Divinity

"Randy Clark has again blessed and challenged us with his new compilation, *Supernatural Missions*. It helps to fill a huge gap in mission literature, applying the theory and theology of mission in the Spirit's power to world mission, including short term missions. Randy's accumulated wisdom and experience in doing supernatural mission around the world fills the book with convincing examples. His book is enriched by similar applied theology from others involved in supernatural mission. You will be informed and inspired. We have added this book to our mission text books in our degree program."

- Dr Geoff Waugh, teacher of revival at Christian Outreach Centre School of Ministries in Brisbane, Australia

"When Randy Clark asked me to check out *Supernatural Missions*, the subject grabbed my attention. I do not know a more qualified person to put such a book together than Randy, who has lit fires all over the world for Jesus and the supernatural. I am excited about the impact this book can have on world missions. We live in the days of the greatest outpouring of the Holy Spirit ever (Joel 2). What an exciting time to live for Christ! Many have yet to hear. Let's get to work!"

- Mark R. Anderson - Evangelist, teacher and author of Humility the Hidden Key to Walking in Signs and Wonders, as well as other books.

globalawakening
1451 Clark Street
Mechanicsburg, PA 17055
www.globalawakening.com
1-866-AWAKENING

TABLE OF CONTENTS

INTRODUCTION:

This book began with a perceived need brought to my attention by one of our students at the Global School of Supernatural Ministry. The student asked to remain anonymous because of her intention to do mission work among Arab nations upon graduation. The student was already well-trained with a degree from a reputable Christian school. The concern was that there wasn't a textbook that dealt with doing missions primarily from the perspective of power evangelism combined with presence evangelism and presentation evangelism. I was told a book was needed that could be used as a text in Christian training schools, ministry schools and in missions classes in other schools. This book is written to answer the question, "How does the supernatural work of the Holy Spirit impact the way we understand and do missions?"

When I first received the completed manuscript, I was moved to tears by the Holy Spirit. I believe the anointing of God is on the truth presented to us by so many writers from so many parts of the Church. It is my prayer that this book will find its way into the classrooms of Christian colleges, seminaries, and divinity schools and that even liberal and cessationist scholars will find it instructive and important to make their students aware of another perspective on Christian mission. I pray that it will become a "pearl of great price" among every Evangelical school that places a high value on the Kingdom of God, the mission to declare its nearness and works towards its advance through missions. I pray that every charismatic and Pentecostal school would require it as one of the textbooks for the study of missions.

1

I was once asked by a leading Argentine Baptist seminary professor, Dr. Carlos Merida, "Does the church of God have a mission or does the mission of God have a church?" After much thought I believe the answer is the mission of God has a church and this church has been endowed by its Creator with the power to carry out its mission! Even so, Come Lord Jesus, come in the power of the Holy Spirit. With gratitude, we continue to receive Your gifts to carry out Your mission. May my generation advance Your mission closer to its consummation!

– Randy Clark

Chapter 1
WHY POWER MAKES A
DIFFERENCE IN MISSIONS

" *In Acts 1:8, before Jesus' ascension, he tells his disciples the means by which they were to fulfill their commission of spreading the gospel and teaching all that He taught them to the world. Jesus said, "But you shall receive power when the Holy Spirit has come upon you; and you shall be witnesses to Me in Jerusalem, and in all Judea and Samaria, and to the end of the earth." Acts 1:8 NKJV*

The church has often focused on fulfilling the great commission given by Christ in Mt 28:19-20, to make disciples, but does not connect the need for the power of the Holy Spirit to fulfill it. It is as if we forget that Christ showed the people as well as taught the people with words about the Kingdom of God. When the power of the Holy Spirit is connected to the commission to advance the Kingdom, it is accomplished exponentially. It is the healings, deliverances and other signs and wonders that demonstrate that the Kingdom of God is at hand. As we look throughout church history and the recent past, we can see how the Holy Spirit's power is integrally connected to missions. Read the following pages to see how God changed the lives of people and nations by the power of the Holy Spirit. Power is the difference in missions. **"**

- Randy Clark

A Classic Modern Day Example of Missions and the Difference Power Makes

In September 2005, I led a team to Imperatriz, Brazil to work with the Assemblies of God denomination. While there we needed more translators. There was an American family there, the Baileys – David, Diane and their four children - who were fluent in Portuguese. They had been raised in Brazil as missionaries, where three generations of their family had worked with the Krikati tribe. The grandfather had pioneered the work with this unreached tribe in 1960. The father was continuing this missionary work with his wife and adult children. They had been trying to evangelize this tribe and establish a church for over 40 years. Extremely dedicated, they were deeply committed to Jesus and His call on their family, living sacrificial lives for the gospel. They needed money and we needed translators. They were so helpful to us as translators.

What we didn't know was that they were cessationists - they believed the gifts of tongues, interpretation of tongues, healings and working of miracles had ended with the death of the apostles. This caused an internal struggle, especially for the father, because we were preaching and ministering in these gifts, declaring that God wanted to heal and deliver people. The family was translating messages that they didn't believe theologically. Furthermore, not only were we declaring these things; they were happening right in front of our translators' eyes! Their long-held beliefs were being challenged by what they were witnessing. The father was very concerned. He began to study the Bible, because the mission agency he worked for required missionaries to resign if they came to believe miracles, healings, tongues, etc. were for today. Changing his belief regarding the "sign gifts" could have very serious consequences. He continued for several days his study of the Bible, all while he was translating for us. His wife and children were also translating for us and witnessing hundreds of healings and some miracles.

By the end of our ministry trip, the family had become convinced by what they had seen, and this caused them to see the

Bible in a different light. They were now certain that the "sign gifts" had never ceased and they asked me to come to the hotel room where they were and pray for them. They wanted to receive an impartation from the Holy Spirit to be able to minister in the power of the Holy Spirit and operate in the gifts of the Holy Spirit.

When we returned to the city in 2007, I met the family again and heard the rest of the story. The father, being a man of great integrity, knew that his new theological position would require him to resign from the mission agency he and his father had worked with for over 40 years. It meant he would not be able to continue ministering to this native tribe. He wanted to honor the agency, so he wrote a letter indicating the change in his theological beliefs and inquired about the process for the transition. The day he notified them of his intention to honor them by resigning, the Holy Spirit was poured out on the tribe and a classic revival broke out. The Krikati people were weeping in public under the power of God's conviction. This was a huge thing because the tribe believed that weeping in public was a sign of weakness and an invitation for evil spirits to attack them; now they were openly weeping and repenting of their sins. They came early to the meetings and stayed until around midnight. They began to pray for the sick, not giving up until the healing occurred. Most of the time, healings did occur. The people even wanted to go on mission trips to reach other tribes. The church grew from an average attendance of about 20-30 people to over 200 in less than a year.

After 40 years of hard, sacrificial labor, the Baileys had 20-30 converts. Then, in less than a year, the church grew to over 200. No longer were the natives referring to "your God;" now it was "our God." One year of ministry in revival accomplished more than the previous 39 years of ministry when there was the absence of the powerful ministry of the Holy Spirit Himself. The question to be asked is, "To what degree was this a sovereign move of God and to what degree was it dependent upon the choices and change in the way the missionaries were thinking about how to do ministry?" I believe we will find that God initiates all breakthrough (Isa. 43:11-12; 45:7). However, human response, human thinking and beliefs are vital to breakthrough and revival (Amos 3:7; Matt. 11:16-19). The problem is often our need for a deeper repentance, in the biblical understanding of the word - "to change the way you think." I hope this book will help us change the way we think about the mission, mandate and means of accomplishing God's mission. The mission is to announce that the Kingdom of God is at hand. In doing so, we heal the sick, cleanse the lepers, cast out demons, raise the dead and announce good news to the poor who are of special concern to God (Matt. 11:2-6). This is the time of God's grace, His acceptance and His forgiveness.

We cannot be content in this book to give information. We must recognize that the Bible is not only a book of wisdom, precepts, and principles, but also a book of the stories of people and how they responded to the "word of the Lord" that came to them. A book without the "testimony of Jesus" would be void of "the spirit of prophecy."[1] The telling of the stories - the testimony of what Jesus has done and is doing in people's lives - brings the power not just to inform, but to inspire. Still, that is not all the stories and testimonies do. They carry a prophetic invitation to enter into the same kind of experience with God. To those who have an ear, let them hear as they read this book. I believe the secret to missions comes from hearing and obeying the Lord. To obey requires that we be empowered to do the impossible.

The Secret of History Makers in the Kingdom of God

Several years ago I had been asking God for the opportunity to speak in universities. A few weeks later, an opportunity came up to speak at Regent University in Virginia Beach, VA. As I arrived at the school and headed into the classroom I asked, "What is the name of this class?" I thought I should try to teach on the subject. I was told it was on leadership. Turning to the board, I wrote what I felt was the secret to becoming a history maker within the Kingdom of God. To become a history maker or a powerful leader, you need two things. One, you need to have a powerful experience with God - a personal encounter with the living God. You need to have an impartation, whether you call it being filled with the Spirit, sanctified by the Spirit, baptized in the Spirit or a less controversial term - blasted by the Spirit. Secondly, you need to know your purpose. You need to have certainty regarding your destiny and a strong call from God. If you have these two things, then you will have the third necessary ingredient to be a history maker. You will have the grace and power not to quit when the cost to carry out the mission becomes very high. Without the first two you won't have persevering grace or faith to fulfill the call. My greatest heroes of the faith have been revivalist-evangelists, evangelistic pastors and missionaries. A large number of the revivalist-evangelists were also healing evangelists. There was a great advance in missions in the middle of the 20th century related to the role of healing evangelists who were touched in the revival of the late 1940's and early 1950's. Their stories are amazing - they heard the "word of the Lord" to go and do what He told them to do. These heroes of the faith heard and obeyed. The hearing of "the word of the Lord" gave them faith to do mighty exploits in "the name of the Lord."

Revival and Missions

I teach three different "Schools of Healing and Impartation" around the world. In the first school, the first two lectures are on the relationship between revival and church growth. I focus on some of the strange manifestations that have historically occurred with regularity during awakenings or revivals. In another lecture, I teach that awakening at a national or regional level will always produce an increase in missions and a growth in the churches, as well as a greater concern for the poor.[2] Revival is characterized by the power of God (Thes. 1:5; Acts 1:8; 2:1-4). Unusual manifestations often occur in periods of God's visitations: i.e. deep conviction, tears, holy fear, trembling under convicting power, sometimes laughter and powerful, lasting conversions (Jer. 23:9; Gen 17:1, 3, 17; Ezra: 3:12-13; Neh. 8:6-9).

These visitations, revivals and awakenings touch people so powerfully that they yield their lives to the purposes of God. The fruit of these "outpourings of the Spirit" is multiple: the planting of new churches, commitment to cross-cultural missions, salvations, beginning ministries to the poor, restoration of gifts and concern for impacting or transforming culture. These types of endeavors were the fruit of the following outpourings:

- The First Great Awakening

- The Second Great Awakening

- The 1858 Prayer Revival

- The 1904 Welch Revival

- The Pentecostal Revival of 1905 in India and Chile

- The 1906 Azusa Street Revival

- The 1907 Korean Revival

- The 1932 Shantung Baptist Revival in China

- The late 1940's Revival

- The 1947 Latter Rain Revival

- The 1948 Healing Revival

- The 1949 Revival connected to Billy Graham

- The Charismatic Renewal of 1960

- The Jesus Movement of 1968-1974

- The revivals of the mid 1990's: the 1993 revival with pastor Carl Schrader and Evangelist Rodney Howard Browne in Lakeland, Florida

- The 1994 Toronto Blessing with Pastor John Arnott and Evangelist Randy Clark

- The 1995 Brownsville Revival in Pensacola, Florida with Pastor John Kilpatrick and Evangelist Steve Hill

- The 1996 Smithton Outpouring with Steve Gray in Smithton, Missouri

- The 1996 awakening among college students at evangelical colleges

- The 1996-1999 Regent University student revival

As a result of these visitations ,where the Face of God was revealed in the power of the Holy Spirit, millions of people were born again into the Kingdom of God. Hundreds of thousands of churches were planted around the world. Whole new denominations were birthed. The gifts of the Spirit were restored with healing and deliverance once again becoming, as in the book of Acts, major reasons that people came to Christ. Ministries were launched with a special purpose to help the poor. It was the power of God in the lives of these men and women that enabled them to dare to do what seemed impossible. The motivation, the faith and the ability all came from the power of God, which was rooted in the "rhema" word of God – the call on their lives.

Defining Power

Power can be the result of having been touched and affected by the Holy Spirit. The consecration and faith level of the person has an affect on whether or not the power is used for the Kingdom of God or ends in the experience, becoming only a fond memory. Power encounters don't take the place of consecration or sanctification of our lives unto Him. But they can, and are, the primary source of such consecrations and sanctifications. Most of the people I know who received powerful impartations and became history makers were already consecrated, called servants of God. There are some exceptions, such as Randy McMillan of Cali, Columbia and Cesar Castellanos formerly of Bogata, Columbia and now in Brazil. Both men are modern day apostles. Neither were committed Christians when God spoke audibly to them and sovereignly called them to Himself and to His mission. I share their stories later in this chapter.

Jesus made the connection between power and mission right before his ascension. In Acts 1:8 (NIV) Jesus declared,

9

"But you will receive power when the Holy Spirit comes on you; and you will be my witnesses in Jerusalem, and in all Judea and Samaria, and to the ends of the earth." The disciples had already received the Holy Spirit on the night of the resurrection when Jesus appeared to them. John 20:21-22 (NIV) tells us, "Again Jesus said, 'Peace be with you! As the Father has sent me, I am sending you.' And with that he breathed on them and said, 'Receive the Holy Spirit.'" This theme of being sent with authority and with the ever-present presence of Jesus through the Holy Spirit is in the Great Commission in Matthew's gospel. Matthew 28:18-20 states:

> Then Jesus came to them and said, 'All authority in heaven and on earth has been given to me. Therefore, go and make disciples of all nations, baptizing them in the name of the Father and of the Son and of the Holy Spirit, and teaching them to obey everything I have commanded you. And surely I am with you always, to the very end of the age.'

Luke's gospel has the promise of the Spirit connected to mission that was fulfilled in his second volume, the book of Acts. Luke 24:45-49 (NIV) says, "Then he opened their minds so they could understand the Scriptures. He told them, 'This is what is written: The Christ will suffer and rise from the dead on the third day, and repentance and forgiveness of sins will be preached in his name to all nations, beginning at Jerusalem. You are witnesses of these things. I am going to send you what my Father has promised; but stay in the city until you have been clothed with power from on high.'" This was fulfilled on the day of Pentecost when the Holy Spirit was poured out upon the disciples.

Having considered the very strong witness of the Gospels and Acts regarding the importance of power for mission, let us now consider what this power looks like. Let us try to define it. First, it is a delegated authority from Jesus to the disciples and those who would become believers through the ministry of the disciples.[3] Second, the power is connected to the glory of God (Paul uses the words "glory" and "power" synonymously in Cor. 15:43. John 2:11 connects Jesus' first sign – one of the terms for a miracle or healing in John - with the revealing of His "glory"). Third, it is done by the Holy Spirit. He is the source of this power. Fourth, it is done by the energy of God working in us. In Col. 1:29 (NIV) Paul states, "To this end I labor, struggling with all his energy, which so powerfully works in me." Paul understood where the power came from. Romans 15:17-19 (NIV) says:

> *Therefore I glory in Christ Jesus in my service to God. I will not venture to speak of anything except what Christ has accomplished through me in leading the Gentiles to obey God by what I have said and done - by the power of signs and miracles through the power of the Spirit. So from Jerusalem all the way around to Illyricum, I have fully proclaimed the gospel of Christ.*

This encounter with the Holy Spirit produces compassion, love, faith, enabling grace and perseverance. Also, it brings fruit of supernatural accomplishments, or at least accomplishments greater than the person had prior to the encounter with the Holy Spirit.

What are some illustrations of how this power is manifested both in the Bible and today? The Bible records supernatural dreams (Matt. 1:20; 27:19), visions (Acts 10:11-17; 16:9), impressions, angelic visitations (Isa. 6:1-8; Acts 1:10-11), trembling, falling, loss of strength (Dan. 8:17-18; 10:9; Matt. 28:4; John 18:6) and the audible voice of Christ (Acts 9:4-5). In addition, there were fillings of the Spirit, sanctifications by the Spirit and baptisms in the Spirit (Acts 4:8, 31; 7:55; 8:17; 13:9, 52; 19:6; 1 Co. 6:11). I believe all these references to experiences of the Spirit would fall under the two elementary teachings of Apostolic Christianity found in Hebrews 6:1-2, which refers to "the doctrine of baptisms and the laying on of hands." It would also include power encounters with sorcerers/shamans and those moving in divination (Acts 13:6-12). This power would cause manifestations, which would cause others to think they were drunk (The accusations in Acts 2:13 that the disciples "had too much wine" suggest that the disciples looked drunk, sounded drunk and acted drunk). Most important for the mission were the gifts of healings and discerning of spirits, which would be helpful in the ministry of deliverance. Dr. Gordon Fee said (and I am paraphrasing him), "The Holy Spirit gives us power to work miracles and power to persevere when the miracle doesn't happen."

Does the Power Make a Difference?

Having defined power, after considering a few of the passages where Jesus or the Apostle Paul connected power to mission, and discussing the importance of power to become a "history maker in this land," the question still remains: "In what way does power make a difference in missions?"

I now meditate on the question, "Do the power and the gifts (which make the power of God so real to people) exist for the Church or for the mission?" I believe they exist primarily for the mission and are done through the Church. Christ died for the Church. However, the Church's job is to find the "other sheep" and bring them into the fold.

A second question regarding power is, "Is this power primarily to make us better, more moral people and to experience more of the fruit of Galatians 5: love, joy, peace, patience, kindness, goodness, faithfulness, gentleness and self-control? Or is the power to make us bolder in our witness and better equipped for evangelism? It is both, but the latter emphasis has the highest priority. However, any form of holiness that has no emphasis on evangelism and mercy ministry is not biblical holiness. Is the primary purpose of the power of God to bear witness to the Apostles and their teaching as evidence of correct doctrine? Or is the primary purpose of the power of God to display the compassion, love, and nature of God? Are accompanying signs an integral part of the proclamation of the gospel of the Kingdom? Again, I believe the primary purpose of the power is the latter rather than the former. God's power is to be a continuing revelation of His love and an integral part of the presentation of the gospel (Matt. 14:14; Rom. 15:18-19). The power of the kingdom and a gospel that is proclaimed with signs following should be normative rather than exceptional in this time in the history of the Church. The qualification in the last sentence is to note the historical context of the Church and its leaders. It is not right to hold people to our standard today when they lived in a time period without the same revelation or understanding of gifts that now exists in the Church. It isn't fair to judge other great and consecrated leaders in the Church whose ministries occurred when there wasn't a belief in the continuation of the gifts of healings and miracles in their time. The theology they held limited their expectation and faith in what could be expected as available to believers. Until the early part of the mid 19th century, cessationism was the belief held by the vast majority of Protestants. Now, however, we are more than 100 years past the latter day outpouring of the Spirit upon His Church. Furthermore, we are more than 125 years beyond the beginning of Protestants rediscovering the ministry of healing.[4]

Power does make a difference. It makes the gospel relevant to the present needs of people who must deal with disease, demons and natural disasters. It says, "our God can help you now, not just when you die." This gospel we preach can bring healing to the sick and deliverance to the demonized. You don't need to consort with shamans to get help with evil spirits.[5] The power allows us to evangelize and do missions the way the apostolic Church (33-90 A.D.) did, the way the Ante-Nicene Church (90-325 A.D.) did, the way the Ante-Chalcedon Church (325- 81 A.D.) did, the way the Church of the first millennium (481-1,000 A.D.) did and the way parts of the Church have done throughout its history.[6] However, it is true that in its second millennium the Church did not operate in the same degree of power it did during its first 1,000 years.

Thankfully, this all changed around the beginning of the 20th century. Some healings occured within Protestantism in the 19th century, but in the 20th century the outpouring of power and gifts was similar to the power in the earliest years of the church. During the last half of the 20th century and the first part of the 21st century, there have been even greater things happening than in the first centuries. The world has seen more healings, more miracles, more people raised from the dead, more martyrdoms and an unprecedented growth in the numbers of people becoming Christians. This should not surprise us. If all I had was the United Nations' chart of the population growth of the world and one verse, John 3:16, "For God so loved the world that he gave his one and only Son, that whoever believes in him shall not perish but have eternal life," I would have expected the power of God to be poured out at the start of the world population explosion - the beginning of the 20th century. Prior to 1900, the population growth of the world was very slowly moving upward in the chart. However, when it reached 1900, the line turned sharply upward.

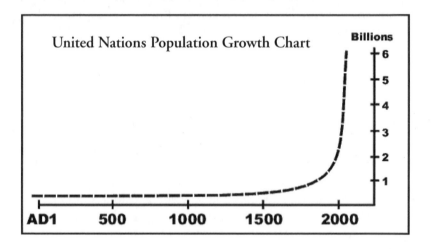

So, what do I mean when I say the power makes a difference? Power reveals the glory of God, the compassion of God and causes people groups who already have their own holy books to believe in the gospel. As in the disciples' day, people today often don't believe in the gospel because of what the Bible says. Instead, they believe in the Bible because of first believing in the gospel. They believe in the gospel because it is backed up with more power than the shaman or cleric of their religion could manifest. Simon the Shaman of Acts 8, for example, lost his hold on the people of Samaria and even himself comes to faith because of the greater power of God flowing through Philip. This results in whole people groups coming to

Christ. Like in the Early Church, today many people come to Christ in families, villages and whole regions, rather than just one person at a time. I personally know a number of people who have witnessed the vast majority of a village come to the Lord at once as a result of seeing the power of God manifested in healing, signs and wonders. These signs often accompany the preaching of the gospel or the viewing of a Jesus film, when Christains immediately ask for the sick to be brought up to the platform where they are healed.

The difference is in how the gospel is presented. The apologetic for the faith is not based so much on reason, but on the power of God (1 Cor. 2:4-5). It is a return to the strategy of the Apostle Paul. He wrote to the Thessalonians, "because our gospel came to you not simply with words, but also with power, with the Holy Spirit and with deep conviction."[7] With this strategy the Church has once again become a world Church. What it had obtained by 800 A.D. when it was in Europe, Africa, the Middle East, and Asia, it is once again.[8] Today, it is on every continent, except Antarctica. Only in a few places - like its birthplace of Israel, in Muslim lands like Turkey and in Japan - does it have little strength. Millions of Christians over the course of 1,000 years were persecuted and martyred in these lands where Christianity is now such a small minority. At one time, this was where the Church was the strongest and had the most adherents.

For centuries the Church was strong in Israel, Turkey, Iran, Iraq, and in Central Asia. The Church was stronger there than in Europe until about the 10th century. Over the next ten centuries of repeated massacres, genocide against Christians, occasional severe persecutions and the constant humiliation of being relegated to unequal, second-class citizens of an empire or country, the Church in those lands was essentially destroyed. The Nestorian Church and the Assyrian Chaldean Church of middle Asia underwent a thousand years of persecution before they were virtually wiped out.[9] At one time, the Church was prospering in Japan and becoming a large minority within the country until a severe genocide against Christians decimated the Church.[10] Before the 20th century, the Church made three major attempts at evangelizing China, all of which ended prematurely at the hands of persecution and genocide. Even the severe persecution of the Communist's Cultural Revolution in the 20th century has not stamped out this fourth push into China over the last 50 years, however.

Do you believe it is in the heart of God to establish His Church again in middle Asia, a place where so many martyrs have spilled their blood? Can we believe that what God did in China can be repeated? The "yeast" has yet to leaven the whole lump, but the leaven is at work. The mustard seed has become the biggest plant in the garden, but not all the birds have come to roost in it yet (see the parables on the Kingdom of God in Matthew's gospel 13:31-33). How can the gospel possibly penetrate the Muslim world once again? It will not happen by rational arguments but by signs and wonders. This is how Muslims are coming to Christ in Mozambique, Pakistan and other countries. I believe that is how God intends to win them in the 21st century; the way the Church expanded in the first few centuries is how it will expand in the 21st century. The Church will come to understand that the gospel has not been fully preached unless we add the "what we have done" to "what we have said." Notice again what Romans 15:17-19 (NIV) says:

> *Therefore I glory in Christ Jesus in my service to God. I will not venture to speak of anything except what Christ has accomplished through me in leading the Gentiles to obey God by what I have said and done - by the power of signs and miracles, through the power of the Spirit. So from Jerusalem all the way around to Illyricum, I have fully proclaimed the gospel of Christ.*

May the land of the former Eastern Roman Empire, the Byzantine Empire and its neighboring nations once again see the glory of God in the gospel with signs following. May the largest church buildings in the world, buildings that became mosques after severe persecution of the Christians, once more become churches for the worship of Jesus Christ.

Still, we must learn lessons from history - crusades are not God's way to victory. They actually deeply hurt the cause of Christ in these lands and caused greater persecution of the Christians. We must allow the power of God to demonstrate the love of God to the people in places like Turkey and other nations of the world. It is by our love, not our wars, that they are to know Him.

Power Led to the Christianization of the Roman Empire

Ramsay MacMullen, Emeritus Professor of History and Classics at Yale University, set out to find the answer to the question, "How did the early Christians who had no money, institutions, little education and whose religion was illegal, conquer the other gods of the Greco-Roman pantheon? How did Christianity become the official religion of the Roman empire in 300 years?" His research as a secular historian resulted in quite a surprise. The Church's success was not primarily due to great preaching or convincing apologetics, but to healings and demonic deliverances performed in Jesus' name.[11] MacMullen documents numerous conversions from the first four centuries through Christians demonstrating with power encounters the supremacy of Christ over false gods that the people had formerly worshipped. This discovery of the preeminence of power evangelism in the first centuries of the Church was not the conclusion of a Charismatic Christian historian trying to prove a point, but that of a secular historian from Yale! The Great Commission was being fulfilled because the disciples had been filled. The disciples in turn, believed that their disciples were supposed to be filled with the Holy Spirit, even as they had been. Unfortunately, many modern day Christian historians either scarcely cover or completely ignore this reality of how evangelism was done.

The Power Then and Now

I want to conclude this chapter with testimonies of how God has used healings, deliverances and other demonstrations of the power of God to advance the kingdom from around the world. I have cited historical figures, along with a few personal friends, who have been used by God in bringing in the harvest.

17

Europe

Germany - Johann Blumhardt

Johann Blumhardt (1805 - 1880) was a German Lutheran theologian who lived in the Black Forest of what today would be Germany. After a two-year battle against a demon that was tormenting a young woman, Johann cast it out. When it left it yelled, "Jesus is Victor!" which could be heard over a mile away. Immediately, the spiritual atmosphere changed and people began to come to his house asking him to hear their confessions. Many were in tears, broken over their sins. A spiritual awakening came to the entire area and Blumhardt was thrust into a healing ministry. Eventually, religious authorities asked him to stop praying for healing, since so many were being healed and subsequently leaving their churches to join his church. However, even the jealousy of religious leaders did not stop him from continuing in his ministry of power evangelism for years.

Great Britain

George Whitefield and John Wesley

George Whitefield (1714 - 1770) and John Wesley (1703 - 1791) were greatly used by God in what was termed the Evangelical Awakening in England. Whitefield and Wesley, along with about 30 others, had a powerful experience with the Holy Spirit. This experience would propel both of their ministries. At a meeting on Fetters Lane at about 3:00 A.M. while taking communion, they were all overtaken by the Holy Spirit and fell under the power. Upon arising, there was a new power in them for reaching the poor and the lost of England. Wesley placed a strong emphasis upon experiencing the power of God to give victory to walk in perfect love and holiness. One secular historian stated that if England had not had the great revival under Whitefield and Wesley, England would have had a revolution like France where the blood ran down the streets filling the gutters.

Although Whitefield was initially concerned about reports of physical manifestations in Wesley's meetings, he eventually saw many fall and shake under God's power in his own meetings. After Whitefield's first encounter with people falling in his own meeting, Wesley wrote, "From this time, I trust we shall all allow God to carry on His work in the way that pleases Him."[12] Whitefield, in turn, convinced Wesley to move beyond just preaching in churches and into the fields for open-air crusades. In one meeting, Whitefield held for a Presbyterian group in Cambuslang, Scotland, over 20,000 people met for an open-air annual communion service. People were deeply impacted by the Holy Spirit as thousands fell to the ground under His power. Many were unable to get up, well into the night. Loud cries and weeping as well as shouts of joy were heard throughout the night. Many accepted Jesus as their savior and remained faithful in the church for years to come. Whitefield would eventually make 11 trips to the mission field of the American colonies where the Church was in a state of decline and compromise. About 3% of Americans were going to church in the colonies at that time. In comparison, this is about the same percentage that attends church in Europe today. With his passionate preaching and ministry, Whitefield helped usher in the First Great Awakening.

C. T. Studd

C. T. Studd (1860-1931) gave up his career as a famous cricket player for a life on the mission field. After serving with Hudson Taylor in China, Studd ministered in India, the United States and Sudan. Eventually, grieved by the lack of Christianity in central Africa, he moved to the Belgian Congo in 1913. During his many years in the Congo, Studd experienced a great revival, seeing churches planted and an extensive missions outreach established. Supernatural manifestations accompanied his meetings. Studd remarked in one particular gathering in 1914:

The whole place was charged as if with an electric current. Men were falling, jumping, laughing, crying, singing, confessing and some shaking terribly… As I led in prayer, the Spirit came down in mighty power, sweeping the congregation. My whole body literally trembled with the power. We saw a marvelous sight, people literally filled and drunk with the Holy Spirit.[13]

It is true that most of the European missionaries and evangelists of previous times did not see miracles and healings in a normative way, as they are occurring today. Once again, we do not hold them responsible for things that were not happening in their day. Still, they did experience power to live lives of hardship as they preached the gospel. Through them God convicted, converted and convulsed many with His power in those days of His outpouring.

Ukraine

Henry Madava

Henry Madava was born in Zimbabwe but relocated to Kiev, Ukraine to study aeronautics. While there, the Lord began to speak to him about the need for a strong church, which would be open to all in Kiev. After about a year of struggling to accept his call, Madava began Victory Church with the help of five friends. Since then, his church has blossomed into a thriving congregation of over 19,000 worshippers. Henry has developed a lifestyle of sensitivity to the Holy Spirit and places a strong emphasis on worship in his church. The power of God has been present to heal the sick in his crusades around the world, bringing hundreds of thousands to Christ. He told me that it is the power of God to help people with their lives that draws the people to Christ. Also, he told me that he received an impartation for himself and his church during our first trip to his church, which gave him the courage to begin his crusades.

Sunday Adelaja

Sunday Adelaja was born in Nigeria in 1967. While still young, he was abandoned by his mother and subsequently raised by his grandmother alongside his uncles and aunts and other abandoned children. His difficult childhood included the death of three of his grandmother's four children in a one-year period, followed by his grandmother getting cancer. After years of bitterness and rebellion, Sunday's life was changed at 15 after the death of his grandmother. He was struck by the level of his Christian grandmother's sacrifice for him, even when others had told her to give up on her embittered grandson. He quickly went from a poor student to an excellent student. Four years later he gave his life to Christ, which he says felt like "220 kilograms of weight had been lifted from me."

In 1986, six months after his conversion, Adelaja moved to the Soviet Union state of Belarus on a scholarship to study journalism. For five years he would experience harassment and constant monitoring by university officials and the KGB due to his Christian faith and involvement in the underground church. During this time, the Lord gave him a prophetic dream of preaching to masses of white people. When the Soviet Union fell, Adelaja and his wife went public with their church, planting the Word of Faith Bible Church in Kiev, Ukraine. Despite their many efforts, they saw little fruit. However, when the Lord redirected Adelaja to reach the drug addicts and go "where preachers don't go," a thousand people came into his church in one year. Through his boldness and message of faith, thousands more have been saved and many miracles have occurred in his church. He now oversees more than 700 churches in over 45 countries, including 30,000 members in his original church in Kiev - the largest Evangelical church in Europe. His ministry has also planted over 3,000 drug rehabilitation centers and feeds over 1,000 people a day. For his impact on social issues, he has been welcomed by the United Nations as well as meeting with other presidents and world leaders.[14]

The Future of Europe

Today, Europe needs to be re-evangelized. The birth rate needed to sustain a culture in a developed country is 2.1 children per woman, but the European rate has fallen to 1.5 children per woman. Several studies show fertility rates of Muslims in Europe at least twice that of native Europeans. While fertility rates of Muslims generally decrease as they adapt to European culture, their current birthrates still far exceed that of native Europeans. Muslims who strictly follow Islam have significantly higher fertility rates than secular Muslims.[15] Fertility rates and high immigration rates have led to significant increases in the European Muslim population. One study determined it would only take 12 years for the Muslim European population to double.[16]

This immigration strategy was used by Muslims in the Middle Ages to not only establish itself in formerly Christian countries, but also to ascend to the majority of the population. Muslims could potentially accomplish today what the horror of centuries of battles fought and lives lost could not accomplish in Europe. Europe could be lost not by death but by birth- not with the pain of war, but with the joy of sexual procreation. Today, Europe is a mission field with neo-paganism and Islam quickly becoming a larger portion of the population. For the Church to do evangelism for the next 50 years as it has been done in the last 500 years is to invite the loss of Europe as a Christian continent culturally, if not spiritually. The only thing, in my opinion, that can stop this is a combined effort on two fronts. First, the self-centeredness that is at the root of the decline in European birthrate must be replaced with a value on children and Christian families. Second, European Christians must return to a New Testament form of Christianity- one that has power and not just institution or form. We can no longer afford to have a form of godliness but deny its power (2 Tim 3:1-5).[17]

Middle East

Several years ago a missionary from the Sinai Peninsula came to me with a very interesting story. He told me that a meeting had been held with all the missionaries on the Sinai Peninsula. At this meeting it was discovered that not one of them had led a Muslim to the Lord unless the person had first had a dream in which Jesus appeared to him/her, had a vision, experienced a healing, or saw a miracle. It was signs and wonders that caused each Muslim to accept the Lord. This was among a collection of missionaries who had served between 2 to 38 years in the Middle East.

This was a wake up call for these Evangelical missionaries. They eventually sent a delegate to ask charismatic scholar Jack Deere if he would come and minister to them. Jack told the delegate he should talk to either Bill Johnson or myself. I invited this man and his friend to join me for a pastors meeting in Phenom Pen, Cambodia. At the meeting, both were powerfully touched by the Holy Spirit and they returned reenergized for the difficult work of serving Christ on the Sinai Peninsula.

Asia

Myanmar/ China/ Southeast Asia

Along the border of Myanmar (formerly Burma) and China resides a people group called the Wa. In the 1800's this headhunting tribe of about 100,000 was feared by neighboring tribes because of their savagery. In the 1880's one of their own, Pu Chan, claimed that the one true God had sent him to tell the people to stop their headhunting and other attempts to appease spirits. He also prophesied that the true God would soon send "a white brother with a copy of the lost book," and that they were to be very careful not to miss this opportunity. Eventually, Pu Chan sent out a pony and told his followers that if they followed the pony wherever it went, it would take them to the white messenger with the lost book. These devoted disciples followed the pony 200 miles over mountainous trails to the village of Kengtung in Western Burma near the borders of China, Thailand and Laos. The pony stopped at a well, but there was no trace of a white messenger or a book.

The disciples heard noises from inside the well and looked down to find a white man digging. The white man was American missionary William Young. "Have you brought a book of God?" they asked excitedly. Willaim climbed out of the well, telling them that he had a book from God. They were overcome with emotion and fell at his feet, begging him to come back with them. Young told them that since he had thousands of the local Lahu people coming to him to learn about this God, he could not leave. Instead, he offered accommodations for these and other eager disciples and spent several years teaching them about the God of the Bible. Young's son Vincent grew up learning the Wa language from the disciples who would come to their base to be trained. As Vincent grew older, he made many trips into the Wa mountains to teach the gospel and eventually translated the entire New Testament into their language. After several years the Youngs found themselves with 60,000 baptized Lahu people and 10,000 baptized Wa who, in turn, continued to spread the Gospel throughout Burma and China. This is just one of countless testimonies of how God uses supernatural means to reach even the uttermost regions of the world with the Gospel.[18]

Thailand

I recently had the opportunity to take a team to minister in northern Thailand. While there, we visited a rural village in the mountains named Om Koi. For several years, the people of Om Koi have experienced healings, miracles and even numerous children being taken up to heaven. As a result, the church is growing faster there than in any other part of Thailand. Although they are a small, rural people, many believers across Thailand believe that God will bring revival through the people of Om Koi to the entire nation.

Korea

One of the greatest revivals in the last hundred years has occurred in the nation of South Korea. Many times the rapid church growth in Korea has been preceded by intense fasting and prayer. One of the unique aspects of the revival in Korea has been that the mainline denominations have been profoundly influenced by the charismatic movement. It is common to enter a Methodist or Presbyterian church and find people prophesying, healing the sick and performing miracles. It is no coincidence that both the largest Methodist church and the largest Presbyterian church in the world are in Korea. Also, David Yonggi Cho's Assembly of God church has around 850,000 members, making it the largest church in the world. For decades healings and miracles have been an integral part of the church's growth.

China

Dennis Balcombe is an American missionary sent out over 40 years ago by a Latter Rain church in California. He has fully dedicated his life to China and the spread of the gospel there. He even asked his own children to only speak Chinese in the house. When the time came to marry, he asked them to only marry Chinese spouses.

While in China, I met with seven house church leaders who oversee 25 million believers. They told me that 80% of these believers came to the Lord after 1988. Naturally, I asked them, "What happened in 1988?" They answered, "Dennis Balcombe brought us the Holy Spirit." They also estimated that an additional 60 million Christian have been powerfully impacted by Dennis.

Although he was blacklisted by the communist government and prevented from entering mainland China for many years, Dennis was permitted to travel extensively throughout mainland China beginning in 1988. Church after church experienced an outpouring of the Holy Spirit as signs, wonders, miracles and great joy followed the preaching of the gospel. Dennis even told me that, while I was experiencing an outpouring of revival in Toronto, Canada in January of 1994, the exact same things were taking place in his ministry in the Shandong (also written Shantung) province of China. With no knowledge of the events in Toronto, thousands of Chinese fell, cried and laughed as the Holy Spirit moved in their midst. Speaking in tongues is a normative part of the Christian life in the churches in China that Dennis oversees.

Also, I heard from an evangelist in east Russia that he too independently experienced in January 1994 the exact things we saw in Toronto and Dennis saw in China. When the local believers in Russia were asked who told them to do these things, they answered, "We read the book of Acts!" They went on to explain that just as it appeared as if the disciples were drunk when the Holy Spirit came upon them in the book of Acts, so too it appeared as if they were all drunk when the Holy Spirit came into their meetings.

Another American missionary, David Hogan, also saw the same things we saw in Toronto among his top indigenous leaders in rural Mexico shortly after revival in Toronto broke out. When Hogan heard about Toronto, he didn't know if it was of God or not. He figured that if the things in Toronto were really of God, God could do them among his pastors without outside missionaries trying to replicate in his churches what they saw in Toronto. As a result, he strictly forbade any foreigner to mention the events of Toronto to any of his Mexican leaders. One day he came back to his place of meeting and over 30 of his normally stoic leaders were laughing, rolling on the floor, and praising the Lord. This was proof enough for him. I believe that the evangelist leading the meeting was Bill Brizinski.

Africa

Kenya

A few years ago, I had the honor of speaking at Elim Bible Institute in Lima, New York. While I was there, Elim's former president told me a fascinating story. Many years back a western missionary had been prophetically sent out by God to minister among the tribes of Kenya. Despite having been called by God, he saw very little fruit from his ministry. After several years of frustration, he cried out to God, "God, you have to do something!" Soon after, while in prayer, he heard a funeral procession pass by his house. The Holy Spirit told him to go pray for the dead person in the coffin. He obediently ran up to the coffin and began to pray for the man's life to return. Those carrying the coffin soon heard a loud knocking from inside the coffin. They opened it up and the dead man jumped out of the coffin! News of this amazing miracle spread throughout the area. This one event was the impetus of a great revival. An estimated 10,000 churches sprang up after this incredible miracle.

Central and South America

Brazil

I often call Brazil my land of anointing. Over the last 10 years, I have seen more healings, miracles and overall fruit in this nation than any other. One church where I ministered, International Restoration Ministries in the northern city of Manaus, has seen great fruit from the power of the Holy Spirit. Several years ago, when this church was a 700 member Baptist congregation, they experienced a visitation of the Holy Spirit. Many fell down and began speaking in tongues during the services. As a result, the church was kicked out of the Baptist convention. However, rather than reject this move of the Spirit because of persecution, Pastor Rene Terra Nova chose to continue to press in for more of what God had for them. From that point on, they committed themselves to pursuing the gifts of the Holy Spirit and to the cell church growth model (which I describe in more detail below). The church grew from 21,000 members when I first visited in 2000, seven years after being kicked out of Brazil's Baptist Convention, to 48,000 when I came back in 2003. It now has 60,000 members in one local congregation as well as other partner churches in the area. I share more from my visit to that church in my Short-Term Ministry chapter.

I visited another church in Goiania, Brazil led by Pastor Aluizio with 3,000 members. This was a church committed to fasting, praying and healing the sick. However, they almost never saw healings. When we went there, our team trained them in words of knowledge, how to pray for the sick and had an impartation service. When we went back the next year, I asked the pastors what had been the fruit of our meetings. They said, "Before you came, we hardly ever had healings. But since you and your team came, not one Sunday has gone by that people haven't been healed in our services. Not one week has gone by that people have not been healed in our cell groups." The last time I went to the church, it had grown to 30,000 members in two locations. The church grew from 3,000 to 30,000 in ten years.

Lagoinha Baptist Church in Belo Horizonte, Brazil

Lagoinha Baptist Church is the largest Baptist church in the nation. It is a charismatic church and operates in the gifts of the Holy Spirit. The pastor's son and daughter both graduated from the late Gordon Lindsay's Christ For the Nations Institute in Dallas, Texas. I personally witnessed many healings and miracles when my team ministered in this great Baptist church. The church has a strong emphasis on worship and has concerts with up to one million people in attendance praising the Lord.

Quadrangular Church in Belem, Brazil

While in a prayer service in South Bend, Indiana in the first decade of the 20th century, two Swedish immigrants, Gunnar Vingren and Daniel Berg received a prophetic word to go to a place called Para. After researching and finding that this was a province in northwest Brazil, the two set out for Brazil. The two arrived in the Para town of Belem in 1910 and began prayer meetings in the basement of a Baptist church. After tension arose over manifestations of tongues and healings, the two began a church called "Assembly of God" (four years before the founding of the Assembly of God denomination in the United States). The Assemby of God congregations in the city have since grown to over 30,000 members.

Pentecostal churches have become the largest Protestant denomination in Brazil with over 13 million members. In recent years, many traditional denominations have participated in a movement, called "Renovation" in which, for all practical purposes, they have become Pentecostal churches. Many of these churches from mainline denominations even have the title "Pentecostal" in their name. Additionally, the charismatic movement has swept through the Catholic Church. Brazil currently has both the largest Catholic and Pentecostal population of any nation in the world.[19]

Argentina

Tommy Hicks

In 1951 the Argentine church was mired in a state of spiritual apathy. Adding to the problem, First Lady Eva Peron was spurring on a spiritist movement that was sweeping the country. Meanwhile, her husband, President Juan Peron, continued to extend his dictatorial reign as he usurped increasing political power. In the midst of this difficult spiritual climate, small pockets of believers began to intercede for hours at a time for a spiritual awakening to visit their nation. Healings, salvations and angelic visitations became commonplace in these prayer gatherings. The numbers impacted by these meetings were limited, however.

In the midst of this atmosphere, unheralded American healing evangelist Tommy Hicks approached a "pro mass-evangelism" committee in Argentina, requesting to do a stadium-size healing evangelism crusade. The committee considered this idea preposterous since the nation never had a stadium crusade and there were not many evangelicals in the country or much interest in the healing ministry. The committee recommended aiming for 2,500 people, but Hicks insisted on a 25,000-member stadium with widespread advertising by radio and the press. He reasoned that God could both draw the crowds and overcome the strict religious censorship of Peron's reign.

After prayer, Hicks concluded that a face-to-face meeting with Peron was the only way to accomplish what God had laid on his heart. Against impossible odds that an unheard of minister could meet with the president, Hicks took the situation to the Lord in prayer. Still convinced this was the Lord's will, he set out to find someone who would grant him the access to the president. At the president's headquarters, Hicks encountered a security guard and began to tell him of the healing power of God. After listening intently, the guard asked, "Can God heal me?" A few moments later, the power of God was surging through Hicks' hands into the guard's body. "All the pain is gone!" he declared in astonishment. Within minutes Hicks had an appointment set to meet the president.

The next day, president Peron listened intently as Hicks told of the miraculous power of God and the need for a citywide healing and salvation stadium crusade with full press and media coverage. At the time Peron was suffering from a progressively worsening eczema which no physician could cure. Amazed by Hicks' testimonies of a wonder working God he asked, "Can God heal me?" "Give me your hand," Hicks answered. Hicks prayed a simple prayer of faith as the power of God flowed into Peron's body. Before all present, the dictator of Argentina's skin was made whole. Peron wiped his face and exclaimed, "My God, I'm healed!" Hicks was soon granted everything he requested.

Hicks began his crusades, demonstrating night after night the healing power of God. Within days it became apparent that the 25,000-seat stadium was too small. Hicks moved the meetings to the 180,000-seat soccer stadium which had never been filled. People flocked from neighboring countries and crowds waited for hours just to get in. For weeks healings, miracles and demonic deliverances spread from the stadium to many parts of the country. God used a Latter Rain American evangelist with little fanfare and a lot of faith to visit Argentina in a sovereign way.[20]

Eduardo Lorenzo - Baptist Congregation in Suburb of Buenos Aires

Several years ago I met with a young man named Victor in Buenos Aires, Argentina. Victor told me the story of his father, Eduardo Lorenzo, who was a key leader in the Baptist convention.

When Lorenzo began pastoring a small church outside Buenos Aires, almost the entire church consisted of people outside of the community. Victor told me that they would routinely see people from the community get out of their cars, come up to the door of the church and then turn around, get back in their cars and leave. Pastor Lorenzo was perplexed as to what was going on.

One day he was faced with a demon manifesting through a woman in front of him. He was caught off guard, having had no training in deliverance, but was eventually able to cast it out. The church leaders realized that they needed more training in spiritual warfare. After inviting several experts to train them in deliverance, they began to see more demons manifest along with various spiritual attacks against the church. They followed this up with an extended period of strategic intercession and fasting, during which they identified the territorial spirit over the region. Later, during the final hour of a five-day fast to break the power of this spirit, the 200 intercessors in the room felt a release in the spirit realm. The power of the principality had been broken. This encounter with the power of the Holy Spirit confronting and overcoming the power of darkness led to significant spiritual breakthrough in the community. The church has experienced significant growth. Victor said that the majority of the church is now composed of people from the community.

Omar Cabrera

I was present at a meeting in Argentina when Omar Cabrera was being honored for his pioneering work as a healing evangelist. This award was well deserved. Nearly forty years ago, Cabrera began a new denomination, Vision de Futuro, in response to a specific word from the Holy Spirit. His church was built on the power of the Holy Spirit, healing and is strongly dependent upon words of knowledge.

Cabrera pioneered Strategic Level Spiritual Warfare. He specifically committed larger amounts of money for crusades in the cities where he had a definitive breakthrough in prayer. Identifying the strongholds over the city gave him a strategy and authority to temporarily bind the strongman over the area. It led to blinders coming off the eyes of the unbelievers, resulting in many more miracles and thousands more saved. He preaches to crowds of up to 50,000 people and now has hundreds of churches in his Vision de Futuro network.

Carlos Annacondia

Carlos Annacondia was a successful businessman when he gave his life to the Lord at an evangelistic crusade in Buenos Aires in 1979. The Lord soon called Annacondia to preach the gospel. By 1981, he had an evangelistic ministry of his own. He began his work by preaching throughout the poor villages of Buenos Aires and later moved on to stadiums in many countries across five continents. It is believed that millions accepted faith in Jesus Christ during his crusades. Annacondia even arranged for evangelistic meetings to be held in a 4,000-member high security prison. Hundreds came to Christ and the prison eventually developed a Christian floor with 800 inmates. This floor held around-the-clock prayer meetings with 180 praying at any given time. For years, prisoners continued to get saved after being transferred to this floor. Over a five year period, 600 men completed their sentences and only one was re-arrested- an extremely low re-arrest rate for high security prisons.

The most distinctive aspect of Annacondia's ministry is the ministry of deliverance after people accept the lordship of Jesus Christ. This ministry is conducted in deliverance tents specifically set up for the demonized at his meetings. Annocondia's meetings are often characterized by the healing anointing, people being "slain in the Spirit" (or falling under the power of the Spirit) and people's teeth being filled with gold and platinum.

Uruguay

Jorge Marquez was a successful architect while attending a church of 100,000 people in Buenos Aires. At the Lord's leading, he retired from his job, took all his retirement money and invested

32

it into planting a church in Montevideo, Uruguay. At the time he arrived in February 1991, no protestant church in Uruguay had more than 500 people in one congregation. Jorge began to build his church with physical healing and deliverance as foundational building blocks. He told me that many drug addicts had been delivered and are now preaching in his church. He added, "If their hearts are in the right place, I can teach them and then they can preach. But if their hearts are not in the right place, I can't teach them." Through his perseverance in healing the sick and delivering the oppressed, Jorge has seen his church grow to 3,000 people. Their church has water baptized over 11,000 people and planted churches in a number of other cities in Uruguay and Brazil.

Honduras

A number of years ago, I was invited to minister in a church in Oklahoma City. As is typical in my meetings, I laid hands on many people for impartation after the message. One man had been a missionary to Honduras for 30 years. I laid hands on him and he fell to the floor but did not have any particularly strong physical manifestations (which often accompany times of significant impartation). However, I later heard that when this missionary went back to Honduras, he saw more miracles and healings in the next three months than he had in his previous 30 years of missionary work.

Johetebeche Methodist Church, Santiago, Chile

In 1902, American physician and Methodist missionary Willis Hoover watched as a holiness movement emphasizing sanctification swept through Chile. At the time, he had been overseeing approximately 6,000 members of the Chilean Methodist church. Although Dr. Hoover supported the move of God in Chile, he hungered for more. In 1905, his hunger increased upon reading reports of an unusual revival at a girl's school in India characterized by prophetic experiences, trances, visions and speaking in tongues. Soon after, a man in Hoover's church had a dream in which the Lord told him, "Go to your pastor and tell him to gather the most spiritual people of the congregation. They are to pray together every day. I intend to baptize them with tongues of fire."

Within several days, a move of God unprecedented in Chilean history ensued. These freshly empowered believers hit the streets proclaiming the Gospel and declaring the mysteries of God and a coming revival. Visions and miraculous healings were commonplace. An early leader described the event: "It was an astonishing scene never before seen in Chile. The brothers were inspired to dance, to have spiritual visions; they spoke in angelic languages, prophesying about this great spiritual revival. The Holy Spirit took them into the streets. The authorities took them to the police stations as arrested prisoners, but they continue to dance in the stations, speaking with other tongues and prophesying to the same authorities."

The Methodist church soon grew weary of Dr. Hoover and the Pentecostals. In September of 1909, the Methodist Missionary Society excommunicated Hoover and 37 leaders. Undeterred, Hoover admonished his congregation to preach in the streets every Sunday. Street corners and bus stations nationwide became perfect preaching grounds. Today, the resulting denomination, the Pentecostal Methodist Church, has over 600,000 members. One of its churches, the Jotabeche Church in the capital of Santiago, has grown to over 100,000 members. With Pentecostals comprising nearly 15% of Chile's population, Chile can be considered the most Pentecostal nation in the world.[21]

Columbia

Randy MacMillan

Randy MacMillan was a backslidden university student in Florida. He was also the son of a prominent lawyer, which made for a privileged and comfortable life. In addition, Randy was a descendant of the pastor of the nation's first Presbyterian church in Jamestown, Virginia.

One day when he was in his dorm room packing up to leave for a Christmas vacation trip to New York, he turned around and saw Jesus standing there. Randy stared at him for about half a minute before falling to the floor, weeping deeply and confessing his sins to the Lord. Still being touched by God and unable to talk, his friends carried him to the car to leave for their vacation. Since Randy was still so "out of it" his friends decided to drop him off at his parents' house in Virginia.

On the way, the audible voice of God told him that he would be a prophet with a word from God in a country that did not speak his language. When he got to his parent's house they were concerned with the drastic change in their son and thought that he might have been brainwashed. This led his dad, a lawyer, to cross-examine him in a hotel room for two days. His parents did not believe that Jesus could appear today and especially would not do so to someone living a life of drugs and partying. Finally, after a few days, his family decided they should be careful about what they said to Randy in case this was really God. Within six weeks Randy was prophesying and seeing healings on campus.

After several years, God led Randy and his Columbian wife to move to Cali, Columbia. One day while in his room, a demon appeared to him and said that he had principality over Cali and commanded him to leave immediately. Randy responded, "Jesus called me here...I will not leave unless Jesus himself comes and tells me to leave this city and leave this country." Eventually, this spirit and a host of other spirits left the room, but Randy ended up sick for two or three months.

During this time he reasoned that if this principality really wanted him out of Cali and Colombia, God must have a great plan for the city and the nation. God soon began revealing his vision for the whole body of Christ in the city of Cali. Randy would become a driving force behind arranging all night stadium prayer meetings. Even the entire professional soccer team in Cali came to Christ. Eventually the stadium was too small, so they moved the all night meetings to a park where up to 80,000 people would gather. Randy has spent his life ministering in Columbia. He even prophesied the now famous G12 church growth movement, popularized by Cesar Castellanos, before it happened. Randy is currently an apostle overseeing around 70 churches.

Cesar Castellanos

Cesar Castellanos was a nominal catholic and regular drug user as a young man. One night, Jesus appeared to him. Cesar was terrified by the Lord's presence, especially since he was in the middle of a drug trip. He told the Lord that if he would come back tomorrow at a certain time, he would be straight and would listen to what the Lord had to say to him. The next day he waited in his chair and, at the exact time Cesar specified, the Lord appeared to him again. As a result, he was powerfully converted. The Lord later showed him a vision of a model of discipleship, called G12, patterned after Jesus' example of discipling 12 people at a time. This cell group based model for discipleship and church growth has been a foundational component in many of the largest churches in the world throughout Latin America, Africa and Asia. Cesar's church in Columbia is the largest in the hemisphere with 200,000 members in his main church in Bogotá. Randy's and Cesar's testimonies both demonstrate how sometimes people are simply sovereignly chosen by God. These encounters often lead to dramatic conversions and a lifetime of great fruitfulness.

North America: United States

TL Osborn

TL Osborn was a pioneer in going to open fields in non-Christian nations to preach the Gospel. As part of his presentation of Christ, Osborn declared that the miracles that would follow were proof of the validity of the Gospel. Many preachers have followed in his footsteps and open field meetings have become a standard procedure in third world gospel crusades. He has preached in over 70 countries to crowds of up to 300,000. Osborn was committed to producing "Documiracle" films to testify around the world of the healing power of Christ. The Osborns supported approximately 30,000 native missionaries leading to around 150,000 churches.

Oral Roberts

Oral Roberts was born in 1918 as the son of a Pentecostal preacher whose family was often ridiculed for their beliefs. Oral ran away from home at 15. Two years later, he was brought back by his basketball coach after collapsing on the gym floor from tuberculosis. One day, while his health slowly deteriorated, his sister came and told him of healings at a local crusade. She assured him, "Oral, God is going to heal you." His family took Oral to a healing meeting where he was miraculously healed of both tuberculosis and a life-long stuttering problem. He immediately began preaching to whoever would listen.

In 1947 after 12 years of little success, Roberts held an evangelism crusade and prayed that God would bring over 1,000 people and heal at least one person. Around 1,200 people attended and a woman with a shriveled hand was able to open her hand again at the end of the meeting. Roberts was soon preaching to much larger crowds and seeing countless miraculous healings as part of the Healing Revival of the late 1940's. Roberts reported that in 1957 alone, he saw one million people give their lives to Christ. He noted that there was often a direct correlation between the amount of healings and the amount of salvations - more displays of healing led to more salvations. After seeing the miracle power of God in his meetings, many unbelievers would give their lives to Christ. Roberts eventually founded his own university (Oral Roberts University) with the intent of incorporating prayer and the gifts of the Holy Spirit in the context of a quality education.

Lester Sumrall - United States and Philippines

In 1953, American preacher Dr. Lester Sumrall had an encounter with demons while ministering in Manila, Philippines. A woman, Clarita Villanueva, was being tormented by what commonly became known as "The Thing." "The Thing" was actually a supernatural force that no one could see, yet there would be physical marks on Clarita's body as it attacked her. These attacks were so terrible and were such a curiousity to the city that journalists had written articles in the newspapers about Clarita's torment.

God spoke to Dr. Sumrall's heart and said, "If you will go to the jail and pray for her, I will deliver her." After some divine connections through his friendship with the mayor of Manila, he got an appointment to go and pray for her. The woman was completely made whole by the power of God. It is said that this one deliverance opened up the whole city to the gospel of the Lord Jesus Christ.[22]

Conclusion

These are but a few examples of the people who were changed by the power of God and brought revival and movements throughout history. History continues to be written as God moves with demonstrations of His power through men and women who are proclaiming the gospel message every place on the globe. As healings, deliverances, signs and wonders are done through sons and daughters of God, lost souls are coming to Christ. It is no longer just the message that needs to be preached, but a demonstration of power that will convince the doubter to believe in Christ. God is looking for families, tribes and nations to come to believe in Christ. It is His desire that none should perish, but that all may have life and more abundantly.

Endnotes

[1]Revelation 19:10 "the testimony of Jesus is the spirit of prophecy"

[2]The First Great Awakening (1730's -1740's) produced thirty thousand conversions in New England in a three-year period. In the same period at least 50,000 were converted in all the colonies. An awakening today with similar percentages compared with the total population would result in more than 5 million conversions. The Second Great Awakening (1780's to around 1812), which had its most powerful local expression of revival at Cain Ridge, Kentucky, saw the number of Presbyterians double, the Baptists triple and the Methodists quadruple. On the heels of this movement, Adoniram Judson, the first Protestant missionary sent from North America, set sail for India and Burma in 1812. The great Protestant Missionary movement ensued. The late 1940's Latter Rain revival that began in Canada and the United States caused a Revival to break out in Argentina, the Philippines, Kenya and Angola. Missionaries were sent out to Europe, Africa, Turkey, India, Japan, New Zealand and Australia. Also, Elim Bible School in New York and Calvary Bible College in Australia were founded by those touched by this move of God.

[3]Matthew 28:19-20: "teaching them to obey all things I have commanded you." The "them" is the same "them" who were to be baptized. John 14:12-13 (NET): "I tell you the truth, *the person who believes in me will perform the miraculous deeds that I am doing,* and will perform greater deeds than these, because I am going to the Father." (The Greek word *erga* ("works") in John 14:12 denotes miraculous works in the Gospel of John, in most cases healing miracles: BDAG, p. 390). Mark 16:17-18: "And these signs will accompany those who believe: In my name they will drive out demons; they will speak in new tongues; they will pick up snakes with

their hands; and when they drink deadly poison, it will not hurt them at all; they will place their hands on sick people, and they will get well." Note that this power was not limited to the Apostles because the evangelist/deacons Philip and Stephen also worked healings and miracles (Acts 6:8; 8:5-8), as did the scattered disciples who went to Antioch because of the persecution (Acts 11:21: the "hand of the Lord" refers to the powers of the Spirit in signs and wonders, as Acts 13:11 shows). And healings and miracles were also worked by ordinary believers like Ananias (Acts 9:17-18; 22:12-16), and congregations like the Corinthians (1 Cor. 11:1; 12:9), the Galatians (Gal. 3:5), the Philippians (Phil. 4-9), the Thessalonians (1 Thes. 1:5-6), and all Jewish Christian congregations (Heb. 6:1-2 and James 5:14-16).

[4]The Faith Cure Movement began around 1873 and saw numerous healing ministries and conferences spring up. Physical healings became commonplace for the first time in centuries. The movement was eventually absorbed into the Pentecostal movement after Azuza Street in 1906.

[5]From discussions with professors at evangelical seminaries who spent years on the mission fields, I learned that the reason there was such a problem on the mission field with syncretism (mixing Christianity with the religion they had prior to accepting Christ) was that the gospel presented to them was of a cessationist nature. The gospel offered them no power to deal with the demons they lived in fear of. The westernized gospel (not the New Testament gospel) had been influenced by liberal theology and cessationist theology. It taught that demons were actually part of the superstitious worldview of the indigenous people. As a result, the people would return to shamans to get help with the demons. See Dr. Charles Kraft, "The Power of the God for Christians Who Ride Two Horses: Communicating and Ministering the Power of the Gospel Cross-culturally," in Dr. Gary Greig and Kevin Springer, eds., *The Kingdom and the Power* (Ventura, CA: Regal, 1993), pp. 345-356.

[6]For more on miracles in the first 1000 years of Christianity, see our School of Healing and Impartation: Empowered manual.

[7]1 Thessalonians 1:5a.

[8]John Philip, *The Lost History of Christianity: The Thousand-Year Golden Age of the Church in the Middle East, Africa and Asia - and How it Died.* (New York: HarperOne, 2008).

[10]Ibid.

[11]Ramsay Macmullen, *Christianizing the Roman Empire: A.D. 100-400.* (New Haven: Yale University Press, 1984).

[12]Clare George Weakley, Jr., The Nature of Revival (Minneapolis, MN: Bethany House, 1987) p. 79, quoting Nehemiah Curnock, ed., The Journal of the Reverend John Wesley (London: Charles H. Kelly, 1909), entry dated July 7, 1739.

[13]Winkie Pratney, *Revival: Its Principles and Personalities.* (Huntington House Publications, 1994).

[14]Valerie Lowe, "The Unlikely Ambassor," *Charisma Magazine*, 2007.

[15]Eric Kaufmann, "The Demography of Islam in Europe." http://www.sneps.net/RD/uploads/1The%20 Demography%20of%20Islam%20in%20Europe.pdf.

[16]Mary M. Kent, "Do Muslims Have More Children Than Other Women in Western Europe?" *PRB*, http://www.prb. org/Articles/2008/muslimsineurope.aspx.

[17]Omer Taspinar, "Europe's Muslim Street." *Brookings*, http://www.brookings.edu/opinions/2003/03middleeast_ taspinar.aspx.

[18]Don Richardson, Eternity in Their Hearts: Starling Evidence of Belief in the One True God in Hundreds of

Cultures Throughout the World. (Ventura, California: Regal, 2006).

[19]Vinson Synan "In the Latter Days: The Outpouring of the Holy Spirit in the Twentieth Century. (Xulon Press, 2001).

[20]Edward Miller, Cry for me Argentina: Revival Begins in the City. (Sharon Publications, 1988).

[21]Synan, pages 59-62.

[22]Lester Sumrall, *Demons: The Answer Book*. (Whitaker House, 2003).

Chapter 2

FINISHING THE UNFINISHED TASK

" *If we are to complete the task Jesus left for us, the task of discipling all nations, we must align ourselves with God's priorities. This includes allocating people and resources strategically, sharing God's passion for the least-reached people in the world. It also involves being aware of what God is doing in this particular season so that we can partner with His plan to spread His Kingdom throughout the earth.* "

- Leif Hetland

Alignment and Assignment

I am amazed by the way God choreographs our lives. As believers involved in the Kingdom of God, there are moments and events that align us to what will be needed to finish the task God has assigned for our lives. These events are moments of convergence. The New Testament word is "Kairos," which is the Greek word that means "opportune time." It is a "time" when God orchestrates things in such a way that there can be great momentum and acceleration. It is a time of shifting, aligning and bringing things in order for our assignment. If we properly respond to these "kairos" times, then we will find ourselves thrust forward in a new place with a new power. When Peter gave explanation of what God was doing in regard to healing the lame man at the Gate called Beautiful, he connected the event to an outpouring from God that related to the unfolding of the redemptive purposes of God that He had planned from the very beginning. Hear Peter's words as an encouragement for your own life:

Acts 3:19-21 (NKJV)

> *Repent therefore and be converted, that your sins may be blotted out, so that times of refreshing may come from the presence of the Lord, and that He may send Jesus Christ, who was preached to you before, whom heaven must receive until the times of restoration of all things, which God has spoken by the mouth of all His holy prophets since the world began.*

These refreshing, renewing encounters are always pregnant with the purposes of God. God moves with intention toward what is in the very core of His heart - redemption and restoration. His passion for people is global. He is still doing this all over the world and He will do it in your life. Your life fits in the cosmic puzzle that God is piecing together. You have a need for alignment to fulfill your assignment. Many times it is in an outpouring of God's power that people experience such a season (Kairos) of refreshing. When these times occur, they become memory stones in our lives of occasions when we know we have experienced God's presence and power in a life-changing way. These are occasions when God aligns our heart with what is on His heart. We have passion ignited, gifts stirred up, improved hearing and a stronger resolve to do the will of God. We begin to discover that the will of God for our lives becomes clearer and more defined for us.

One of the major points of this convergence has to do with reaching the unreached wherever they are. In a moment of encounter, God can capture a person's heart and it redirects their whole life. History reveals that this is how men and women have been consumed to reach a people in a place they have never been. Think about it! God moves on a person's heart and they become ignited with a passion for a people in a foreign land they have never seen. The heart becomes gripped by God and filled with a love for the unreached. It has happened so many times with world-changing results.

Lottie Moon is a well known missionary among Southern Baptists. On December 22, 1858, her heart was moved upon by God through the power of the Gospel. She ended up leaving behind her aristocratic way of life and spent 50 years ministering in China. One of her quotes demonstrates the passion that filled her heart. She said, "If I had a thousand lives, I would give them all for the women of China." This is what happens to a heart that is filled with the things that are on God's heart.

One of these great heart-gripping convergences happened to me on June 4, 1995. Oh yes, I still remember the exact date! At the time, I was a Baptist pastor in Sandnes, Norway. I was struggling, trying to find my way forward as a pastor, doing what I knew to do. I loved God. I read my Bible. I prayed. I loved the people. I had a burden for missions. As I look back, I realize that so much of what I did, I did to prove my love for God to the people or to prove my love for people to God. Gratefully for us all, God knows what we need and sets us up to get it.

It was during those days that I attended a conference in Halgesund, Norway at which a man by the name of Randy Clark would be ministering. News of how God was using this man had been buzzing through ministerial circles. I decided that I would slip in to the conference and check it out. God was putting a desire I could not even understand at the time in my heart and I was somewhat blindly stumbling toward it. I sat in the conference watching and listening. I was just Mr. Norwegian Nobody, slipping into a service with a hungry heart. I had no idea that life as I knew it was about to experience a huge change. It was Kairos time for Leif Hetland! Out of nowhere, Randy Clark summoned me to the front of the auditorium. With the comfort of the pew now behind me, I went forward, clueless as to what was about to transpire.

There before God and everyone else, he began to pray and prophesy over me. He began speaking of how I would be a bulldozer into some of the darkest places on earth and that there would be a multitude following where I went. He even used the word "Apostle" in regard to what God was going to do in my life. As he continued praying, an incredible flow of power began to course through my being. It was like wave after wave of electricity pulsating into the very core of my being. I was being overwhelmed by God's Spirit. My body crumbled under the weight of it all. I found myself lying on the floor in body, but internally I could see a bulldozer plowing through what I would describe as the jungles of the Amazon, clearing a path to get to people who were in the untouched areas. This experience was setting a course for my life. I could see and sense it. I was being Divinely stirred and resourced for my destiny (assignment). God imparted something to me that day during a two hour encounter with Him. Apart from the supernatural ministry of the Holy Spirit inside me that day, there is no explanation for what happened or the change that followed as a result of it.

Though I had slipped into the meeting, what God had planned was not to be hidden. The newspaper reported the conference the next day and the unusual events that took place. They even included a photograph of the meeting on the front page of the paper. Guess who was in the picture of Randy Clark praying for someone as they began falling to the ground? You got it - Mr. Norwegian Nobody. So much for sneaking away to a conference. There I was on the front page getting zapped by God. That newspaper photo is now in my office as a memory stone for me to remember the goodness of God. At the time, I honestly feared it would be evidence the enemy could use against me, since such things were not common or even desirable among many of my brethren. Now, however, it is seen as a powerful testimony of something life-changing God did for me.

The week after the conference with Randy Clark, I started experiencing the gifts of the Holy Spirit operating in my life. I could sense the supernatural presence of God with me in a tangible way. Something had changed. Something was different. At the time, I did not understand what was taking place. It was like I was awakening to a new environment. I now realize that I was experiencing the Kingdom of God. I was being prepared for the destiny God had for me. A new mantle had come upon me and I was learning how to wear it.

A few months after this shift, a Pastor from a Muslim nation came to visit the church I was pastoring. As he passionately shared about the great need for people in these nations to hear the Gospel and how dangerous it was to preach it, I felt my heart being connected to these unseen people who have never heard. It is hard to explain, but my soul was moved toward them. It was as if I could feel their pain and desperation. Please understand, I had been burdened for missions for a long time. I had been doing mission trips for a while. I knew about the need to get the Gospel to every nation, but this was another convergence of God's plan for my life. What I knew in my head about the Great Commission, now flooded my heart. Something else inside of me shifted. Inside of me was placed a desire with more power than the fear of death. I knew I had to go to these people in response to their heart cries, even if they did not really know what their hearts where crying for. This was the clarifying of God's assignment for me.

It was during this season of having my heart fueled with compassion for the unreached people groups of the world that the Scripture out of Psalm 2 became so life-giving to me.

*Ask of Me, and I will give You The nations for Your inheritance,
And the ends of the earth for Your possession (Psalm 2:8 NKJV).*

Up until this event, I had been looking at the nations as a problem we needed to resolve. God began to show me that they were a promise to be received. I often teach now on Islam: A Problem or A Promise? You see, through our position in Jesus Christ, the nations are a gift to be received. This created another paradigm shift for me. You cannot achieve a gift, you receive a gift! Trusting began to replace trying in my attitude toward the Great Commission. I decided, based on what God was revealing to me, that I would ask for God's grace to help me to stop performing for a promise. I started asking for the nations, understanding they were Jesus' inheritance as the Beloved Son of God. In Him, the nations are our inheritance as well. We go forth to receive the inheritance of our King Jesus among the nations.

Among us Baptists in those days, we had been learning from the teaching of Henry Blackaby that it was important to find out what God was doing and join Him in what He was doing, instead of asking Him to bless what we were doing. So my prayer life began to focus on getting God's heart for a people and discovering the ways that God was working or wanted to work among a particular people group. This became a key to unlock inheritance. It is His will, not our zeal, that makes the difference.

Not long thereafter, the first call came for me to go into the world of Islam. My heart became so burdened and filled with an indescribable love for the people of Ishmael. I said "YES," and as a result of that "YES" I found myself experiencing history and destiny colliding in my life; what God said He wanted to do in me and God was actually doing in me came together.

What difference did all this season of convergence make in my life? One year after it all started, I found myself in the middle of the 10/40 Window in one of the darkest nations where the enemy is working greatly to keep the light of the Gospel from shining. What was happening? Something I can say I have seen numerous times in numerous nations around the world, especially in the unreached areas of the world. Standing before tens of thousands of people who have never heard about Jesus, I saw thousands giving their lives to Jesus Christ. I saw crippled limbs healed, blind eyes opened and demonic shackles broken as the Gospel of Jesus Christ was proclaimed in demonstration and power. I heard a multitude saying an eternal "YES" to Jesus. My faith became sight through the grace of God and the power of His Holy Spirit.

Since that first journey into the places of darkness, I have seen over 750,000 people who have said "YES" to Jesus when He was preached to them. Most of these precious souls live within the 10/40 Window amongst people who have never heard a clear presentation of the Gospel of Jesus Christ. Many have never even heard of Jesus.

I do want to add at this juncture that what I share with you is to the glory of God and to demonstrate how He orchestrates and choreographs things in all our lives to see His purposes fulfilled on this earth. I have simply shared with you a few things that happened to me from my own perspective. The part we cannot see is the untold army of intercessors who are praying around the world for the Kingdom of God to come into Earth as it is in Heaven. Among these intercessors are people who pray for us all. I completely realize that the global prayer force was a strategic part of preparing circumstances that brought a life-changing convergence into my own personal life and so it is with yours as well. It is about the big picture, brothers and sisters. The inheritance for our Christ is huge and the fields are ripened unto harvest. He is praying, intercessors are praying and Father is answering those prayers. Workers are being called, equipped, and sent into the harvest field.

Let me share a particular story that took place on my first missions' trip to Pakistan in 1996. I had an incredible life-altering experience. As I looked out from the platform across a sea of faces, my heart was both stirred and troubled. Stirred by the hunger I saw in many faces and concerned by the hatred I saw in others. Among the audience were protestors angered by the fact that foreigners were proclaiming Christian beliefs in their city. But surrounding the minority of protestors was a massive crowd pressing in to hear about Jesus and His great love. The Gospel was preached in word and then it began to be demonstrated in power. For the first time, my own eyes saw miracles of God occurring in the crowd. Blind eyes were opened, deaf ears were opened and many other miracles were happening in the crowd.

One of them marks my memory very vividly. In the crowd was a paraplegic who was being carried by other men. His limbs were mere bones with a thin covering of skin. Suddenly, people started shouting and moving back away from the man. He had stood up and was supporting himself on two legs that had not functioned in years. As he stood there with trembling legs crying out in joy, the crowd around him erupted into a symphony of jubilation. The eyes of the collective crowd were exploding with amazement at what God had wrought. Other miracles began happening and waves of souls began to repent and give their hearts to Jesus. I was dumbfounded. I had believed in a great God of miracles, now my faith became sight. But there was one more thing that occurred in that first Pakistani Crusade that stands out even more.

At the conclusion of the service, a Pakistani woman came up to me. She had experienced a healing in her body, but more importantly she had experienced the grace of God's salvation through Jesus Christ. She did something that certainly could have landed her in trouble in her community; she lifted her veil in my presence. Why would she do such a thing? She wanted me to see the smile on her face. It is forever etched in my mind. She was aglow with the glory of God. She shared how she had been saved and healed. This radiant woman continued with her story and her questions. She shared how she had lost her father, her mother and a brother, as well as other friends and family. After she had heard about Jesus, she was greatly desiring that they had heard also. She asked me, "What will happen to them because they never heard this message?"

My heart was deeply moved by her words. Before I could begin a gentle answer to her question, she asked me, "How long have you known about this Jesus?" My mind stumbled with the answer as I told her that basically I had heard about him all my life growing up in Norway. We Norwegians were brought the gospel message over a thousand years ago. I shared that in America, where I live, everybody has the opportunity to hear about Jesus. When she realized that this message had been known by others for such a long time, she then asked a question that rocked my world and I am still shaken by it every time I think of it. She asked, "Why did you not tell me this before?"

Like this woman's family members, who died without ever hearing about Jesus, today 55,000 people around the world will die without ever hearing about Jesus. If we could hear the voices beyond the grave, I wonder if we would hear a huge multitude crying out, "Why did you not tell us?"

Our Willingness

We must humbly confess that more has not been done because the church has not been willing to do it. In the days when God was moving so greatly in the heart and life of J. Hudson Taylor, the great missionary to China, an event took place that demonstrates the willingness needed among people today to reach the unreached. One day J. Hudson Taylor received a visit from a Scottish school teacher by the name of George Scott. George Scott limped in on one leg and made it known that he wanted to go to China to be a missionary to reach the Chinese people. He was asked by Taylor, "Why do you want to go to China, when you only have one leg?" The humble man replied, "Because those with two legs aren't going." He was accepted and sent to China.

As we have all heard, it is our availability, not our ability that God is interested in. The operative word of Jesus' last mandate to the Church is "Go!" He has not changed his mind about our mission. We must all work together through praying and giving to help those who are actually doing the going.

I once heard a neat little preaching nugget that sums up the big picture concerning the mission of the Church:

The Lord went up!

The Spirit came down!

The church went out!

The sinners came in!

This little summation reveals the major challenge to today's church. It is the third line about the church going out. Just as Jesus said to His disciples that it was expedient for Him to go to the Father so that the Comforter could come, it is also expedient for the church to go out, so that the sinners will come into the family of God. There are still so many waiting for someone to come to them. They don't know that their heart hunger is to hear about Jesus, but we do!

I am so grateful for all the wonderful things that are happening globally in our day. The Holy Spirit is moving mightily. People's hearts are being stirred to go to the nations and claim Christ's inheritance. Advances are being made toward the fulfillment of the Great Commission, but there still remains much work to be done, especially in the darkest places on the Earth. Though the challenge is great, I am greatly encouraged. Why? Because:

Our Ascended Lord is still on the throne!

His powerful Holy Spirit continues to be poured out!

A new generation of believers are being filled with a passion to go out!

An unparalleled number of unbelievers are being birthed into the Kingdom of God!

Look Among the Nations

In one of the more obscure books of the Old Testament, the Prophet of God, Habakkuk, declared a prophetic promise that stirs my heart each time I hear it. It stirs me because it is such a bold and promising Word from God. He declared, "Look among the nations, and see; wonder and be astounded. For I am doing a work in your days that you would not believe if told" (Habakkuk 1:5 ESV). Later in Habakkuk 2:14 (ESV), an additional promise is heard from the Lord through Habakkuk:

> *For the earth will be filled with the knowledge of the glory of the Lord as the waters cover the sea.*

Our generation needs to realize that God is doing these same things in our day, though there is still much more work to be done in our generation. God is at work among the nations and His glory is being poured out. We only need to open our eyes to see and our ears to hear. The Spirit of God is inviting us to look and see what He is doing in our time and how we can participate with Him in reaching the unreached. He is doing a great work among the nations. Consider the following statistics:[1]

- There are 16,788 people groups in the world today.

- Unreached/least-reached ethnic people groups - 6,900.

- Christian radio broadcast covers approximate 81% of the world's population.

- There have been approximately 5.7 billion viewings of the Jesus Film and it is available in languages known by over 90% of the world.

- 4.6 billion people in the world have heard the Gospel message, while another 2 billion have still not had any Gospel message preached to them at all.

While enjoying a tasty fast food meal during your 60-minute lunch break, here's what took place on God's globe:

2,738	people died from starvation
342	people died from malaria
$2,088,751,996	personal income was earned by church members (0.01 percent of church members' income was given to reaching the unreached)
20	Christians were martyred

Is this prophetic promise from Habakkuk 2:14 for our time? Many would argue that prophecies of this sort should be put on the shelf to be claimed only in what Theologians call "the millennium." But I say they are promises we should claim now and that people are claiming now. God is intentional, purposeful and sovereign. Every generation is presented with the same promise. Our awesome Heavenly Father desires to astound us with His mighty works, which go beyond our ability to imagine. He loves to reveal His glory and nature among the nations. Are we willing to embrace this promise? He wants us to take part in this glorious endeavor. As His beloved children, His witnesses, we are called to walk in obedience to the Holy Spirit in declaring the Gospel of the Kingdom and proving of His Nature.

Jesus is the Desire of the nations. It is His nature to reveal Himself as the Desired One of all the peoples. In the unveiling of His Nature to every tribe, tongue and nation, He wants us to co-labor with Him. It's time that we rise up to testify of this truth and be the living witnesses, the extension of His Nature and the very proof of His superior Kingdom. He believes in us completely. He is convinced the Church can *finish the unfinished task* of reaching all the nations!

Many are looking, but not all are seeing the mighty works of God among the nations. There are so many reasons for this problem. The major one is our tendency to be caught up in our own little concerns and issues blocking our sight to what is God's Cosmic Agenda and heartbeat - His Kingdom demonstrated and expanding to all the nations.

He made a covenant with Abraham and said:

> *I will make you a great nation; I will bless you and make your name great; and you shall be a blessing. I will bless those who bless you, and I will curse him who curses you; and in you all the families of the earth shall be blessed (Genesis 12: 2, 3 NKJV).*

He has never forgotten this promise. He is intentional and He is in relentless pursuit of the 'Abrahams' of today who will say, "Yes, Lord, my friend, I believe in Your promise. I will go to the land and the people You will show me and be a witness of Your goodness to them."

In case we have forgotten the uniqueness of the time we are in, I want to inspire us that we are living in the most exciting time of the history of the Church. This generation is the only generation that could see the finish line. We are in the last of the last days and things are getting better and better! This is how the peace and the reign of the Kingdom of God expands through all the earth, from one level of glory to another.

> *Of the increase of His government and peace there will be no end, upon the throne of David and over His kingdom, to order it and establish it with judgment and justice from that time forward, even forever. The zeal of the Lord of hosts will perform this. - Isaiah 9:7 NIV*

No one will be able to stop the expansion of His Kingdom - His Government of Peace, among the nations.

The levels of understanding and the revelation that the Church corporately is now receiving and beginning to live in are just phenomenal. The depths of the corporate desperation in the hearts of His people for His manifest Presence, the subsequent and progressive unveiling of His glory, all of these are just mind-blowing and altogether overwhelming. We are undeniably hearing the sound of the abundant rain of the Holy Spirit coming about to flood the nations of the world.

There's a steadily rising tide of the move of the Spirit of God throughout the history of mankind, from the First Century Church up to this generation. This accumulated move of God has now, in our generation, become a "spiritual tsunami" in magnitude and power, a wave that's about to sweep the whole earth with God's glory. It is a great privilege to be standing on the threshold of the unfolding of these things. Around the world, God is moving and this space does not allow sharing even a small fraction of what He is doing. For example, just witness some of what is happening in Asia.

China, according to an article in the Pew Forum, now has over 130 million Christians.[2] Interestingly enough, this growth has come through small meetings in houses. Groups usually no larger than 25 people meet to worship and pray. In 1949, only 1% of the population were Christian when the communists took over. The Church in China has exploded. Though impoverished, the Chinese Church is filled with power.

In Asia, there are over 800 million people living on less than one dollar per day. Yet, it is among the Chinese where the "Back to Jerusalem" initiative is being acted upon by tens of millions of Chinese Christians who are praying and ignited by burden and desire to see the Muslim world brought to Christ. Large numbers of them are learning to speak Arabic and to teach the Bible in order to go to the descendents of Ishmael with the Gospel of Jesus Christ.[2]

The seed of the Gospel is powerful. Think of the nation of Mongolia. Just twenty years ago, there were only four known Christians who lived in Mongolia.[4] Today there are believed to be over 10,000 indigenous believers of Jesus Christ living there. People were made to hear the message we have been given to proclaim.

Here in the United States, people have heard so much so often that it seems "old hat." But for those who have never heard, it is like water to a man dying of thirst.

Around the world today God is orchestrating a mighty invasion of heaven on earth through the Church. We might not yet be fully aware of it now, but as the days unfold we will be hearing news of revival fires sweeping nations, cities and communities, transforming every aspect of society and the gathering of the end-time harvest in places where the strongholds of the enemy are situated. In regions of deepest darkness, the glory of God will shine through His Church.

The Unfinished Task

Yet, while we truly rejoice in what God is doing among those being saved, we cannot do so to the exclusion of those who have not yet heard. Yes, let's party and celebrate what God is doing. But let's remain committed, serious and prayerful about what He has called us to do. What we have done does not negate what we are to do.

The challenge to *finish the unfinished task* is still before us. Coca Cola has made it to the areas where the Church has not yet gone. Cell phones are bringing the messages of the world to the places where the message of the Gospel remains largely unheard. I do not write these things to discourage, but to awaken. This is our hour! We have never been presented with so much opportunity and so many resources to see the Gospel carried to every person in every nation.

Today, while most of us who are part of the renewal movement enjoy our spiritual renewal conferences, drive down the road listening to our favorite Bible teacher, or sit down to enjoy the latest best seller about the Holy Spirit, there are 55,000 people who will die in unreached people groups without ever hearing the Good News of the Gospel of Jesus Christ. Their lips, which were created to confess His name, go silent without ever hearing His name. They will be placed in their graves with knees that became calloused from bowing to other gods because they never heard about the True One. This grieves my heart and fuels my desire to see the Gospel carried to those who still have their hearing and can hear about Jesus and His great love.

Last year's grapes may already be in the bottle, but next year's wine is still in the field. The field with the most grapes perishing on the vines is called the 10/40 Window. Over 4.45 billion people live in this geographic window located between 10 and 40 degrees north of the equator. The Window forms a band encompassing Saharan and Northern Africa, as well as almost all of Asia (West Asia, Central Asia, South Asia, East Asia and much of Southeast Asia). Roughly two-thirds of the world population lives in the 10/40 Window.

The 10/40 Window is populated by people who are predominantly Muslim, Hindu, Buddhist, Animist, Jewish or Atheist. Many governments in the 10/40 Window are formally or informally opposed to Christian work of any kind within their borders.[5]

The term "10/40 Window," coined in 1990 by missionary strategist Luis Bush, holds the greatest populations of people yet to hear the Gospel.[6] In addition, 85% of the poorest of the poor in the entire world live in the 10/40 window. Over half of the cities of the world who are least evangelized are in this window of need. The socioeconomic conditions of this area and its borders sealed off from access to the Gospel, issue us a challenge to remember that Jesus said He was anointed by the Spirit of the Lord to "preach the Gospel to the poor" (Luke 4:18).

A question for we believers to ponder is this: "Is the current 1.25% of all missions giving that finally makes it to 10/40 window people groups the right appropriation of our missions giving?"[7]

Of course, I am Norwegian and we are not so bad at math. This giving percentage seems like really "bad" math to me. Sowing the least seed where there is the greatest need seems to be opposite of good strategy. Think of it this way. What if you were given the power and resources to build 100 new restaurants that would feed people free of charge day and night, with directions from the person funding the restaurants that you were to find the places with the most hungry people and build the restaurants there? One year later you meet with this benevolent individual and you show him the map and statistics of what you have done and how you used the funds that continued coming in. The individual looks over the map and stats and quickly sees that you only built two restaurants in the 100 most needy areas. The other 98 are in areas that did not make the top 100 list. Would you be given a "Well done, my good and faithful servant?" The answer is obvious, yet this is our current trend of giving to missions to *finish the unfinished task.*

Behind the desert curtain and the veil of Islam the descendents of Ishmael are crying out for water, as did their ancient grandfather, Ishmael and his mother Hagar, who were refreshed by the angel of the Lord as the Lord opened their eyes to see a well of water. The role of bringing water to them is upon us. The role of opening their eyes is still upon the Lord. Let's read the account of this again:

> *And she went and sat her down over against him a good way off, as it were a bow shot: for she said, "Let me not see the death of the child."*
>
> *And she sat over against him, and lift up her voice, and wept. And God heard the voice of the lad; and the angel of God called to Hagar out of heaven, and said unto her, "What aileth thee, Hagar? fear not; for God hath heard the voice of the lad where he is.*
>
> *Arise, lift up the lad, and hold him in thine hand; for I will make him a great nation." And God opened her eyes, and she saw a well of water; and she went, and filled the bottle with water, and gave the lad drink (Genesis 21:16-19 KJV).*

I find it interesting that the above passage points out that it was the voice of the lad that God heard. This little lad had the blood of Abraham coursing through his veins. Ishmael's descendents have indeed become a great nation. It is time for them to be called into the promises made to Abraham in Christ Jesus.

The desert curtain may seem unbreakable, but with the power of the Holy Spirit unleashed through the prayers of the people of God, He is still sending answers to the hearts of "Ishmael" who are crying out to Him. We must use everything at our disposal to get the Gospel to the unreached. The lingering message of our Ascended Christ is still, "Go into all the world and preach the Gospel to every creature" (Mark 16:15 NIV).

Technology allows us to do today what would have taken a lifetime not that long ago. Daniel said at the time of the end, travel would be accelerated and knowledge would be multiplied (Daniel 12). Not that long ago, messages from foreign countries were delivered by walking, riding a horse and sailing in a boat. Now we can instantly communicate with each other globally. As a matter of fact, many of our messages go out into space and then back to earth instantly. Anyone can fly half way around the world in a matter of hours. Our space shuttle astronauts orbit the entire earth in 90 minutes.[8] Think of it! There are human beings out there traveling completely around the earth in less time than it takes you to watch your favorite movie in a theatre. Compared to what Paul had to do to go to the nations, we have it made! We must use all means at our disposal to get the Gospel to the nations.

The promised consummation of history rests upon this Unfinished Task. Jesus said, "And this gospel of the kingdom will be preached in the whole world as a testimony to all nations, and then the end will come" (Matthew 24:14). Never before has there been such momentum for missions in the history of the church. The global surge of the Holy Spirit is undeniable. Although the prognosticators of doom and defeat are raising their voices to a decibel level that is almost deafening, the life changing power of the Gospel is advancing and gaining ground. The past two decades of human history are filled with the account of a tremendous outpouring of the Holy Spirit seen in the largest gatherings in the history of the world for corporate prayer, evangelistic meetings, and revival. Seemingly, the church world remains largely ignorant of these great advances. You may ask, "Where are these things of which you speak?" The simple answer is, "In the nations!" Prophetically, Messianically, and in Kingly language, as I mentioned earlier, the Psalmist declared:

> *The LORD has said to Me, "You are My Son, Today I have begotten You. Ask of Me, and I will give You the nations for Your inheritance, And the ends of the earth for Your possession. You shall break them with a rod of iron; You shall dash them to pieces like a potter's vessel" (Psalm 2:7-9 NKJV).*

It is the nations that King Jesus, God's beloved Son, is after. He will rule, reign and triumph over all His enemies. His message of grace carried by a Bride infused with His nature and Spirit, is presently heralding His claims on the people of the earth for whom He died.

Never has the Church done as much to reach people as she is doing today. Never have more people been reached than are being reached today. As the planet swells in population, the Church keeps advancing. She goes girded with the strength of God's mighty Spirit and fueled with the passion of her Bridegroom within her. Yet there is so much more potential than she has yet realized. It will be an astounding sight to witness and an awesome sound to hear, when she stands in the fullness of her destiny and gives that final push to usher in the end of the age. The peoples of the earth will give the fruit of praise and thanksgiving to the One Who gave His all for them. *Will You?*

Will you pray more than you have been praying for the unreached to be reached and the Unfinished Task to be Finished? Will you give more than you have been giving to bring the Gospel to the people who have never heard? And will you have the courage to go to one of these people groups and share Christ, if the Holy Spirit issues such a call to you? There is such a need for this level of courage.

In the mid 1800's, David Livingston, who was a Scottish medical missionary, made it his life's aim to penetrate the heart of

Africa, carrying the Gospel as he went. Ultimately, he was placed in his grave there. During this time, a missionary society wrote to David Livingstone and asked, "Have you found a good road to where you are? If so, we want to know how to send other men to join you." Livingstone wrote back, "If you have men who will come only if they know there is a good road, I don't want them. I want men who will come if there is no road at all."[9]

May our great God give us all courage to do all we can do to continue carrying the light of the glorious Gospel of Jesus Christ into the darkest places where people are dying to hear. By the grace of God, we will *finish the unfinished task*!

Endnotes

[1] www.joshuaproject.net

[2] "The pew forum on religion & public life." http://pewforum.org/Topic/Religious-Affiliation/Christian/?filter tax = 118&filter date=all&filter add=0.

[3] (http://www.slideshare.net/chrisdat/global-church-today-gerald-wheaton-presentation).

[4] Howard Culbertson. "Christian Missions: A church for every people and the gospel for every person," http://home.snu.edu/~HBULBERT/.

[5] "What is the 10/40 window?" http://www.joshuaproject.net/10-40-window.php.

[6] Luis Bush. "The Challenge Before Us," http://www.lausanne.org/documents/lau2docs/058.pdf.

[7] Howard Culbertson. "Christian Missions: A church for every people and the gospel for every person," http://home.snu.edu/~HBULBERT/.

[8] www.nasa.gov.

[9] David Livingstone. *Missionary Travels and Researches in South Africa* (Keffmann Press, 2010).

Chapter 3
THE BIBLICAL BASIS
FOR WORLD MISSIONS, PART 1

" *An understanding of missions must be grounded in scripture, since our desire to bring all people into reconciliation with God springs from the same desire in His heart. The story of God's redemptive mission begins in the Old Testament. Here we learn of God's original intentions for human beings and of His plan to restore their relationship with Him, now broken through sin. We also discover the significance of Israel as God's chosen people, the vehicle to bring the blessing of redemption to the world.* "

- Bill Jackson

The Old Testament

Introduction

It seems like a century ago when I heard Dr. Christie Wilson, former missionary to Afghanistan, do a lecture on Matthew's account of the Great Commission. He pointed out that when Jesus told His apostles to "disciple all the nations" the word "nations" actually means "people groups," those who share a common ethnic, cultural and linguistic heritage. He quoted Jesus' words, "When this gospel of the kingdom is preached as a witness in every 'nation' the end will come" (Mt 24:14). Suddenly, he had my attention. The world mission of the church was tied to the end of the world! But he wasn't done yet. He then asked, "If we are to reach every people group with the gospel of the kingdom, how many groups are there and where do they live?" I sat up. Here was something tangible, something with Velcro® on it. Who were they and where did they live? I wanted to know so I could go!

As if he knew what was on my mind, he said that research on people groups was only in its infancy (this was 1981). I was now dismayed. It had been 2,000 years and people group research had only just begun? Of the 23,000 ethnolinguistic groups estimated at the time, Christian missionaries had only penetrated 5,000 groups to date. 5,000 groups? The math was simple. Almost 17,000 people groups had never heard that Jesus had come! That couldn't be. I'd thought the Great Commission was on the downslide.

Everyone else left the lecture hall, but I couldn't move. I wasn't able to wrap my brain around what I had just heard. What I didn't realize was that I wasn't the only one in my generation hearing these statistics. They became a piece of grit in our souls and initiated a world Christian movement that has reached more groups in twenty-five years than in all of church history combined. The website, www.joshuaproject.net, now lists the total groups at 16,349 with 6,644 groups unreached, leaving us with the job 40% yet unfinished.

The last bastion of unreached groups lies within the "10/40 Window" that makes up the Middle East and Asia, the most dangerous places on earth for authentic followers of Jesus. For such a time as this

God is now speaking to this generation. I believe that he will raise many of you up in a tsunami of the Holy Spirit to carry His story to the ends of the earth - and some of you will die. But as Jim Elliot, the famous missionary martyr from my parent's era, once said, "He is no fool who gives what he cannot keep to gain what he cannot lose." Jim found a story worth dying for and we did too. What this story is I pass on to you because it's your turn now.

In the Beginning…

In the beginning Elohim, God, created "out of nothing" everything that existed - and He did it simply by speaking (Gen 1:1-2). He was showing that He was infinitely more powerful than the other "gods" of the Ancient Near East. To make a mockery of the battle imagery basic to pagan cosmology, the text says that the Spirit (the word "spirit" means "breath" or "wind") of God was "hovering" (bird imagery) over the waters and, out of the Spirit, God simply spoke (thus "breathed") over "the deep," the supposed realm of evil powers, and spoke light into being. He then proceeded to create the earthly forms and fill them with life. These He called "good" (Gen chapters 1-3). The pinnacle was God's creation of Humankind as male and female, Adam and Eve. The Bible says that they were created in God's very image, living pictographs of the godhead. Now the text said it was "very good" (Gen 1:31).

God set Adam and Eve in a garden in a land called Eden (Gen 2:8). Here they walked with God and tended the garden with Him. This garden is a picture of the first temple with the garden as the "inner chamber" where God's Presence was available to His people. Adam essentially functioned as the first king and priest ministering before God and serving Him. Later, the same Hebrew word for "tend" is used by the priests ministering before God in Israel's temple.[1] The text makes two assumptions about Adam and Eve: 1) they had a right vertical relationship with God because they walked and worked with him every day and 2) they had a right horizontal relationship with one another as they were naked and not ashamed (Gen 2:25). On this foundation of a right, vertical relationship with God and a right, horizontal relationship with one another, God gave them three assignments: 1) to multiply his image through child-bearing, 2) to fill the earth with that image, and 3) to rule the earth as God's ambassadors (Gen 1:28). To ensure their success God "blessed them." We don't know what this blessing was but later in the story God's blessing was mediated through the impartation of the Holy Spirit.

The text doesn't tell us why God did all of this, creating the universe and the world and human beings to reproduce until He could see a reflection of Himself as He looked down on the earth. Later the prophets would say that when all is said and done the knowledge of the glory of the Lord would cover the earth as the waters cover the sea (Hab 2:14). The Bible is very clear that God does everything for His glory but is not remiss or arrogant in any way (Rev 4:11). This must imply that there is no other being in the universe with whom to be more delighted, so it is only right that God should do all for His glory and revel in those human beings that worship Him. The New Testament will show that Jesus is the eternal reflection of the Father, preexistent with Him (Jn 1:1; Col 1:17). It is Jesus who will not only correct the problem of sin, which we will see entering into the story very soon, but also show us the Father (Jn 14:9). The Spirit of God, then, seems to reflect the power that the Father and Son have for one another. From this New Testament perspective we could surmise that God created the world that it might reflect Him and multiply His Trinitarian joy.

As we jump back into our story we remember that Adam and Eve, on the foundation of the two assumptions, were given a blessing to fulfill the three assignments: to multiply God's image, fill the earth with it (and so multiply God's joy) and rule the earth as "Kings and Queens of Narnia." In essence, they were to expand the borders of the Garden of Eden until it filled the whole earth. One might call this great work the Eden Project. In the garden, they were at perfect rest because every one of their needs was met perfectly in God and this rest was to span the globe. As David would later write, "He makes me lie down in green pasture" (Ps 23:2). Now here was a purpose for the ages! God was so sure that the Eden Project would be completed that He Himself sat down to rest. He would not need to create another thing (Gen 2:1-4).

After God's rest, however, came man's test. Satan, in the form of a serpent, visited Adam and Eve and tempted them to attempt to carrying out the Project on their own, without God. It didn't work and Humankind - as well as the Project - fell into the deep darkness of sin. God said that because they had asserted their independence, Adam and Eve would surely die, just as a branch dies (Gen 2:17; 3:3) when broken from the vine. Was God's plan now null and void? Would He need to get up from His rest? No! The same God who had created out of nothing had the capability to satisfy His justice by issuing the death penalty to man but then raise man back to life. Bringing life out of death…this is how God would solve what appeared to be an impossible dilemma. The Project could be completed after all!

But wait - the man and the woman didn't die for their sin. God substituted the death of animals for them and used the skins of those substitutes to cover their nakedness (Gen 3:21). Furthermore, God told the woman that she would have a male child who, though incurring a wound in battle, would crush the serpent's head and destroy his works. As a sign that he was a vanquished foe the serpent would slither on its belly all its days. God said that He would put enmity, or war, between the seed of the woman and the seed of the serpent (Gen 3:15). The storyline of the Bible traces the war between these two seeds and, despite all Satan's attempts to stop the Eden Project, God's purpose would prevail because, as Creator, God spoke everything that exists into being and, as King, rules over His realm.

How the World Got the Way It Is

Humankind, however, would from this point forward become a mixture of digity and depravity because of the power of sin; dignity as those created in God's image have capacity for great beauty and creativity, and depravity because the default nature of men and women would now be rebellion and sin resulting in, to quote Robert Burns, "man's inhumanity to man."[2] Indeed, of the first two sons born to Adam and Eve, Cain murdered his brother Abel and it had only just begun (Gen 4:8).

Genesis 6 begins with the most agonizing description of the results of sin anywhere in the Bible. It was so powerful that, despite advances in population and culture, the writer says of the people in that era, "...*every inclination of the thoughts of their hearts was only on evil all the time* (italics mine). The Lord was grieved that he had made man on the earth and His heart was filled with pain" (Gen 6:6). The same righteous God who had been true to His character and judged sin in the garden stood once again against sin. How patient is our God! Brought to the brink, God's wrath finally spilled over in a reenactment of the return of the earth to darkness and the waters of chaos at Creation. It rained for forty days and forty nights, so long that the whole earth was covered with water once again (Gen 7:12).

To preserve the seed, however, God's grace saved a man named Noah and his family (Gen 6:8-10). Just as the man and the woman had been kept from judgment and their nakedness covered, so now Noah was protected from certain death and shut into the ark by the Lord as it rained for forty days and forty nights. As the waters receded, God reiterated the same commands to Noah that He had given to Adam. Noah's loosing of a dove to search for dry land depicts the dawning of a new creation (note the connection between the bird and new creation, an allusion to Gen 1) and Noah and his seed proceeded to repopulate the earth, albeit now multiplying a fractured image that defaulted to sin despite amazing potential for creativity (Gen 6:8-9:7).

To preserve His plan, God made a covenant to never destroy the earth with a flood again. God, who is light, put a "bow" in the sky as if to say that He had set His war bow on His heavenly mantle (Gen 9:8-17). We can still see the colors of His light after a rain, reminding us that God will bring the Eden Project to completion. This is the first of seven covenants in the Bible. Each covenant reflects the way that God deals with human sin step by step. Since the Creation sequence took seven days, the number seven is the number of completion or perfection in the Bible. That there are seven covenants means that God's plan will perfectly deal with sin, thus removing the barrier that keeps humans from knowing God and fulfilling our destiny as image-bearers and kingdom ambassadors who will complete the Eden Project.

As we return to our story, we now find that Humankind has settled in one place, rather than scattering throughout the earth as God had commanded. Speaking the same language, they sought to make a name for themselves, rather than for the Creator, and defiantly began to build a tower so high it seemed to reach the heavens (Gen 11:1-4). Strangely, they covered the tower in waterproof pitch, probably as flood insurance - they weren't buying the sign of the rainbow in the sky! The Eden Project had now been rejected for the Asphalt Project and the people built their urban jungle ever higher.

God knew that if they continued in their rebellion it would be almost impossible to reach them. To prevent this, He caused them to speak different languages so they couldn't communicate. This, of course, put an instant stop to the tower. That place came to be called "babel," the Hebrew word for "confusion" (Gen 11:5-9).[3] The Asphalt Project would ultimately fail and is depicted in the book of Revelation in the fall of the great city of "Babylon" (Rome), the writer, John's metaphor for the fall of Satan's typological system of evil and ultimately a picture of the crushing of the serpent's head (Rev 12).

Speaking different languages, the people were forced to migrate outward in their nations, their clans and their languages to the lands God had established for them. The reader might be wondering how the Eden Project would ever be completed with the world now divided the way it was, each national group standing as racists and thinking that their cultural standards and language were at the center of God's world. They seemed farther from God's purpose than ever, but God had a plan that nothing could stop.

Blessed to Be a Blessing

God then appeared to a man named Abram, a seemingly random face from among the arrogant and racist peoples of the earth. God told Abram to leave his land and people and migrate to the place that God would show him. If he did this, then God would bless him and give him a great name (remember that the Asphalt Project people were attempting to make a name for themselves). God would cause Abram to multiply into so many descendants they would outnumber the stars of the sky. Not only this, but every clan on the earth would be blessed with Abram's blessing (Gen 12:1-3). Now, at last, the reader discovers why God broke the world up into different language groups. He took a large, seemingly impossible task and broke it into smaller tasks. Abram and his seed would become God's people for the sake of the world, the puzzle piece that would tie the Eden Project together.

After God had built Abram into a people He would later commission them to go to another people to extend the image and kingdom of God. From there God would raise up others to go out from that people, and so on. The Old Testament is clear that the Gentiles had always been intended to be a part of the Project team (Isa 42:5-9), even though their full inclusion would await a Jewish missionary by the name of Paul. To a people, through a people, from a people - that was the plan. In the Old Testament the clans would come to Zion to find God, while in the New Testament God's people would go out from Zion until the knowledge of the glory of the Lord covered the earth as the waters cover the sea (Hab 2:14).

At the heart of the mission was the dissemination of the divine Word about how God was going to deal with the problem of sin that would remove the barrier between God and men and restore the Eden Project: remove and restore - that's where things were headed. The removal of sin would center on the male child who would pay for man's sin and be raised from the dead because only God had the ability to create out of nothing. With sin removed, the Project would be back in play and its restoration would be energized by a new impartation of the Holy Spirit. With the seemingly impossible task broken down into smaller, more doable tasks, God's people would go to a people, through a people and from a people until all the clans on earth could join in being God's image and taking dominion over the earth. As God said through Isaiah, "For my own sake, for my own sake I do this...I will not yield my glory to another" (Isa 48:11). God would be glorified. The prospect of the finished Project is so breathtaking that it is the only vision worth giving one's life to. With the Project's foundation laid, let's pick the story up a bit and follow the story of those who understood what it meant that humans were "crowned with glory and honor" and gave their lives to reach out to apprehend the future by faith (Ps 8:5).

The cast in Genesis foreshadows the world mission of the church by portraying over fifty different nations interacting with the people entrusted with the Project. There was one problem, however - Abram and his wife, Sarai, were barren (Gen 15:2). God told Abram that if he would take the name "Abraham" (father of nations) by faith (Gen 17:1-8), the couple would have a child in their old age. Abram believed God and God credited it to his account as righteousness (Gen 15:6). From that time on, Abram was called Abraham and Sarai was called Sarah (princess) (Gen 17:15-16). They were now royalty, typological king and queen of a new nation that would be known in history as the Jews, or Israel. In their faith, Abraham and Sarah did have a child in their old age, when their bodies were "as good as dead" (Rom 4), and they called the child of the promise "Isaac" (laughter) because nothing could stop them from siring a progeny that would outnumber the stars of the sky, as God had promised (Gen 21:1-7). The seed would transfer from generation to generation against all odds, from Adam to Noah to Abram to Isaac, and now to Jacob. Jacob would then pass the blessing to his son, Judah. At the end of his life Jacob prophesied that out of Judah's seed would come a king whose rule would never end. He would be a lion of a man, the Lion of the tribe of Judah (Gen 49:8-12).

The Exodus: the Salvation Paradigm

Driven to Egypt by a famine, God rescued the twelve sons of Jacob and their families from sure extinction through Jacob's son, Joseph, whom his brothers had sold into slavery out of jealousy (Gen 42, 47). God, however, raised him up from his lowly position to sit at the right hand of Pharaoh himself (Gen 39, 41). In this way, God preserved Jacob's seed for the sake of the Project. After Joseph died, the Pharaohs to come forgot Joseph (Ex 1:8) and the sons of Jacob and they became slaves for four hundred years (Ex 12:40-41). When it couldn't get any worse, God's people cried to the god of their ancestors for deliverance (Ex 2:23). The Bible says God "remembered" His covenant with Abraham, Isaac and Jacob, whose name God had changed to "Israel," meaning "struggles with God" (Ex 2:24-25). From this point forward God's people would be known as Israel and the ways of God would be a constant struggle for them. Isaiah would later say, "For my thoughts are not your thoughts, neither are your ways my ways" (Is 55:8). The foundation had been laid. It was time to redeem the sons of Israel and form them into the missionary people for the world.

We see in the exodus a picture of God coming to rescue humanity from slavery, typifying our bondage of sin. How did He do it? He raised up a deliverer, a type of Christ, to issue a series of ten plagues, each one a defeat of one of the Egyptian gods. The only reason that Israel was not judged by God along with the Egyptians - for they were just as sinful since they were human - was that they trusted in God's provision of a sacrificial animal slain on their behalf. For any, Israelite and Egyptian included, that put the

74

blood of the sacrifice on the doorposts of their house; when God's death angel visited the firstborn sons of the land that night, they would not be touched (Ex 11-12). Not even the son of Pharaoh was a god. In this tenth and final plague, God was declaring victory over all the cosmic powers. God alone was King!

As a picture that they were not to linger in the land of sin and slavery for one more second, they ate what would come to be known as the Passover. It was a meal with unleavened bread, since there was no time to let it rise, and with their staffs in hand, their shoes on, and their cloaks girdled up so they could run, run away from sin and slavery toward the divine Presence lost in the Garden. When the morning came there was wailing for the firstborn sons of Egypt and Pharaoh finally relented and gave Moses permission to follow his god out of Egypt. Israel went up with a "mixed multitude." Many of the Egyptians had been convinced by the "signs and wonders" of Israel's god and came to believe that he was God (Ex:11-12). To go up out of Egypt with their former slaves suddenly became the smartest thing to do! From Israel's inception as a nation, then, we see God's people fulfilling their missionary calling to be a blessing to the nations; the true Israel, then, has never been an issue of racial heritage but of faith.

As if to make it doubly obvious that it was God who was redeeming them from Egypt, he brought Israel to the edge of the Red Sea with no place to go. We are taken right back to the opening verses of Genesis, where the deep represented chaos, the alleged realm of evil. Once again, God sent His breath and blew back the waters so His people could walk "through the valley of the shadow of death" to a "table prepared before them in the presence of their enemies" (Ps 23:4- 5). When they passed through the waters up on to dry land, Pharaoh, having now come to his senses, realized that he had just let his entire labor force go and presumptuously tried to follow them into the deep. But once again God drew upon the ancient battle motif and released the waters simply by withholding His breath and swallowed those who dared to curse Israel (Ex 14:5-31). The Israelites rejoiced at God's just judgment and sang from the opposite shore, "the horse and rider fell into the sea" (Ex

15:1). It was then that they finally saw it. Yahweh had just defeated every foe. Yahweh, the God who was "ever present for them" (the probable meaning of the Hebrew consonants YHWH) was also Elohim, the Creator (the name for God in Gen 1), King over the entire universe! In the first explicit reference to the Kingship of Yahweh, the mixed multitude declared, "Yahweh will reign forever and ever (Ex 15:18).

God brought the people He had created and redeemed to Mt. Sinai (Ex 19), the mountain of His Presence and a type of the Garden of Eden. This time there was no walking with Adam in the cool of the day. The shroud of sin was over the earth and the new Adam, the Prophet Moses, had to climb up to find God amidst thunder and lightning and thick darkness (Ex 19:16-19). The people stayed at a distance, weak at the knees, while God gave Israel her formal missionary call. God had brought them to Himself on eagle's wings and they, among all the peoples of the earth, were to be His treasured possession (Ex 19:4-6). They would have a regal calling - to be a kingdom of priests that would mediate between God and the other clans to bring them the news of God's substitutionary sacrifice in fulfillment of the promise to Abraham. They would also be a holy people that would model for the rest what it looked like to be the image of and rule for God, and to reflect back to Him the joy of His own glory.

To get them ready for their mission, God gave them a field manual called the Law that gave explicit instructions about how to approach Him in the proper manner through the administration of a system of substitutionary sacrifices. The blood of bulls and goats would point to the male child who would one day come as the final sacrifice and crush Satan's head. The manual taught them how the people of God ought to treat one another with love within their cultural context. What it would look like to image God would need to be contextualized as cultures changed, but the law of love would always be the rule. On that foundation the people of God were to expand the borders of the beatific garden into the weed patches of the earth. That was their mission. It is also ours as the new Israel of God, for the job has yet to be completed.

Most amazing of all was that even though God was King over the universe, He left His celestial home to live among His people and lead them forth into the Project. He would also show them how to fight with light and not with swords. God would lead His people from a humble, earthly palace, a mobile mission tent called the Tabernacle. He presided over the universe from His throne room, the inner chamber called the Most Holy Place. The throne on which He "sat" (later they said it was His footstool) was a box made of acacia wood and covered in gold. Inside the box was the field manual and God would preside over Israel's fidelity to its prescriptions (Ex 25-27).

Disciplinary "curses" would come to those who failed to represent God's image before the nations. Through the sting of those curses it was hoped that those who lacked faith would come to their senses. For those who trusted God and continued to herald the fame of God's name, there would be a continual flow of individual blessings (as exemplified by the book of Proverbs) even though the nation could incur God's discipline for collective disobedience. Those who served God in leadership were given impartations of the Spirit of God to ensure their success. Once, as Moses' leaders prophesied under the power of the Spirit, Moses saw this as a picture of what God wanted for all His people. He "wished" that one day all Israel would prophesy under the power of the Spirit (Num 11:16-29). They would have to wait a long time for this to come true, but it would.

One of the pressing questions for the generation that had come out of Egypt had to do with where they were going and whether there would be any rain when they got there. Egypt had a predictable rainy season with an annual overflow of the Nile that fertilized the delta. The abundance of food was seldom in question. Would their future home have the same certainties? To assure His people God promised to send them to a land overflowing with "milk and honey" that would have two rainy seasons each year (Ex 3:17). The first would be in the fall and would be enough to cause the newly planted seeds of the grain harvest to germinate. The last one - a greater rain - would be in the spring and would bring the harvest to fruition. These would prove to be important promises because other nations would attempt to persuade the Israelites that only their gods could be trusted for rain, especially during periods when God was testing His people with one of His disciplinary curses in the form of droughts (Dt 11:13-17). But as to who would provide for Israel? The God of Israel, Yahweh, was none other than Elohim. It was no contest.

The New Eden

All was now set. God had created a people for Himself and had defeated the gods that had held them captive through the mediating, prophetic ministry of one from the seed of Abraham. Death had passed by God's people through the provision of a substitutionary sacrifice. Then God had resurrected them from certain death on eagle's wings to the mountain of His Presence. There He had commissioned them to bear His image to the nations and set up His palace from which He would rule and lead His people. But to where?

God was going to carve out for Israel a new garden from among the weed patches of the earth, a land called Canaan that would later be called Israel. In this garden God would grow a kind of hybrid seed that would be so hearty it would be able to take root in any of the hostile soils of the earth. The Promised Land, then, was a practice run for the Eden Project. As a sign to them of the land's potential, God had Israel send twelve spies into the land, one for each of the twelve tribes of Jacob. Their job was to scope out the land's bounty from top to bottom and to get a look at those clans that would oppose them. The spies came back to a waiting Israel with huge clusters of grapes and wild honey (Num 13). In a sense, God's people had gone into their future and brought the future back into their present. Later, Jesus would tell His people to pray that this experience would be a regular occurrence when He taught them to pray, "Let your kingdom come on earth as it is in heaven" (Mt 6:10). Before taking possession of cities they had not built and eating of flocks and fields not their own, God would

78

first use His people to pronounce judgment on one of the more persistent Asphalt Projects on the earth. Like those who had been building the tower, these men and woman, called the Canaanites, were like a cancer on the earth and would need to be stopped. If their Project were left unattended, "almost nothing would be impossible for them" (Gen 11:6). Just prior to taking the first city in the new Eden, the Israeli general, Joshua (yeshua in Hebrew, meaning "salvation"), had an encounter with "a man" with a drawn sword. Joshua, no doubt with his hand on his scabbard and his knees squared for battle, wanted to know if the soldier was for Israel or against them. The man identified himself. Here, before Joshua, stood the commander of the armies of the Lord! While the text does not identify who the commander is, we most certainly have here a pre-incarnate appearance of Jesus, "Jesus' is Greek for yeshua and it appears that the Pre-incarnate One wanted to remind His forerunner that Israel had been chosen for the sake of the world. In response to Joshua's question as to whether the angel was for or against Israel, the reply was "neither" (Jos 5:13-15). All that God had been doing with Israel had always been for the world; the blessing given to Abram had been for all the clans of the earth. As God would later say through Amos in order to keep Israel from having a higher estimation of herself than she ought:

> *"Are you Israelites not the same to me as the Cushites?" says the Lord. Did I not bring Israel up from Egypt, the Philistines up from Caphtor, and the Arameans from Kir? (Amos 9:7)*

Israel was not God's treasured possession because she was loved more. She was God's treasured possession because one nation had to be first; Israel's honor is the privilege of place in the Project, not her intrinsic purity. She was never to lose this perspective lest she herself be caught in the clutches of racism and find her fig tree barren of a harvest among the nations at the time of the male child's visitation.

In issuing God's just judgment against the people of the Canaanite's Asphalt Project, God's heart was just as filled with pain as at the time of Noah. To bring the point home, God had Israel renew her commitment to the instructions in the field manual before taking Jericho. God went first into another mock battle, as at Creation, presiding over His people from His mobile throne. Israel followed in worship and the walls of the first Asphalt city came a tumblin' down (Jos 6). The next stage of the Eden Project had begun.

In telling the Old Testament story, a major mistake is often made at this point. It is assumed that at the time of the occupation the new Eden had been secured when the book of Joshua comes to a close. Nothing could be further from the truth. In reality, Israel had only entered Canaan and divvied up the land allotments for the twelve tribes. Unfortunately, God's just judgment on the Asphalt people had only just begun. Throughout the period of the Judges, Israel lived side-by-side with these people and did not press in to finish the occupation. God's Project, therefore, was on hold. The story awaited a true leader who would trust God fully and finish the judgment to secure the borders of the land. Only then could God's plan for the world move forward. Despite a number of judges that had been filled with the Holy Spirit, it seemed like God's true leader would never arise. The book of Judges closes with everyone doing what was right in their own eyes (Jdg 21:25). Every man was looking out for himself, a foundational mentality of the Asphalt Project! No wonder God's people were not finishing the occupation.

As we come into the time of the last judge, a prophet named Samuel, it is clear that God is perfectly capable of leading His people as King. He alone defeats the Philistines and their god, Dagon, shatters before the throne of God's Presence that had been captured and brought into their Asphalt Project temple (1 Sam 5:2). It also seems that God could lead His people through a human if He chose to do. The reader of the book of Samuel now witnesses another defeat of the Philistines as Samuel obeys God's instructions perfectly, just as Joshua had done at Jericho. It comes as a complete shock, then, when the people of Israel ask Samuel to anoint a human king "to be like the other nations" (1 Sam 8:5). To be like the other nations? Israel had completely forgotten who they were and what they were supposed to be doing! They were the people of God, chosen for the sake of the world, and finishing the occupation and securing the borders of the land was necessary for God to cultivate the new Eden with its hybrid seeds that would take root and grow among the hostile soils of the earth. Jesus would later say that, at the end of the age, He would separate the wheat from the chaff and the wheat would be gathered to eternal life while the chaff would be burned and destroyed forever (Matt 13:24-30). Under His sovereign and mysterious purposes God gave Israel the kind of human king they were looking for. God instructed Samuel to anoint a tall, impressive man by the name of Saul as Israel's first, human king. While Saul was impressive on the outside, he was insecure and full of himself on the inside, even to the point of building a monument in his image (1Sam 9-10). His was the DNA of the Asphalt Project. The reader wonders when another prototypical male child would be raised up, like Moses, who would understand who Israel was in the world and who would put the fame of God's name first? It was now! Samuel anointed the last of the sons of a man named Jesse, a shepherd boy by the name of David, to be the next king of Israel (1Sam 16).

The Davidic King

After his anointing by the Spirit, David was introduced to Israel as he brought supplies to his brothers, who were fighting in Saul's army. The Israelites were defending the valley of Elah, a key valley for the protection of the high country. Above lay a Canaanite city known as Jebus. For forty days, the biblical number of testing, the Philistine champion, Goliath, taunted the armies of Israel. As David assessed the scene, he realized that Goliath stood as a type of those among the nations of the Asphalt Project that would curse Israel, just as God had predicted in His initial encounter with Abram. Dressed in his scaled armor, Goliath also had the appearance of that serpent of old, Satan, who had defied the very person of God. Taking it all in, David must have had a moment of revelation - God would curse those who defied the armies of the living God. Drawing upon the weapon of a shepherd, David felled

Goliath with one smooth stone from his sling. Just as the horse and rider had fallen into the sea, Goliath fell before David. Cutting off Goliath's head with his own sword as a prophetic picture of the child who would one day crush the serpent's head, David then did an interesting thing with Goliath's head. The text says that he brought it outside the gates of the city Jebus crested on the hills above. What did he do with it? The ancient writer doesn't tell us (1 Sam17). What we do know is that later, when David reigned as king, he issued God's just judgment on the Canaanites in Jebus and chose their city as his capital. He renamed it Jerusalem, the city of Peace (2 Sam 5). Later, called Zion, it became not only David's capital, but the city of God's Presence in the land of the new Eden.

It was David, then, a man after God's own heart (1 Sam 14:14), who obeyed God by faith and finished the occupation. In typical Ancient Near East fashion, the conquering king wanted to build his god a temple in which to rest, the animal skins of the traveling war tent having no doubt disintegrated long ago. As David brought the Ark of God into Jerusalem, he put on priestly garments and danced before the Lord (2 Sam 6:14). In doing so, he was typologically another king and priest as Adam had been.

Through the prophet, Nathan, however, God told David that it was not he, David, who would build a house for God but God who would build a house for David. God would establish David's family line forever. It was not David, therefore, who would build the temple but a son of David (1 Chr 17). David's job had been to finish God's judgment against the people of the Canaanite Asphalt Project and to secure the borders of the land. The son of David who would build the temple would be a man of a different calling. He would be a man of peace. As a sign of His amazing grace, God chose Solomon to be king, the son of David's tragic relationship with his wife Bathsheba (2 Sam 11). The name "Solomon" is derived from the Hebrew word shalom. Shalom refers to the full experience of the Eden Project, the kingdom of God.

The traveling war tent would now give way to an edifice that was not more worthy, but more appropriate to Israel's new circumstances. It was time for God to teach His people how to tend the new garden in preparation for the day when they would go throughout the earth preparing the soil and planting the hybrid seed. God would now preside over the Project from the temple that Solomon would build on Mt. Zion. As always, He would judge Israel according to her fidelity to the field manual and her progress toward the goal of making God's name famous among the nations of the earth.

In the first ten chapters of the book of 1 Kings, we see that all that God had planned seems to come to fulfillment. Solomon, the son of David, was established as king and built the temple. The structure was so magnificent that it was considered, along with Solomon's gardens (note the garden motif), as one of the seven wonders of the ancient world. Functioning as a picture of the abundance of Solomon's kingdom, 1 Kings 4 describes what life in the new Eden was like. The text says of God's people that, "they ate, they drank, and they were happy" (1 Kgs 4:20). Furthermore, it says that "each man had his own vine and fig tree" (1 Kgs 4:25). As a nation, Israel also had peace on every side.

But it wasn't just the nation. Solomon himself had an immense deposit of the Kingdom upon him. He was a prolific songwriter and a skilled scientist, researching everything from biology to zoology to botany (1Kgs 4:29-34). His daily table was so immense that it is almost cartoonish to read about. Each day, thousands of loaves of bread were eaten and hundreds of animals consumed (1 Kgs 4:22-23) in what was certainly the most choreographed kitchen in the history of the world. All of it was a picture of life in the Eden Project. From this point on, the banquet motif would stand for the ingress of the kingdom of God and prefigure the great kingdom banquet at the end of the age when the Eden Project would be completed and God's Presence would become all in all. The Passover meal foreshadowed this great meal and Jesus would use it as the Last Supper, redefining its symbols in light of His own body and blood that would be shed for all.

With everything working on all cylinders, the reader is not surprised when, in 1 Kings 10, the Queen of Sheba in North Africa visits Israel because she has heard of God's fame. The writer tells us that she is so overwhelmed with the God of Israel that she put her trust in Him (1 Kgs 10:6-9). One might now expect that the nations would begin streaming to Zion, but that didn't happen. The Asphalt Project had crept in and threatened to destroy the new Eden.

In Deuteronomy 17, Moses had prophesied that one day there would come a generation in Israel that would want a human king. When they did, Moses listed the kinds of characteristics that such a king should have. He mentions that the king should not build a big military, lest the nations get the wrong idea about Israel. Nor should he have a large harem, lest his wives cause his heart to stray from God. Neither was he to accumulate large amounts of silver and gold with all the traps along that path. Interwoven into the description of Solomon's immeasurable kingdom in 1 Kings 4 is, unfortunately, the mention of exactly these kinds of things. The text says that Solomon had many chariots. Modern archaeologists' uncovering Solomon's stables attests to how many horses he had to drive them. Israel was primarily hill country. Chariots, on the other hand, were the tanks of ancient warfare and were fit for offensive strikes on flat ground. Solomon should have been witnessing to the nations, but instead he embittered them by subjugating them for taxation to build up his wealth. And, just as Moses had predicted, Solomon's 300 wives and 700 concubines swept his heart away from God (1 Kgs 11:1-4).

The practice run for the Eden Project was beginning to wither. Apparently the temporary removal of the sin barrier through the system of sacrifices had not really solved the root issue. Human beings were sinful creatures and always defaulted to the arrogant independence of the Asphalt Project. Only when God's sevenfold covenant had played itself out would sin be removed once for all. Only then would the plan that nothing could stop get back on track.

The Kingdom Divides and the Prophets Speak

God didn't judge Solomon's kingdom out of His love for David but Solomon's son, Rehoboam, was a court brat and within a matter of years the twelve tribes burst out in civil war (1 Kgs 12:19- 20). It was at this time that God raised up men called "the Prophets." Their main job was to call Israel back to fidelity to the field manual. Without it, God's name would not be imaged properly to the nations. It was a critical time for the Eden Project.

The ten tribes that had annexed to the north would have twenty kings before it was all said and done. Not one of them listened to God's messengers, the Prophets. As God had done at the time of Noah, at the time of the tower, at the time of Egypt, and at the time of the occupation, when His patience had worn thin, He stood up to defend His glory. God raised up the mighty Assyria, the world power at the time, to execute judgment on the northern tribes because they had demonstrated such hardness of heart that they rejected every attempt to coax them back to faith. While some from each northern tribe snuck back to the south, thus preserving the twelve tribes for posterity, most were devastated by Assyrian might and were dispersed as booty among the peoples of the Mediterranean basin (2 Kgs 17:5 ff). Here would begin the great Diaspora, the scattering that eventually produced Jewish ghettos in every city in the empire. In God's sovereign plan, as He had done with the dispersion of the peoples at the tower, He once again forced His people to fan out in all directions. In the bigger plan of God, these Jewish ghettos and their synagogues would await a man in the New Testament by the name of Paul, God's apostle to the Gentiles, but that's getting ahead of our story! Those left in the land by Assyria would intermarry with foreigners, develop their own religion, part Jewish and part pagan, and become their own, peculiar people group living in Samaria. We will know them in the New Testament as "the Samaritans."

The two tribes to the south proved to be more faithful than their brothers and sisters to the north. While they too had twenty kings, eight of those kings listened to the Prophets and the country experienced revivals during their tenures. Even these weren't enough, however. The power of sin once again sucked them into the vortex of the Asphalt Project and brought judgment down on their heads. The rising world power now was Babylon and, as was true at the time of the tower of babel, this nation would typify Satan's system of evil in the Biblical narrative. The Babylonian's were smarter than the Assyrians, however, and rather than dispersing their captives for cash, they took the best and the brightest back to Babylon to enrich their own culture and workforce (2 Kgs 24:13-16). Israel found herself in captivity for seventy years and longed for the day of release back to the land. Even bigger was the question as to whether the Project was still on. If it was, had Israel lost her call as missionaries to the nations or had she lost the privilege of being the people of God for the sake of the world? The Prophets said it was all still a "go" and predicted that there would be a new exodus. Israel would be restored to the land and fulfill her mission to reach the nations (Jer 25:9-12; 29:10).

As was noted above, it was during the time of the Divided Kingdom, with God's worldwide plan on the line, that God raised up the Prophets. These men were filled with God's Spirit to call Israel back to obedience to the field manual and its prescriptions for how to worship God and be His image to the nations. Many of their prophetic oracles spoke directly to the restoration of Israel and the reinstitution of her missionary role. We will now back up to highlight some of their greatest prophesies as the story of the Old Testament comes to a close.

In the ninth century, the issue of rain was back on the table. At the word of the Lord, the prophet Elijah had shut up the heavens dry as dust for three years (1 Kgs 17:1). Instead of repenting and turning back to the Lord, the people turned to the gods of the Syrians, Baal and Asherah, his female partner. It was said that when they had sex their seed would fertilize the earth and bring the harvest. To hedge their bets on the fertility of this insidious pair, Israel adopted the practice of temple prostitution to "turn on" the gods so they would send the "seed." It was the ancient version of a pornographic movie. This was so dishonoring to God that Elijah called a showdown on Mt. Carmel (carmel means "God's vineyard," a metaphor for the people of God) to show His vineyard who the real God was, just as had happened back in Egypt. Lightening swallowed up Elijah's sacrifice and the heavens were shaken in such a manifestation of God's power and affirmation of the prophetic word that it calls back to God's revelation of Himself at Mt. Sinai (1 Kgs 18:19-40). It was clear that Yahweh, the God of Israel, was Elohim, the Creator of the Universe. He alone was God.

The first writing prophet appears to be Jonah in the 8th century. The book is a living parable, acting out Israel's racial prejudice and rejection of her role as missionary; Jonah refused to preach a message of repentance to the Assyrian capitol, Nineveh (Jonah 1:3). God was giving Assyria the opportunity to turn from her wickedness some years before she would turn back to her wicked ways, and God would use her to bring judgment on Israel, a deed that would then bring them under judgment later. What should have been seen as an opportunity to enact the promise to Abram, to be a blessing to the nations, became a moment of shame and horror, not only for Jonah (anyone want to be swallowed by a great fish?) but for Israel as well. After being spit up on the seashore, Jonah, now in the frame of mind to obey God, preached repentance to the Assyrian capital. Nineveh did, in fact, repent and averted disaster for the present (Jonah 2 & 3).

It was Amos who realized that Israel had become so complacent that her empty, religious rituals meant nothing to God. It was so bad that Israel's privilege of being the people of God for the world was in serious jeopardy (5:21-27). Amos saw that a day of darkness was coming, but it would not be for the nations. If Israel did not change her ways, she would be judged along with those who cursed the true seed of Abram. Joined by both Micah and Hosea, these prophets, speaking to the tribes in the north, saw their predictions of annihilation come at the hands of the now ripe-for-evil Assyrians in 722 BC. The Asphalt jungle seemed to be spreading everywhere.

Though still the 8th century, the prophet Isaiah focused his work on the two salvageable tribes to the south. The most notable of these was Judah, out of whom Jacob had said would come the lion King who would reign forever. Through Isaiah, God said to the Judean king, Ahaz, "I will give you a sign." This sign was intended to show the king that his fear of those from the Asphalt Project would come to naught. God would cause a virgin to be with child and she would call His name "Immanuel," meaning "God with us" (Isa 7:14). The child would come from David's line and would be a living temple, the typological fulfillment of God's traveling war tent. He would have a seven-fold (i.e. full) endowment of the Spirit of the Lord (Isa 11:1-2)and lead His people forth to crush the head of the serpent and all his works. Furthermore, in the future God would honor the backwater area called "Galilee of the Gentiles" (Isa 9:1). At the time of the male child, Galilee would be a mixed area comprised of both Jews and Gentiles and would prefigure Israel's missionary role among the nations. Through this future son of David, God said that those living in darkness - the nations - would see a great light (Isa 9:2).

In Isaiah's collection of prophetic oracles, chapters 40-66 appear to be written some time after Israel had been taken into exile in Babylon. In these prophesies Isaiah offers Israel "comfort" (Isa 43:1)by drawing parallels to their being in exile and their time of slavery in Egypt. Just as they were captive in a foreign land in Egypt, they were now captive in Babylon. And just as God had delivered them from Egypt, Isaiah prophesied that a "way," a new exodus, would be coming, when once again God would lead them out of the wilderness (Isa 43:19). As He did in the first exodus, God would send a messenger/angel who would cry out in the wilderness to prepare the way for the Lord (Isa 40:3). Arrogant people would be humbled and broken people would be raised up so that the Lord's way would be straight. The word "way" will go on to have a very important significance; Jesus would say that He was the "way" (Jn 4:6). Furthermore, the early church would be called the "way" in the early stages of their movement out into the world (Acts 9:2).

This way, or "day", of deliverance would be a day of "glad tidings" (Isa 40:9). The word for "glad tidings" in the Greek Old Testament is "euangelion,"meaning "good news."[4] It is this word, usually rendered as "gospel," that the New Testament writers will use to announce the coming of Jesus and the kingdom that He would bring. Fortuitously, it would be a word that communicated to the Greeks and Romans as well, but that is again getting us ahead of our story.

How would this new exodus come to pass? God was going to raise up a "servant." Without the full reading of Isaiah's oracles about this servant, one might think that the reference was to Israel (41-42), Cyrus, the king of Persia God's "anointed" would be a Gentile (43- 48), or the remnant of Israel (49-51). Indeed, all these were servants of the Lord for a time, but the true Servant is identified in chapters 52-53. This one would be the Servant, par excellence, and would be a Savior for the sins of the whole world. In Him the sevenfold covenant would deal with human sin once for all. And how would it happen? God would put His Spirit on this Servant, thus empowering Him differently than the servants of old. This Servant would be highly exalted, yet would suffer as one who was numbered with transgressors - a very odd picture indeed. He would be pierced for our transgressions and carry our infirmities, yet by His wounds, "we" would be healed. Though He would be assigned a grave among the wicked, He would see the light of life and be satisfied.

Somehow, in this manner, the suffering Servant would announce "glad tidings" to the poor, give liberty to the captives, sight to the blind and proclaim the year of the Lord's favor for humanity (Isa 61:1-3). All of these are signs of the ancient Jubilee and ultimately the dawning of a new creation. As we will read in the New Testament, no one except Jesus would know how it all fit together. Nevertheless, as those who were in exile heard these prophetic oracles, they would have surely taken great comfort in them and longed for their fulfillment. In the distant future, the true Servant and Messiah would echo Isaiah, saying, "Blessed are those who mourn For they shall be comforted" (Mt 5:4 NKJV).

It was Jeremiah who finally saw it and he saw it out of his pain. God confirmed Isaiah's word to him; out of David He would raise up a righteous Branch. Here He was not building on His prophetic tradition, not even expanding it, but bursting it wide open. God showed him that the time was coming when He would make a new covenant with His people (Jer 31:31).

Using the exodus as his backdrop, just as Isaiah had done, Jeremiah predicted a new exodus from exile (Jer 29:10). In this new exile, Jeremiah said the new covenant would not be like the covenant God had made with their Jewish forefathers. This time the field manual, the law, would not be written on tablets of stone, but on the tablets of Israel's heart (Jer 31:31-33). There would be a New Jerusalem, the fulfillment of the Project that would reflect God's image. God would "refresh the weary and satisfy the faint" (Jer 31:25). Furthermore, all would know Him, from the greatest to the least, and their sins would be remembered no more (Jer 31:34). Only in this new covenant - the seventh - would the problem of sin finally be removed. Jeremiah was so sure of this that on the eve of the Babylonian captivity he bought a field and staked his claim in the new Israel (Jer 32:9). Joel realized that the return from exile would not come without the outpouring of the Spirit seen by Isaiah. After a devastating locust plague, one of God's disciplinary curses designed to bring Israel back to the image-bearing instructions in the field manual, Joel predicted that the outpouring would come not only on the Servant, but on all God's people (Joel 2). Moses' prayer would come true. All God's people would prophesy, not just the prophets, thus indicating that the barrier of sin had, indeed, been removed and that God's people had been welcomed back into the Presence of God. Through the power of the outpoured Spirit, two-way communication with God would be restored and it would be as Adam had experienced it in Eden.

Meanwhile, exiled in Babylon, prophetic figures Ezekiel and Daniel loomed large in seeing a glorious future for God's downtrodden but missional people. While Ezekiel had seen in a vision that the glory of the Lord would tragically depart from

God's temple in Jerusalem just prior to its destruction by Babylon (Eze 10:18), it must have been encouraging when God told the prophet that He would be with His people no matter where they found themselves among the nations. God had not scattered His people randomly. He had strategically placed them among the nations (Eze 36) because the original mandate to Adam had been to multiply God's image until the earth was filled with God and the beauty and justice that would come in a world ruled by royal ambassadors.

Daniel saw that one like a son of man would go into God's Presence, just as the high priest did on the Day of Atonement, and receive an eternal Kingdom that He would bring to the earth. This Kingdom would shatter all the kingdoms of this world and would become a mountain that would fill the whole earth (Dan 2:44-45). The Eden Project would come to fulfillment and God's Presence and Garden would be all in all. On that day, all the dead would rise, people from every nation. Those who had blessed the missionaries from the faith seed of Abraham would be welcomed into eternal life, but those who cursed the missionaries and Abraham's blessing would be thrust away into utter darkness.

In fulfillment of Isaiah's prophesies, one of David's descendents, named Zerubbabel, did lead God's people back from Babylon to the land of Israel (Ezra 2; Hag 1), albeit still under Persian rule. Under the encouragement of the prophets Haggai and Zechariah, a smaller, scaled down version of the temple was rebuilt and the sacrificial system reinstated. Nehemiah rebuilt the walls of Jerusalem to keep the people safe and they rededicated themselves to the instructions in the field manual and their calling to be God's image to the nations. Despite the fact that Haggai prophesied that the glory of the latter house would be greater than the former house, the writers never record the return of the glory of the Lord to the new temple (Hag 2:9).

The prophet Malachi, standing with Isaiah, said that all these things would come to pass with the return of "His messenger" who would prepare the way of the Lord. Malachi identifies this messenger as Elijah (Mal 4:5), the prophet that had stood for the Word of God against Baal four hundred years earlier. Since Elijah had not died, but had been taken up to heaven in a fiery chariot, Malachi was saying that he would return to finish his ministry and inaugurate the next event on the eschatological time calendar for the people of God: "the great and terrible day of the Lord" (Mal 4:4). On this day God would, at last, return to His temple. For the people of the Asphalt Project who sought to make a name for themselves, this day would be like a fiery furnace, but for those who revered God's name, the "sun of righteousness would arise with healing in its wings" (Mal 4:2).

The Old Testament closes as a story looking for an ending. When would the male child come who would crush the head of the serpent and lead God's people to the fulfillment of the Project? When would the son of David arise and the son of man usher in God's eternal kingdom? When would the outpouring of the Spirit occur and the year of the Lord's favor come to the peoples of the earth through the seed of Abraham? So many questions, and all await answering.

Chapter 4
THE BIBLICAL BASIS
FOR WORLD MISSIONS, PART 2

" *God's mission of redemption is further clarified and brought toward fulfillment in the New Testament. Cross-cultural missionaries follow in the footsteps of Jesus, who left His home in heaven to bring good news to lost people in an environment very different from His own. In the record of the early church, we see God's story continue as the gospel takes root among Jews and Gentiles, spread by ordinary believers whose lives are marked by God's supernatural power.* "

- Bill Jackson

The New Testament

Between the Testaments

As we turned the last page of the Old Testament, we left a story awaiting an ending. According to Malachi, the next chapter on the eschatological time calendar would be initiated by the return of Elijah. He would prepare the way of the Lord and usher in the great and terrible day of Yahweh. He would judge those who sought to make a name for themselves but bring healing to those who longed to make God's name and renown the desire of their hearts (Isa 26:8). Four hundred years later Jesus would identify John the Baptist as the Elijah of Malachi's prophecy (Mk 1:1). He would be God's sovereign choice to usher in the next phase of the Eden Project.

As we open up to the pages of the New Testament, however, we notice immediately that the landscape has drastically changed. No longer is Israel ruled by Persia but by the new world power, Rome (Lk 2:1). Jewish political parties like the Pharisees debate over the minutia of field manual interpretations. Other parties, like the Sadducees and the Zealots, have more divergent agendas. Aramaic is now the language of Israel but the language of the marketplace is Greek. And then there is the matter of that huge temple on Mt. Zion. Where did it all come from? The events and changes in the ancient Mediterranean world that occurred during this time period, a period strangely absent in the Protestant canon of the Bible (the Catholic Apocrypha is comprised of books from this era), are absolutely critical for understanding the world of the New Testament. For brevity's sake we offer here simply a sketch.

In 333 BC a young Greek named Alexander the Great conquered the Mediterranean world in a ten-year period. Even though he died prematurely, Greek culture and language changed the world, so much so that even the Jews began to adopt Greek ways (some more than others, as we shall see). This produced fierce debates among the older generation about how to fight against these dangerous and ungodly trends. Their various opinions would give rise in the New Testament to the Pharisees, Sadducees, Zealots and a separatist movement, later known as the Essences.

While Israel was under the control of Syria, a despotic ruler known as Antiochus IV thought he was a god and called himself "Epiphanes" (God made manifest). He hated the Jews and vowed to destroy their culture, even to the point of desecrating their temple by sacrificing a pig in God's throne room and sprinkling its blood on God's throne, the Ark of the Covenant. He made Jerusalem a police state and rededicated the temple to Zeus. A young Jew named Judas, later nicknamed "maccabee," the hammer, came to the rescue and led a rebellion against Syria, recaptured Jerusalem, and rededicated the temple to Yahweh three years to the day after it had been desecrated. This began a period of Jewish independence led by the descendents of Judas. It would not last long.

Antiochus Epiphanes stands in the long line of those from the seed of the serpent - those that arose to become the Asphalt People - that have sought to annihilate God's missionary people and stop the Eden Project. He is a type of the Pharaoh, Goliath, Tiglath-Pileser III of Assyria, Nebuchadnezzar and many more down through the history of the church. There is, indeed, "enmity" between the seed of the woman and the seed of the serpent (Gen 3:15), but as God said through Isaiah, "My purpose will stand and I will do all that I please" (Isa 46:10). Nothing was going to stop the plan of God. As a matter of fact, when the Roman king of the Asphalt People, Caesar Augustus, subjugated Israel in 63 BC, God used the changes he initiated to make the final adjustments necessary for the birth of the Christ (Christ is Messiah, "the anointed one," in Greek).

Under the leadership of Augustus, the Roman Empire expanded as far as Gaul to the west, Germany to the north, Arabia to the east and Ethiopia to the south. His great accomplishment was that he brought peace to the ancient world for the first time in history and, because of this, he was called the "savior of the world." He went on to establish the Pax Romana, the peace of Rome, and built a new road system that connected the major centers of the

Empire. By dispatching Roman soldiers at strategic points along the roads he ensured safe travel for Roman citizens.

Initially Rome ruled Israel through local rulers called "kings." The king of the Jews at the birth of Jesus was an Idumean known in history as Herod the Great. It was Herod that built the magnificent temple that we find in the gospel stories. It was also Herod who killed all the babies in and around Bethlehem when he learned from the Magi from the East that this was where it had been prophesied that the Christ would be born (Mat 2:16). The Magi represented those from among the Gentiles that would join the Eden Project through the witness of God's missionary people. They were among the first fruits of what would become a worldwide harvest.

In Galatians 4:4 Paul writes, "In the fullness of time God sent His Son." The Greek word for "time" used here does not mean the ticks on the clock but when all the factors have come together. It was time to see how God had prepared the world for the birth of the Christ. We saw at the beginning of the story that the power of sin was so great that when the people of the world unified, as they did when they built the tower, God saw that almost nothing could stop the rebellion of the Asphalt Project (Gen 11:6). He initiated a plan to deal with sin and fulfill the Eden Project and the knowledge of the glory of the Lord would one day cover the earth as the waters cover the sea (Hab 2:4). He confused their languages, scattering the Asphalt People around the globe, and creating a worldwide mosaic of rebellious and racist people groups. God then chose one man, Abram, from among these rebellious people and blessed him; with the blessing came responsibility. Abram was blessed to be a blessing to all the peoples of the earth. God warned him, however, that while some would welcome the good news heralded by the Jews, some would reject the blessing and curse it. The seed of the woman would continue to be at enmity with the seed of the serpent, all the way to the end of the age.

God then gave this people, the Jews, a revelation of His great Name and a field manual to show them how to be His image on the earth. But, because the power of sin was in God's people too, they also rebelled. To humble them, God scattered them everywhere, thus creating Jewish ghettos in urban centers throughout the earth, each with a synagogue, each with a field manual, and each praying prayers of repentance such as had been prayed by Nehemiah and while they waited for God to fill the temple in Jerusalem with His Presence once again (see Neh 1). The Jews between the testaments thought that God would restore Israel to her former glory and the nations would flock to Jerusalem to become Jews and find God. This was their perception of how the Eden Project would be fulfilled, but God had other plans, as we shall see. Two Gentile nations would change the world and prepare it for God's time of visitation.

When Alexander the Great conquered the world, he unified it under one language. For the first time since the tower, those who knew Greek could not only buy and sell in any city of the world, but also communicate with those from other people groups. After the Hebrew Scriptures were translated into Greek, both Jews and Gentiles had a Bible to prepare them to receive what was about to come.

Significantly, the Roman period created a short period of peace in the empire, forming a period when it was safe to travel. With the Pax Romana there was a guarantee of safe travel for any Roman citizen on Roman roads. Here, then, is how the plan comes together. God was going to call and anoint with the power of the Holy Spirit a Pharisaical Jew from the Diaspora who was born a Roman citizen and fluent in Greek. It was this man, Paul of Tarsus, that God would send around the empire on Roman roads, with police protection, to Jewish synagogues where he would read from a Greek Bible with the word that the Scriptures had been fulfilled by a Jew from Galilee. This Jew, Jesus, had been crucified for our sins but had risen from the dead and ruled the universe from God's right hand (Eph 1:20). He was calling all men to repentance and new life by the Spirit of God who would write the field manual onto the human heart. No longer would sin rule because in Christ

God had thrown sin as far as the east is from the west. He was accepting anyone who would come, Jew or Gentile. And so the world was prepared. In the fullness of time God sent His Son.

The Gospels

The Birth of the Christ

Probably sometime in the early winter, AD 30, God's Spirit overshadowed a young, Jewish virgin named Mary and she became pregnant with a male child (Lk 1:26-38), *the* male child that the biblical story had all along anticipated. It would be this child who would crush the head of the serpent but would also bruise His heel. Mary was instructed to name the child Jesus because He was going to save His people from their sins (Lk 1:31). According to Jeremiah, this would be in fulfillment of the seventh and final covenant, in which the barrier of sin separating humankind from God would be done away with once and for all. John's gospel says that Jesus was not only with God but was God (Jn 1:1). He was the God who became flesh and dwelt (the Greek word means "tabernacled") among us (Jn 1:14). From the perspective of theology, in the event of human rebellion, the Trinitarian God had organized a rescue mission before the dawn of time in which the Son of God would become a Son of Man. He would recapitulate Adam so He could pay for the sins of all humankind; Jeremiah said that He would remember our sins no more.

In both Matthew and Luke's genealogies it is evident that God's plan from the beginning had been to rescue all peoples from their sins. Matthew's list includes Gentiles in Jesus' lineage. David's own grandmother, Ruth, was from Moab. While Matthew's genealogy traces the line back to Abraham (Mt 1:1-16), it is Luke's gospel that traces Jesus' heritage all the way back to Adam (Lk 3:23-38). God had chosen the Jews not only to be the people out of whom God would bring the sin-bearer, but also to be the missionary people for the world. It is for this reason that Matthew includes the story of the Magi from the east pursuing whatever prophetic revelation God had given the seekers among their people, a revelation that led them straight to the Jews. They would have the answer...and so they did. When they found the child, Jesus, they offered Him gold, the gift of kings, incense, a gift signifying a new relationship with God, and myrrh, an embalming spice foreshadowing how the King would redeem Humankind through His own, sacrificial and substitutionary death (Mt 2:11).

The Galilee Jesus

It is Mark's gospel that connects us quickly to the Old Testament story by quoting from Isaiah 40 that God would raise up a voice crying in the wilderness to prepare the way for the Lord. John the Baptist, the Elijah of Malachi's prophecy, announced that the Day of the Lord had arrived with the advent of the Christ, Isaiah's anointed one (Mk 1:1-4). John said that He was the "Lamb of God who would take away the sin of the world" (Jn 1:29). It was time to repent and believe the good news.

Just as Adam received a blessing prior to receiving his marching orders, Jesus too received a blessing at the beginning of His mission. Mark tells us that at His baptism the heavens were torn apart, indicating that a new era in redemptive history had begun, and God said, "This is my beloved son. With Him I am well pleased" (Jn 1:11). In these two statements, God was saying that in Jesus both the vertical ("this is my beloved son") and horizontal ("with Him I am well pleased") dimensions that had been ruptured in the Garden had been repaired. He received the blessing as the Holy Spirit descended on Him in the form of a dove, a symbol denoting new creation (Mk 1:10). In this, Jesus would fulfill Adam's three assignments, to multiply, fill and rule (Gen 1:28). Jesus had in His sights nothing less than the glory of God's name being made known through disciples bearing His image that He would raise up from the seed of Abraham, the one who had been blessed to be a blessing to all the peoples of the earth.

After Jesus' anointing for ministry, Mark's gospel shows Jesus immediately choosing disciples so that He could multiply God's image within them. Interestingly, He chose most of His twelve disciples from Galilee, a racially mixed area in northern Israel. This is also the area where He was raised and inaugurated His ministry (Mk1-2). Given Mark's intentional connection in his gospel to Isaiah's prophesies, it is not surprising to find that it would be Galilee of the Gentiles that would launch Jesus' ministry. A people walking in darkness would see a great light (Isa 9:2). Galilee was a racially mixed area and was the perfect launching pad for the one who would be the King over all peoples. It would function as a snapshot of the Jews fulfilling their missionary calling.

Mark shows Jesus identifying the real enemy when He encounters a demonized man in a synagogue in Galilee (Mk 1:21-28). The enemy this time was not Pharaoh, nor Goliath, nor Nebuchadnezzar, nor Antiochus, nor the current antagonist, Rome. No, it was Satan. With a word Jesus cast out the demon with authority. The future image-bearers were watching; this would soon be a part of their ministry as the Eden Project expanded through their words of authority around the world.

Luke also chooses to begin Jesus' public ministry with a pivotal story illustrating God's heart for the world. Jesus had already garnered considerable fame in Galilee when He was invited to address His "home church" in the little Galilean village of Nazareth of His childhood. The scroll on the lectern that day happened to be the one written by Isaiah. Jesus opened it to the section we would call today "Isaiah 61" and began to read that the anointing of the Spirit had come upon him and that He was the one about whom Isaiah had prophesied who would proclaim liberty to the captives, give sight to the blind and proclaim the year of the Lord's favor (Lk 4:18-19).

They all marveled at Jesus' words until He added a midrash (preaching commentary) that mentioned two Gentiles that had been recipients of God's favor in an earlier time. During the time of Elijah it was not to the Israelites that the prophet was sent during their time of famine, but a widow from Sidon. Moreover, there were many lepers in Israel during the time of Elisha but it was only Namaan, the Syrian, that received a healing through the prophet. At the mention of Gentiles receiving the favor of the Lord and not Jews, the people Jesus had grown up with suddenly turned on Him, thus exposing the same racism typified in these stories (Lk 4:25-30). As it touches the Old Testament, this event foreshadows a tragic turn in the story. The reader wonders if the people that God had called to be the people for the world had somehow missed their calling. Since it was not yet His time of suffering, Jesus passed right through the crowd that wanted to throw Him off a cliff (Lk 4:29-30). The Eden Project would advance with or without ethnic Israel now that the true Israelite had arrived. He was now about the business of reconstituting the Israel of faith around Himself for all those who had ears to hear. To these He would give the Kingdom of God.

The term "kingdom of God" was a Jewish code term. They understood it to mean that time when God would return to Israel, forgive their sins, cleanse the temple, defeat her enemies and restore the Jews to her Davidic glory. Jewish missionaries would call the nations to come to Zion to find God (and, as we shall find out in Acts, the Jews assumed that this meant that the Gentiles would become Jewish). Jesus, however, redefined the entire meaning of the term. When He called people to repentance because the "Kingdom of God was at hand" (Lk 10:9, 11) He meant that in His ministry the rule of God had returned to the realm of the earth. No longer did Satan have the upper hand. In and through His ministry, Isaiah's prophecy from Isaiah 61 was coming to pass: the year of the Lord's favor was dawning and was for all who put their trust in Him. Jesus, not the temple, was the locus of the forgiveness of sins. In so doing, Jesus was not only King but also Priest of the new Israel, thus fulfilling the types of Adam and David. Moreover, He was now reserving the right to define the members of the new Israel on His own authority. In the mind of the Jews, all these things were enough to get Jesus killed as a false prophet.

In a short parable Jesus said that the kingdom of God was like plundering a strong man's house. First, the strong man had to be tied up and then his goods could be plundered. The meaning of the parable is that, even though Satan had violated the people of the earth and had plundered their goods, Jesus had come to bind up the strong man (Mt 12:22-30; Lk 11:14-26). By forgiving sins, healing every kind of disease and sickness, and freeing the demonized, He was returning to people what had been stolen from them.

Luke describes this process in his account of the healing of a paralyzed man who was lowered down through the roof of a house by some friends into the very room where Jesus was ministering (Lk 5:17-26). Luke tells us that the power of the Lord was present that day to heal the sick, indicating Jesus' submission as a man to the voice of the Spirit during His earthly ministry (He didn't heal the sick out of His deity, but as a human being operating by the power of the Spirit, thus leaving His followers a model to follow in the future). Through the Spirit (Paul would later call these various operations of the Spirit "spiritual gifts") Jesus discerned that the man needed to know that he was forgiven of his sins so, as the great High Priest, Jesus forgave him of his wrongs (one might surmise that Jesus understood the man's sins to be the root cause of his paralytic condition). Immediately, the Jewish leaders in attendance began to judge Jesus in their hearts for the "blasphemy" of presuming to operate as a priest, but Jesus knew what they were thinking (again by the Spirit) and called them on it. Probably operating in what Paul would later called the gifts of faith and healing, Jesus told the man to get up and walk. His legs suddenly had life again because the strong man had been bound. Jesus had given back to this man that which the enemy had stolen.

There was a caveat to all this, however. In John's account of Jesus' visit to a pool where the infirmed gathered, He only stopped to heal one man. Jesus explained these kinds of anomalies, saying that He only did what He saw the Father doing (Jn 5:1-19). In another illustration of the Kingdom's apparent failure to break in, John the Baptist, whom Jesus said was the greatest man who had ever lived (Lk 7:28), had been arrested and was suffering in prison. "How could the Kingdom have come?" he wondered. If there was anyone who should have been experiencing the year of the Lord's favor, would it not have been John (Lk 7:18-23)? Strangely, Jesus Himself taught the disciples to pray that the Kingdom would come, as if it were somehow still off in the future (Mt 6:10).

As we gather this seemingly discordant data, our only conclusion biblically is that while Jesus had inaugurated the end of the age (how else would one account for all Jesus' miracles and the changed lives of people?), the full consummation of the kingdom lay out in the future. Only at Jesus' return will all tears be dried and the shroud of sin over the peoples be removed (Isa 25:7; Rom 8:20-21). It appears that Jesus' followers live "in-between the times," an era in human history when the Kingdom is breaking in all around us, but not in every prayer exchange. We live in an age when the Kingdom "now" is overlapped with the Kingdom "not yet." This is an age of war when we battle in prayer over the lives of people. Some will besaved and healed and others will not. The true kingdom mindset is that if it doesn't happen today, we will show up tomorrow, undeterred and undaunted, because Jesus said, "The kingdom of God is at hand" and could break in at any moment. Authentic followers of Jesus, then, have both a theology of power and a theology of pain; they know why it does happen and why, sometimes, it doesn't. They are the immovable, unshakable ones who continually pray that the kingdom would come on earth as it is in heaven.

Having laid down the basic lessons of the Kingdom of God, Jesus shows His disciples the global scope of the Kingdom activities that would be entrusted to them. John records an incident where Jesus had the audacity to walk through the region of Samaria on the way back to Galilee from Judea. The Jews hated the Samaritans as the lowest of the low; after Assyria had scattered the Jews in 722 BC the recalcitrant Jews that were left in Samaria intermarried with Gentiles and crafted a religion that was part Jewish and part pagan. Stopping at a well, Jesus sent the disciples ahead to get food. While there, Jesus encountered a woman from Samaria who was apparently barren. Jesus knew, presumably by the Spirit, that she had had a number of husbands who were no doubt trying to impregnate her to remove her horrible cultural shame. Jesus' supernatural insight into her life, combined with His acceptance of her as a Jew, broke through her pain. When Jesus told her where to find living water that would quench her thirst forever, she ran back into the village to invite her community to meet this incredible man. She wondered if He could be "the Christ" (Jn 4:1-30).

Both Mark and Luke record the incident when the disciples had their first cross-cultural experience in the Synoptic gospels. Jesus told the twelve to go to the east side of the Sea of Galilee, an area with ten Gentile cities known as the Decapolis. The disciples no doubt wondered why they were going there. From a cosmic standpoint, this would have appeared to be a bad move. Here, in one small boat, sat the future of the human race. It is not surprising that a storm hit them like a hurricane. Jesus was asleep in the stern, resting as God had rested since the seventh day of creation. He was awakened to the disciples' panic, got up, and rebuked the storm, probably meaning the demonic entities behind the natural phenomena. Suddenly, it was very still (Lk 8:22-25). One wonders if the disciples connected this incident with the way Jesus had cast out demons on other occasions. Very soon they found themselves on the eastern shore in the middle of the night, only to be met by a completely demonized man that had been exiled to a remote beach in chains because no jail could hold him. Again, with the spoken word Jesus set this man free (Lk 8:26-39). Probably a Gentile, he appears to typologically represent the demonized nations in the story. The point is clear: though Jesus had reconstituted Israel, Satan was not giving up the Gentiles without a fight! But not even Satan could stop the advance of God's Kingdom to reach every people group with the gospel. Jesus had cast a demon out of a Jew representing demonized Israel as well as a Gentile representing the demonized people groups. Satan's Asphalt Project was going down and the Garden of God would now be filling the earth.

Jesus' ministry was filled with opportunities for the disciples to see the year of the Lord's favor come to the Gentiles as He prepared them for their apostolic call. Matthew records an incident where a Roman Centurion who believed in the God of the Jews approached Jesus about healing his sick servant. The Roman did not consider himself worthy to have Jesus come to his house so he asked that Jesus just heal his servant from a distance (Mt 8:5-13). Jesus saw in this Gentile's faith a picture of other Gentiles that would come from around the world to eat at Abraham's table. Unfortunately, the Jews would miss the party, ironically because of their racial prejudice and their refusal to accept Jesus' redefinition of the Kingdom of God. The Jew's racism is highlighted in a number of gracious encounters that Jesus had with Samaritans. We have already mentioned His dialogue with the woman at the well. He also told a parable of the Good Samaritan, where only the man from Samaria bound up the wounds of the traveler that was beaten. Once again, the Jews wallowed in their spirit of elitism (Lk 10:25-37) and of the ten lepers that Jesus healed, it was only the Samaritan that returned to thank Him (Lk 17:11-19).

When Jesus sent out His twelve followers to proclaim the kingdom in Israel and to heal the sick and cast out demons, they came back with a great report that the Kingdom had come wherever they had gone in Israel. Luke records that shortly after that Jesus sent out seventy on a similar mission (Lk 10). The number seventy appears to be symbolic of the seventy nations listed in Genesis 10 that grew out of the three sons of Noah. Jesus' seventy kingdom warriors represented those faithful Jews that would, indeed, accept their missionary calling and take the gospel around the world.

The Jerusalem Jesus

As the Galilean phase of His ministry came to a close Luke records that Jesus "set His face like a flint" (Isa 50:7) to go to Jerusalem to die for the sins of humankind. It is John's gospel that records the incident that sparked those events. During the late fall of AD 29, Jesus began to stay at the house of Mary, Martha and Lazarus in Bethany, just two miles from Jerusalem over the Mount of Olives (Lk 10:38-42). Throughout the fall and winter of AD 30, Jesus and His disciples went throughout Judea proclaiming the arrival of the kingdom and the Eden Project continued to spread. On one of these excursions, word came to Jesus that Lazarus had become ill. Rather than going back to Bethany immediately, Jesus lingered out among the villages. When He finally did return He found that Lazarus had died. He had been wrapped and then laid in a tomb that had been sealed with a huge bolder; the funeral was now in full swing. After weeping quietly, Jesus commanded Lazarus to come out of the tomb, which he did, grave clothes and all (Jn 11:1-44)! News of Lazarus' resurrection precipitated the events that sparked the Passion of the Christ.

Jesus had already predicted three times that He was going to die (Mk 8:31; 9:32; 10:32). He told His disciples that He would be turned over to the Romans, crucified and raised on the third day (Mt 20:17-19). This was so unbelievable to the disciples that the voice of God spoke to Peter, John, and James again from the heavens saying, "This is My beloved Son. Listen to Him!" (Mk 9:7). Still not getting it, they no doubt joined the adoring throngs waving palm branches that were symbols of revolt looking back to the time of the violent insurrection of Judas the Maccabee. While riding a donkey, a servant animal destined to carry the burdens of others, Jesus crested the Mount of Olives with Jerusalem in full view below (Mt 21:1-11; Lk 19:29-44; Jn 12:12-19). The text says that Jesus wept, this time not the quiet weeping seen at Lazarus' tomb, but a loud wailing (Lk 19:41). At long last God's glory was returning to Israel (remember that the glory of the Lord had not filled the second temple that was rebuilt after the exile). Tragically, Israel was missing the hour of God's return to Zion.

Arriving in Jerusalem, Jesus entered the temple as the Messiah was expected to do. After inspecting the temple, He returned to Bethany and the next day He and His disciples set out in the morning to go back to Jerusalem. Jesus was hungry and, seeing a fig tree in the distance, hoped to find a few winter figs left on the branches, the best tasting fruit of the two fig harvests. Upon inspection He found the tree barren, much like Israel, which should have been filled with the best tasting figs of all (i.e., the Gentile nations) but was barren. He cursed the tree and it withered and died (Mt 21:18-22). Israel would, indeed, go on to become a barren nation, rejecting and betraying her God to a Roman crucifixion. The apostle Paul would later write that

God had given Israel a "hardening in part until the full number of Gentiles has come in," thus making the Jews jealous of the Gentile harvest - note that the hardening was "in part," meaning that some Jews would believe throughout the history of the Church (Rom 11:25). When the "times of the Gentiles" had been fulfilled, God would visit Israel again to honor His "irrevocable covenant with Abraham, Isaac and Jacob." He would forgive their sins and "all Israel would be saved" (Rom 11:11ff; cf. Lk 21:24).

Arriving again at the temple, Jesus burned with holy rage and overturned the money exchange tables and rebuked those that were hawking sacrifices in the outer court of the temple. All three of the Synoptic gospels record Jesus' quotation in Isaiah 56:7, "My house shall be a house of prayer for all nations." What should have been a missionary prayer meeting had now become a "den of robbers" (Mt 21:13; Mk 11:17; Lk 19:46). The tragedy of it all was that the nation that God had redeemed with signs and wonders, whom He had brought to Himself on eagles wings to receive her commission to be the image of God as priests to the nations, had completely missed the entire reason for her existence.

Politically, Jesus was betrayed by Judas, one of the twelve, and was crucified for the crime of insurrection, allegedly claiming to be the king of the Jews and attempting to foment a Maccabean-like rebellion against Pilate. Spiritually, He was the "lamb of God who takes away the sin of the world" (Jn 1:29). Isaiah had seen centuries earlier that though He had done no violence nor had any deceit been in His mouth, Jesus was pierced for our transgressions (Isa 53:5). As our substitute, the Lord laid on Him the iniquity of us all and bore the sins of many (Isa 53:5-6). John would later write that He was the atoning (Greek, propitiation, "bearing God's wrath") sacrifice for our sins, and not only for ours but for the sins of the whole world (1 Jn 2:2). In the ninth hour, while darkness covered the whole world, Jesus cried out, "My God, my God, why have You forsaken me?" This is the only time in the gospels that Jesus addresses God with His formal name and not the familial Father (Greek abba). He is taking the place of sinful humanity where our sin has prevented us from being family with God - the sin-bearer paid for sin, broke down the wall, and has offered people from among every nation the inestimable privilege of relating to God as Papa.

As Isaiah had seen, the grave couldn't hold Him: "after the suffering of His soul He will see the light of life and be satisfied" (Isa 53:11). The Bible says that on the third day, just as Jesus had predicted, God raised Jesus from the dead as the first fruits of the new creation (Acts 13:30). The risen Christ appeared to His disciples and many others as proof that He was, indeed, Jesus of Nazareth. In private, He spent forty days with His disciples reviewing all His lessons about the Kingdom of God under the direction of the Holy Spirit. As the grand finale, He told them to rendezvous with Him back in Galilee, where it had all begun. On a mountain He gave them a commission to disciple all the nations of the earth (Mt 28:16-20). They were to find the Asphalt Peoples created by the dispersion of languages at Babel and expand Eden into any asphalt cracks they could find. They were to baptize (immerse) people into the name of the Triune God and teach them to obey every lesson He had taught them about the Kingdom. And, most importantly, Jesus said that He would be with them as they fanned out around the globe in fulfillment of the promise to Abraham that his seed would carry a blessing for all the tribes of the earth (Acts 1:8). To carry out their mission, however, they would need a blessing such as had been given to Adam, to all the great leaders of the Old Testament, and then to Jesus Himself. Luke's gospel ends, therefore, with Jesus telling the disciples that they should wait in Jerusalem for the empowerment of the Holy Spirit. From there they would preach the kingdom of God to all nations, beginning in Jerusalem. When the job was done, the end would come (Mt 24:14; Lk 24:47). With that Jesus ascended into heaven. When the mission to the nations is completed, He will return.

The Story of the Early Church

Among the gospel writers, only Luke intended to add a "part two" to his account of the life of Jesus of Nazareth. The book of Acts, therefore, begins with Luke explaining that in his former book i.e., the gospel of Luke, he wrote about all that Jesus began to do and teach. The inference is that Acts - and all of church history, for that matter - is going to be about what Jesus will continue to do and teach through the lives of His disciples (Acts 1:1-2). After reviewing all that He had taught them about the kingdom of God, Jesus told them to wait in Jerusalem for the promised Holy Spirit and then ascended into heaven (Acts 1:3-12). Only as the ascended Christ, the one seated in the position of absolute authority at God's right hand, would Jesus pour out the Spirit to empower the Church for her worldwide mission to expand the Eden Project. It would begin in Jerusalem and expand in waves until it reached the "uttermost parts of the earth" and all people groups had received Abraham's blessing (Acts 1:8). Luke appears to have structured Acts around a series of cross-cultural waves of the gospel, beginning with mainstream Judaism, and then moving outward to fringe Judaism. From there it would progress into the Gentile world, penetrating Syria, then Asia, then Europe. Acts ends with the apostle Paul alive in Rome, the center of the empire, and teaching about the Kingdom of God and Jesus as the Christ (Acts 28:15-31). Luke is telling his readers that the gospel will continue to move forward unhindered until the worldwide mission of the Church is complete and the Christ returns.

On the day of Pentecost, the day when the tithe of the harvest was brought to the temple in Jerusalem, the Spirit fell on 120 disciples who were waiting on the Lord. The Spirit manifest as tongues of fire and each one spoke in another language as the Spirit enabled them, thus fulfilling Joel's prediction that God would pour out the Spirit of prophecy in the last days. Intimate, two-way communication with God was available universally for the first time since the Garden! Now, full of the Spirit, the disciples went out into the streets praising God in their new languages. In a clear fulfillment of the strategy of God with the dispersion of languages at Babel, men and women from throughout the Diaspora heard them praising God in their native tongues. At the preaching of Peter three thousand people were converted to Christ as the tithe of the end-time harvest, and each Jew went back to their native countries to share what Christ had done (Acts 2). Despite the fact that most of the Jews were a barren fig tree, those Jews that had ears to hear had the joy of fulfilling their commission to be a kingdom of priests and a holy nation (Ex 19:6).

From here Luke's narrative in Acts chronicles the advance of the Eden Project against an array of obstacles. In the first wave, to mainstream Judaism beginning in Jerusalem, we read of two arrests of the early believers by Jewish authorities, tragically the newest members of the Asphalt Project. In the first case, the arrest of Peter and John for healing a man lame from birth only emboldened the believers in prayer and witness. The two apostles were then released (Acts 3-4). In the second case, the arrest of all the apostles, an angel released them to continue to preach (Acts 5:17-19). The jails of men could not hold back the gospel.

Luke chronicles the story of two believers, a couple named Ananias and Sapphira, who lied about the sale price of some land that they had donated to the church because they had held some money back for themselves. Peter saw right through it and each dropped dead in turn as the truth was revealed to Peter by the Spirit (Acts 5:1-11). The text says that from that time on the fear of the Lord filled Jerusalem and everyone, believer and unbeliever alike, realized that gathering in the Lord's presence was serious business.

In the final episode of the first wave of the gospel to mainstream Judaism, Luke chronicles the potential of the "race card" to thwart the Kingdom's progress. There were many poor widows in Jerusalem and quite a few of them had become believers in Jesus. The church responded by starting a food ministry for them, but the Aramaic speaking-widows native to Israel were given preference over those that had come from the Diaspora and spoke Greek. While it appears that this was Satan's attempt to divide the church over racial lines, the Holy Spirit directed the apostles to appoint seven Greek-speaking men to oversee the food distribution (Acts 6:1-6). What could have been a split became the first opportunity to multiply cross-cultural leadership. Not only was the crisis averted but the appointment of this new leadership looks toward to the missionary movement that is just on the horizon.

The second wave of the gospel to fringe Judaism in Judea and Samaria begins with the arrest of Stephen, one of the seven. He had been doing far more than overseeing the food pantry! His ministry in evangelism is accompanied by great signs and wonders and appears to be the first one that understood that Christianity and Judaism were incompatible in regard to both the temple (Jesus' once-for-all sacrifice had rendered the temple obsolete) and the law (Jeremiah said that God would write the law on our minds and hearts). He was arrested for his teaching and put on trial before the Jewish ruling council. In his defense, Stephen accused the Jewish leaders of being in alignment with those Jewish leaders in Israel's history that had continually rejected the prophets. He was right. They took Stephen outside the city gates and stoned him as the first martyr of the Christian Church. As they did so, they laid their coats at the feet of a young rabbi named Saul, from Tarsus in Asia Minor (Acts 6:8-7:60). In this way Luke subtly introduces the man who would become the next great character in the story.

What could have been a fatal blow, however, turned out to be the flashpoint for the cross-cultural transmission of the gospel by the seed of Abraham. A persecution broke out by the Jews, apparently against the Greek-speaking element in the church. Philip, another one of the seven, was scattered to Samaria, where he preached the gospel of the kingdom accompanied by great signs (Acts 8:1-6). This appears to be a demonic stronghold because many demons were cast out (Acts 8:7) and we encounter the first sorcerer in the story, a man named Simon (Acts 8:9-13). When Peter and John were sent from Jerusalem to inspect Philip's ministry, the Holy Spirit fell on the Samaritans just as He had fallen on the

Jews (Acts 8:14-17). The importance of this event is that God was accepting the despised Samaritans as a people group without their having to become Jews first. With this, both Peter and John preached in Samaritan villages on their way back to Jerusalem.

Meanwhile, an angel sent Philip to a desert road leading south. There he encountered a man riding in a chariot who just happened to be the treasurer who served the Queen of Ethiopia. The man was a Gentile that worshipped the God of the Jews and happened to be reading from the scroll of Isaiah when Philip pulled up alongside his chariot. Philip explained that Isaiah's prophecy had been fulfilled in Jesus, the Christ, and the eunuch was converted and baptized on the spot (Acts 8:26-39). While we have no information in church history about whatever happened to this influential man, it is clear that this is Luke's way of telling his readers that the gospel was being sovereignly planted in North Africa.

It is at this point Luke reconnects us with the young rabbi named Saul. He was a Greek-speaking Diaspora Jew from Tarsus in Asia Minor who also happened to be born a Roman citizen. He had been sent as a Jewish emissary to Damascus to arrest followers of Jesus, but was apprehended on the road by a light so bright that it blinded him and he fell to the ground. It was here that the risen Christ appeared to him, informing him that he was the one appointed to bring the gospel to the Gentiles. Paul was taken into Damascus where his blindness was healed and he was filled with the Holy Spirit. He immediately began to preach in Damascus that he had been wrong about Jesus and that He was, indeed, the Christ who had been crucified and was now risen. Persecution broke out against Saul and after narrowly escaping Damascus, he went to Jerusalem where a man named Joseph, called Barnabas, meaning "son of encouragement," vouched for his integrity before the apostles. He preached freely in Jerusalem until debates with Grecian Jews sparked persecution against him there and he escaped once again, this time back to Tarsus (Acts 9:1-30). He will reemerge later in the story, but for now Luke reconnects his readers with the ministry of Peter.

After accounts of Peter healing a paralytic and raising a young (Acts 9:32-35) girl from the dead (Acts 9:36-43) Luke zeroes in on a Roman Centurion living in Caesarea who was a follower of the God of the Jews. An angel appeared to him and told him that God had seen his devotion and his generous giving to the poor. He was to send for a man named Peter, who was staying in Joppa, thirty miles to the south. This man had a message that Cornelius needed to hear. Messengers were immediately dispatched. Meanwhile, Peter had been staying at the house of Simon, the tanner (considered an "unclean" profession by the Jews), and sat on his roof praying. Suddenly he had a vision of a sheet filled with unclean animals being lowered down from heaven. God told Peter to kill the animals and eat them. Peter was appalled at the thought because, as a Jew, he had never eaten anything but kosher food. The vision happened not once, not twice, but three times. Was Peter getting the point? God was declaring that what was formerly unclean was now clean. At that there was a knock on the door and Gentile servants sent from Cornelius invited Peter to travel with them to the north to see their master. It was now clear to Peter that God was up to something, so off they went (Acts 10).

Upon arriving in Caesarea, Peter was no doubt unnerved to find that Cornelius had gathered together his associates, all Gentiles. As Peter stood at the threshold of Cornelius' home, the entire story of God hung in the balance. Would Peter step into his role as the seed of Abram and bless the Gentiles? Praise the Lord. He did! The ascended Christ was so excited about this moment that as Peter began to preach to the Gentile crowd, He poured out the Holy Spirit upon them and they too received the Spirit of prophecy, just as the Jews and Samaritans had. With the conversion, filling, and baptism of the Gentiles Luke has shown that God wants to save all people (Acts 10:17-48). A lingering question remained, however, and here we are taken right back to Stephen's incendiary assertions that the temple and the law were no longer needed. While it was clear to all now that the temple had been rendered obsolete by the atoning death of Christ, the Gentile's relationship to the law and to boundary markers like circumcision and food laws was anything but clear in the minds of some Jewish believers. This issue eventually came to a head as the church gradually became more and more Gentile in its orientation.

The gospel's transmission to the Gentiles was initiated, as were all the demarcation points in the story, by the Holy Spirit. A church had been started in Antioch, Syria by a multi-cultural missionary team from the island of Cyprus and Cyrene in North Africa. There was such a move of the Spirit there that Barnabas was sent down from Jerusalem to oversee the work. Quickly sensing that he would need help, Barnabas remembered his friendship with Saul of Tarsus from many years earlier. Barnabas went to Tarsus, found Saul, and persuaded him to come back to help him mature the work in Antioch (Acts 11:22-26). Later, as the teachers and prophets of the church were fasting and seeking the Lord, the Holy Spirit spoke to set apart Barnabas and Saul for the work to which He had called them. After fasting, they laid hands on the two men and commissioned them off on what we now call the "first missionary journey" to expand the Eden Project (Acts 13:1-4).

After an encounter with a Jewish sorcerer on Cyprus where the power on Saul is clearly evident, the leadership dynamic on the team subtly changes and from that point forward Luke calls the pair "Paul and Barnabas" (Acts 13:5-12). After arriving in Asia Minor, Paul and Barnabas extend the kingdom into a series of Greek cities, Pisidia, Iconium, Lystra and Derbe. In Pisidia, we find the pattern that Paul will follow in every city in which he preaches the gospel. After arriving in a new city, Paul networked with the local Jewish synagogue and, as a visiting rabbi, was generally invited to address the Sabbath gathering. There he preached the crucifixion and resurrection of the Christ and invited people to become baptized and Spirit-filled followers of Jesus. As a general rule, some Jews believed but most did not and Paul was forced to wipe the dust off his shoes and turn to the Gentile harvest (Acts 14:1-4). Very quickly the church in the Diaspora became predominantly Gentile, creating the cultural problems mentioned earlier. This pattern, "to the Jew first, then the Greek" (Rom 2:10), was the vindication of the plan of God from the beginning:

- Breaking the world up into language groups to scatter them around the globe

- Picking one man, Abram, and giving him and his seed a commission as God's people for the world

- Scattering this people throughout the world at the hand of Assyria

- Unifying the world under one language, Greek

- Translating the Jewish Scriptures into Greek

- Using Rome to bring the Pax Romana, establishing peace, connecting the empire with roads, and guaranteeing police protection for Roman citizens

In the fullness of time, God sent His Son (Gal 4:4). Capitalizing on this timing, God called a Jewish rabbi, also a Roman citizen, fluent in Greek, as the apostle to the Gentiles. Paul later introduces his letter to the church at Rome with the mission statement adhered to by the apostolic team: Through Him and for His name's sake, we received grace and apostleship to call people from among all the Gentiles to the obedience that comes from faith (Rom 1:5).

Paul's increasingly Gentile churches were not required to keep the law, thus precipitating what could have been a highly volatile church council. In attendance were those apostles who could be present, the Jewish-Christian leaders that believed that Gentiles had to become Jewish in order to become full followers of Jesus, and Paul and his contingent, which accepted Gentile peoples as peoples and did not require them to adopt Jewish laws or customs. Paul did not need the blessing of the leaders in Jerusalem because he had received his commission and his gospel from the risen Christ (Gal 1:11). He did, however, desire it for the sake of unity. In the end, the day belonged to Peter as he reiterated that it was God Himself who had poured out the Holy Spirit on the Samaritans and the Gentiles without requiring them to keep the law first. James, the brother of Jesus and now the leader of the

115

church in Jerusalem, blessed the Pauline (law-free) gospel, only asking that Gentile converts be sensitive to Jewish cultural issues to preserve unity. This Paul was glad to do (Acts 15:12-30).

The rest of the book of Acts chronicles Paul's apostolic exploits to fulfill Jesus' prophetic word that the gospel would move cross- culturally from Jerusalem, through Judea and Samaria, Syria, Asia, and then Europe. Interestingly, in Paul's second missionary journey he tried to go east into Asia, but Luke tells us that he was "prevented by the Holy Spirit" from doing so and was sovereignly directed in a dream to go west into Macedonia instead (Acts 16:6-7). This is another hinge point in the history of the world. The gospel would take root in Europe with its high value for reading and writing. This would serve well the dissemination of New Testament manuscripts, giving doctrinal objectivity and direction to the churches. The east, however, with its value on oral culture, was not successfully evangelized and the Bible was not valued in the same manner as in the west. In the vacuum arose Islam circa 600 AD, creating the dynamics of the 10/40 window mentioned in our introduction.

As the book of Acts ends in chapter 28 we find Paul reaching Rome, the center of the empire and the New Testament equivalent of the Asphalt Project's tower of Babel and its urban culmination, the city of Babylon. When Paul arrives, he meets with the Jewish leaders who, interestingly, have never heard of him. When he shares the gospel with them we encounter the Jew's typical response: a few believe and the rest reject. Paul turns to the Gentiles, to the unhindered gospel of Jesus as the Christ and the dawning of the Kingdom of God. The fact that Paul is alive at the end is Luke's way of saying that there will be a chapter 29, 30, and so forth, all the way to the end of the age when the time of the Gentiles will have reached its fulfillment.

The Finale

While a full rendition of the biblical data of the end of the age lies far beyond this brief survey, we make mention of five biblical motifs that find their fulfillment in the book of Revelation.

The first is the completion of the mission of the Church. God's plan to break the world into different languages in a divide-to-reach strategy is vindicated in the vision recorded in Revelation 7:10 where John writes:

After this I looked and there before me was a great multitude that no one could count, from every nation, tribe, people and language, standing before the throne and in front of the Lamb. They were wearing white robes and were holding palm branches in their hands. And they cried out in a loud voice: "Salvation belongs to our God, who sits on the throne, and to the Lamb."

Second, we note that throughout our story we have traced the enmity that God put between the seed of the woman and the seed of the serpent. The reader is always aware that this war will ultimately culminate in a great showdown as the clash between good and evil reaches epic proportions at the end of the age. In John's day, as Christians were beginning to be martyred, John sees Rome as a type of ancient Babylon, the final stages of the Asphalt Project. He also sees that Satan will try to put his finishing touches on the tower with the blood of more Christian martyrs than at any time in the history of the church. Finishing the Great Commission will truly involve, as Jesus said, picking up the cross and following Him, all the way to death if need be. In God's final triumph, Babylon the Great is defeated in one, single day. The horse and rider will be thrown into the sea when Satan, his demons and all who follow him will be judged forever.

Third, just as He said, Jesus will return at the completion of the mission of the church. The rider on the white horse will appear just when all will seem lost, but on His thigh is written: *King of Kings and Lord of Lords*. With one fell swoop Satan will fall and the Wedding Supper of the Lamb will commence as the Bridegroom shows up to redeem a Bride from every tongue, tribe, language and nations that is without spot or wrinkle. She is dressed in white linen, a picture of the righteous acts of the saints. Finally, in Revelation 21, we see the Eden Project coming to its final fulfillment. With the descent of the New Jerusalem, we see a picture of the Most Holy Place filling every corner of the new earth. God's joy is complete and His rest is vindicated as He beholds His image covering the earth as the waters cover the sea. There is no longer a need for the Outer Court, for the prayer for the nations has come to completion. There is no longer a need for the Holy Place, for the job of the priests offering sacrifices passed away with the final sacrifice of the Christ. At the end of the age, God will be all in all. As Daniel saw long ago, all will now rise, some to everlasting life, some to shame and everlasting contempt. God will separate the sheep and the goats and the wheat will be shaken from the chaff. For those from every nation that have trusted in God's provision for sin in the substitutionary death and resurrection of his Son, Jesus Christ, John said:

> *And I heard a loud voice from the throne saying, "Now the dwelling of God is with men, and he will live with them. They will be his people, and God himself will be with them and be their God. He will wipe every tear from their eyes. There will be no more death or mourning or crying or pain, for the old order of things has passed away." He who was seated on the throne said, "I am making everything new!" (Rev 21:3-5 NIV)*

Endnotes

[1] The Hebrew word for " tend or till" is `abad meaning: to work, serve.

There are different meanings and derivatives of the Hebrew word used.

See below.

(Qal)

    to labour, work, do work

    to work for another, serve another by labour

    to serve as subjects

    to serve (God)

    to serve (with Levitical service)

(Niphal)

    to be worked, be tilled (of land)

    to make oneself a servant

(Pual) to be worked

(Hiphil)

    to compel to labour or work, cause to labour, cause to serve

    to cause to serve as subjects

(Hophal) to be led or enticed to serve

Francis Brown, *Brown, Driver and Briggs Hebrew and English Lexicon* (Snowball Publishing, 2010).

[2] Robert Burns, *Poems and Song* (New York: P.F. Collier and Sons, 1909).

3 The Hebrew word for "confusion" is babel meaning to confuse by mixing.

Francis Brown, *Brown, Driver and Briggs Hebrew and English Lexicon* (Snowball Publishing, 2010).

4 The Greek word for "glad tidings" is euanggelion used by the gospel writers to declare the gospel or good news of Christ. There are different meanings of the word:

  1. a reward for good tidings

  2. good tidings

    the glad tidings of the kingdom of God soon to be set up, and subsequently also of Jesus the Messiah, the founder of this kingdom. After the death of Christ, the term comprises also the preaching of (concerning) Jesus Christ as having suffered death on the cross to procure eternal salvation for the men in the kingdom of God, but as restored to life and exalted to the right hand of God in heaven, thence to return in majesty to consummate the kingdom of God, the glad tidings of salvation through Christ, the proclamation of the grace of God manifest and pledged in Christ

  3. the gospel

    as the messianic rank of Jesus was proved by his words, his deeds, and his death, the narrative of the sayings, deeds, and death of Jesus Christ came to be called the gospel or glad tidings

5 Thayer and Smith, Greek Lexicon Entry for Evaggelion, http://www.biblestudytools.com/lexicons/greek/kjv/.

Chapter 5
MISSIONS THROUGH
CHURCH HISTORY

"

A study of the historical ways that Christianity has expanded is valuable for putting present-day missions into perspective. It is important to remember that all church history is missions history, as it relates to the continual advance of the gospel into new people groups, whether in Asia, Europe, North America, or elsewhere. Missionary activity is in no way a new thing, and by learning what has occurred in the past, we are better equipped to understand and participate in what God is doing to expand His kingdom in our day.

"

- Peter Prosser

Introduction

The early Christian church grew from a tiny Jewish sect into the world's largest religion in 2000 years. Why is it that a little-known group of believers grew this rapidly and what caused it to happen? The answer, of course, is the power of God! The believers could not have multiplied so fast without God working in their midst.

The church was sent out by Jesus to be His body in the world. This is the essence of mission, from the latin word "missio", to send. The church is the body of Christ, sent out to win the world to Christ. The last thing that Jesus said was to go out into all the world, preaching the Gospel of Jesus and making disciples of the nations (Greek ethnoi-tribes) (Mt 28:19-20). Jesus promised us that He would confirm the Word with signs following (Mk 16:20). A study of Christian missions is a thrilling task, because knowledge of our past helps us to realize what can be done against great odds, even in our own day. This study can also help us to avoid mistakes made in the past which caused whole movements to shipwreck and become failures. Church history is really a story of God's dealings with people and how they took Christ's gospel all over the world.

Some secular historians have predicted the end of the Christian church, claiming that missions are no longer needed, but this is not true. As long as there is one unsaved tribal group without a Christian witness, missions will always be needed.

In fact, the Christian church is now growing faster and larger than at any time in the last two thousand years! Conversions to Christ are estimated at fifteen thousand per day! Churches are being planted by the hundreds each day, and even if Church growth has slowed down in North America, the church is growing by leaps and bounds in Southeast Asia, Africa, China and Central and South America. The Pentecostal Churches alone have grown from zero in 1900 to almost 700 million by 2010!

So here the story begins, significantly in a stable in Bethlehem with the birth of Jesus the Christ, around 5 or 4 BC.

Jesus and the Founding of the Early Church

When Jesus was born, Judaism had been in a long decline and was not reaching out to the nations around it as God had originally intended.[1] Jesus immediately began His ministry by announcing the Kingdom of God, preaching and teaching the good news of Salvation and deliverance, with signs and wonders following as soon as He had been baptized: so should we!

He chose twelve disciples, then seventy others (besides the women who also followed Him), empowering them to cast out demons and heal the sick. The disciples came back rejoicing that the demons were cast out. Jesus, redirecting their focus, told them to rejoice that their names were written in Heaven (Lk 10). The Lord, in His earthly ministry, shared the power of God to heal and perform signs and wonders in the same way that He had done. This power was to continue in the church after His resurrection and ascension back to heaven (Mt 28:18-20) until the Lord comes back in His Second Coming.

In the book of Acts (Greek praxis), the disciples were practicing the same power of God that Jesus had while on earth. Notice that Acts begins with the sentence, "The beginning of what Jesus began to do and teach" through His disciples (Acts 1:1-2). So the Acts are not just the Acts of the Apostles, but the Acts of Jesus Christ through His apostles. We read that after His death and resurrection, the Church received the Power of the Holy Spirit at the day of Pentecost. Suddenly, from 120 people gathered for prayer in the upper room, Peter's preaching in the power of the Spirit produced 3,000 converts! Days later, this grew to 5,000 (Acts 2:41; 4:4). Within weeks, Luke, the writer, tells us that there were too many to count.

From Judea, just as Jesus had commanded in Acts 1, the movement spread to Samaria (the former territory of ancient Israel). From Samaria, where Philip brought revival, the church began to make converts among the Syrians, Arabs, the people of Lebanon and the Greek colonies.

Under Paul, we learn that the church's strategy was to go from Jewish colony to Jewish colony around what is today's country of Turkey, then on to all the colonies around the Mediterranean Sea. We read that Paul was in Turkey and tried to go further northeast, but the Spirit would not let him. Instead, he went northwest into Macedonia, then Greece, and from there to Athens and on to Rome. At the end of Paul's life we read of him trying to go to Spain in the far west of the Roman Empire.

Everywhere that Paul and the early disciples went, they were greatly helped in spreading the gospel of Jesus Christ by three things which the Roman Empire had done:

One, the Romans had conquered all the tribes around the Mediterranean Sea, from Syria, Palestine and Egypt, all of North Africa and all of what is now Turkey, Greece, Italy, France and Spain, all the way up to and including Britain.

Two, in conquering this territory the Romans had spread peace (or at least had made the tribes peaceful on pain of being destroyed). They called this peace the "Pax Romana", the peace of Rome. They also built a system of good roads all over Europe, North Africa and the Middle East, as far as Basra in Iraq. These roads enabled the Christians to quickly spread the good news of Jesus Christ and to plant churches.

Three, all around the Mediterranean Sea were Greek-speaking colonies. The Romans left these colonies to speak Greek, without forcing Latin on them. The language of commerce and trade and common speech was the common Greek language called "koine Greek". This language is what the apostle Paul and the ancient church preached the Gospel with, planting churches all around the Roman Empire using that common language. It helped spread the Gospel quickly so that at the end of the apostles' lives, around 90 AD (when the apostle John died), the gospel had spread all over the Roman Empire, which covered three million square miles in area. Imagine, the disciples, without radio, television, printing presses, computers or telephones, were able to blanket an area as large as the United States with the Gospel! The church was small, but influential and getting stronger by the year.

In addition, the Roman Empire had no strong belief system. Their old gods were being abandoned and the pagan gods, like Baal, were also being deserted. The world was looking for new beliefs and, in the fullness of time, Christianity had appeared at just the right moment.

By the end of 100 AD, the church had five major centers: Rome, Ephesus, Jerusalem, Alexandria and Antioch. From these strong metropolitan cities, the Gospel spread out. Some important things to note about how the church was successful:

- They were united in one body of believers. There were a large number of Jews and Greeks, but there were members of other tribes as well. There was no racial difference. All were one.

- They were united in the Apostles' Doctrine (Acts 2:42).

- They obeyed the gospel. Each believer became a soul winner.

- There was no false separation between clergy and laity. They had pastors and senior leaders, but these were not considered to be better than any ordinary believer.

- The house churches were centers of teaching and training. All believers were expected to contribute with offerings and all were considered ministers (Acts 2:44-46).

- They all were filled with the Holy Spirit and experienced the gifts of the Spirit (1 Cor 12).

- They all experienced believer's baptism. The church was not perfect. 1 Corinthians teaches us that there were serious problems of a moral and doctrinal nature. These were expected to be dealt with quickly and believers who refused to repent or be corrected were disfellowshipped. This was a serious thing and, once disfellowshipped, it took a period of real repentance and training to be included back in the church.

- The church was serious about its task. As John Wesley once said to his preachers, "You have one task—to win souls."

- The church was persecuted: Jesus had predicted this. If you preach the Gospel properly, you will be persecuted. The Good News is not good news to everyone! Some will get very angry and attack the believers. This is what happened to the early church.

First, the Jews began to attack the Church, then the Romans. In the first 300 years of the Church's existence, there were nine major persecutions. The last and worst persecution was the emperor Diocletian in 303-305 AD. Ironically, the Romans persecuted the early church because they thought that the Christians were atheists! This was because the Romans worshipped visible gods and idols, even worshipping the emperors themselves. These "worship" sessions, such as those around modern Christmas for Bacchus, the god of wine, often ended in drunken brawls and sinfulness. The Christians did not worship idols; their God was invisible. To the Romans this was incredible! If a God was invisible, He could not exist!

As a result, many Christians were killed or imprisoned. The Romans enjoyed cruel gladiatorial sports and put the Christians to the sword or set wild animals on them. Others were set on fire and burned. It was serious business being a Christian in those days! In fact the word "witness", in Greek, means becoming a martyr.

Perhaps the real reason for state persecution was that the Romans really feared the Christians. The slaves were becoming Christians in large numbers, won by other slaves. Potentially over half of all persons in the Roman Empire were slaves - millions of them! These were turning to Christ in very large numbers. Someone once said that Rome got rid of slavery, not because of an explosive revolt, but because the Empire imploded. That is, it fell apart because so many slaves converted their masters and the masters themselves released them from their slavery! The empire, unable to continue enslaving its peoples, had to radically change. The change was to come in 313 AD with the Emperor Constantine's conversion. Church historian Cairnes estimates that at least five and probably fifteen percent of at least 75 million people in the empire had become Christian, a figure of about 10 million! It is interesting to realize that fifteen per cent of a nation could bring about such a change. What about today? How many Christians does it take to change a nation?

313-410 AD - The Church Becomes Accepted and Finally Conquers

The church continued to grow for three hundred years. By 313 AD, a Roman emperor actually became a Christian. His name was Constantine and he said that he had had a vision of the cross shining brighter than the sun. Presumably, he had been a sun worshipper. But afterward, even though he remained a brutal man, he lifted the persecution against Christians and began to push Christianity as a viable religion of the state. Christianity did not become a state religion at this time, as some wrongly assume. Instead, Christianity became a tolerated religion of the state (much as it is today) because it was seen to be a good force for law and order in Rome.

Within a few generations, the old gods of Rome were finished, their temples deserted. Christianity began to look more and more like good sense. And with the emperors themselves becoming, if not believers themselves, then at least influenced by Christianity, many ordinary people began to join the church for political gain. Since so many people began to crowd into the churches who were not converted, the Sunday services became spectacles of color, sound and sight, rather than preaching. The people began to attend and be an audience, rather than participate. The conversion of Constantine allowed the building of churches and the rise of a special clergy, since they were the only ones who could read and write. Pomp took over and the simple people remained unlearned laity, dependent on a special group of clergy who performed the ceremonies. With the increasing numbers of unlearned, unsaved people, the services began to become quasi-magical occasions, ruled by learned persons who interpreted God's will for the unlettered people. In addition, emperors consulted the bishops, giving bishops more and more power.

What happened to the "real church" at this time? It continued, but withdrew to small, out of the way places. The religious communities of monks and nuns date to this time. Believers, seeking true fellowship away from the hordes in the churches, went off into the woods, deserts, mountains and valleys, founding communities of prayer, Bible reading and translating, and evangelism of new tribes. This period of acceptance of Christianity did not last, because the Roman Empire did not last! A storm was gathering on the frontiers of Rome that would sweep everything away. This coming storm was the invasion of the pagan German, Hun and Arab tribes.

375-1060 AD - The Dark Ages

The state of the church crumbles before the Barbarian tribes but missions continue. The invasion of successive German tribes from the North and Eastern frontiers swamped the old Roman Empire. These German tribes, led by the Goths, Franks, Anglos, Saxons, Vandals, Vikings and later by the Huns and Arabs, all radically altered the Roman Empire. The state church faltered and fell under the cruel attacks of the Vandals and Goths, but true Christianity continued.

The religious communities of monks began to evangelize these tribes and eventually, over a period of hundreds of years, won some over to Christianity. The true story of the dark ages is this: small communities of unarmed Christian monks won over whole tribes, usually by converting the tribal chiefs and kings through miracles.

Patrick, a Briton, was taken to Ireland as a slave. Escaping to France, Patrick was converted to Christ and called to preach to his former enslavers. By preaching and healing, Patrick and others converted Ireland from idol worship to Christianity. The country itself became a nation of missionaries. Hundreds of Irish monks and nuns went out to convert Scotland and parts of Britain. Irish monks went to France and Germany, and as far as Switzerland. The pagan Franks were converted and proceeded to send missionaries into Spain. The monks also protected the Bible in their mountain monasteries. They copied the versions down through the centuries for the church to use, right up until the printing press was invented in the 15th century.

A light shined through these dark ages. It was the work of these communities, many of them unknown today, who carried out the evangelism to warlike and bloodthirsty tribes. First the German tribes were converted. (This was to have a significant impact on Protestantism and missions in general, because almost all of the revivals and missionaries came out of Anglo-Saxon and German peoples a thousand years later.) But, even though much good work was done, many pagan practices crept into the city churches. A real hierarchy arose that had little to do with true Christianity. The bishop of Rome was like an emperor, demanding that all the church should obey him. Practices that had more to do with idol worship had also crept in. The people, en masse, were still not evangelized. Their tribal leaders had decided, in the name of the tribe, that they would become Christian, but few had a heartfelt Christian conversion. Instead, many of the quickly baptized pagans had simply renamed their idols and beliefs as Christian. Diana and Venus worship was switched to the Virgin Mary, but many believed exactly as they had always believed in the worship of the earth mother. Pagan gods of the hills, streams and valleys were given saints' names. Sun worship became incorporated into Sunday worship. As Cairns said, "Far too many had been won to the Christian religion too quickly for the church to train them… The church, in attempting to meet the need of the barbarians, was itself partially paganized."

It was at this time, in the dark ages, that the bishops of Rome, now known as the papacy, arose and fell into the grossest sins. The adoption of Roman Latin by the ancient church for its services meant that the majority of those who attended could not understand the language of the service. To these unlettered persons, the service had become "hocus pocus", a quasi magical occasion.[2] It is therefore quite understandable that heresies and quarrels arose in the church that would split it into two halves in 1054 AD, Roman Catholic and Greek Orthodox, and again in 1517 AD, when Protestantism began to split off under Martin Luther in Germany.

1060-1517 AD - Schism, Crusades and more Evangelism

As mentioned in the previous section, the ancient church split in 1054 AD. The cause was really over who was in charge of the church, the pope or head bishops in a plurality.

The popes of Rome had come to believe that they were the only true successors of Christ through Saint Peter. Saint Peter, they believed, had alone been given the keys of the kingdom of heaven by Jesus and that only those recognized by Roman popes were true Christians. The Eastern bishops of the church in Alexandria, Antioch, and particularly Constantinople (Istanbul, Turkey) believed that the keys had been given to all the apostles, not just Peter. Thus, leadership in the church was collegial not singular. All bishops of the church shared this leadership with Christ as the head of the church. While a bishop might be elected as a presiding leader, he was not the sole leader. (Later, in 1854 AD, the popes were to declare themselves infallible when sitting on Saint Peter's throne!) The anger between the Greek bishops and Rome boiled over and led to each side declaring that the others were accursed of God.

Meanwhile, back in the 7th century, Mohammed had arisen in Arabia and started a new religion called Islam (submission to God). He had organized the tribes of Arabia and had begun to conquer the Middle East. In 100 years, the Arabs conquered North Africa, obliterating thousands of Christian churches there, and invaded Spain. By 732, the Arab armies were defeated just outside Paris, France. All of Spain was under Islamic rule for over 100 years and portions of the country were under Islamic control for 700 years. Wherever the Islamic armies went, Christianity suffered. Christians were given three choices: become Islamic, die, or stay Christian, but pay a yearly tax to Islam.[3]

Christianity paid a heavy price for neglecting to evangelize the Arabs. A church leader once said, "If we do not evangelize others, they will evangelize us." Even today, there are not enough missionaries in Muslim countries and those that are often stay in largely evangelized areas. However, the rise in non-missionaries is helping to fill this need.

Fortunately, not all of the church was asleep, and again it was the religious communities who led the way. Groups like the Dominicans and especially Saint Francis and the Franciscans, discovered the simple gospel of Christ and began to live it and preach it. Francis himself is an interesting character. The son of a rich, grasping merchant in North Italy, Francis first wanted to be a knight in shining armor. He was captured in battle and imprisoned as a hard-drinking, gambling young man. Falling ill, he almost died, but had a vision of Jesus Christ telling him to go and preach the Gospel. When he was released from prison, he gave up his old ways, renounced his wealth and began to preach the gospel. Others had done this also, but in Francis' case, he was able to meet the pope, a rascal called Innocent III. "Innocent" this man was not, but he was so impressed by Francis and his followers that he gave orders to let them be and to go out and preach this gospel. Francis was one of the first Christians to advocate the sending of missionaries to the Muslim world. By the time of his death at age 44, thousands of men and women had become Christians in Italy, France and other countries. He remains, even today, one of the most influential of all Catholic preachers.

Other leaders followed, but increasingly they began to attack, and be attacked, by the church. Two of these movements were the Southern French Albigensians (Cathars) and the equally French Waldensian movements of the twelfth century.

The first crusades (military conquests by supposedly Christian groups) were actually launched against the Albigensians. This group, as the Waldensians did, based their initial beliefs in the New Testament. That was where the similarity stopped. While the Waldensians tried to model their lives on the New Testament, the Albigensians departed from it, believing in a form of Gnosticism. The Gnostics believed that a good God had created the soul and spirit, but that a bad god had created flesh. This evil god had received a human body when cast out of heaven and had created the human body to lure people into sin. The world and all matter is evil and only spirit is good. Therefore humans should not procreate, because that would produce more evil beings. Marriage, oaths, war, meat - all were banned. The previously mentioned Pope Innocent III launched a crusade against them and tens of thousands were murdered or burned at the stake. Afterward, the lands were forfeited and given to the kingdom of France, which allied with the papacy.

They more noticeably Christian, sincerely preached a simple gospel. They were excommunicated from the Catholic church in 1184 AD, but carried on preaching anyway. The Waldensians believed that everyone should have access to a Bible. Since the Bible was expensive (the equivalent of a year's salary) and in short supply, small portions of the Gospel were handwritten and given out. Memorized and often set to song, these were then passed on to others. The illiterate learned the scriptures by heart. Tens of thousands of Waldensians still exist in Italy today and parts of South America, forerunners by 300 years of the Protestant Reform of 1517.

Apart from these reformers were military knights who also formed orders of monks. It is hard to say if these were true Christians or not. Certainly there would have been Christians among them. Three major orders were the Knights of the Hospital of St. John, the Knights of the Temple of Solomon, and a far more influential order called the German or Teutonic Knights. The Knights of the Hospital, Temple and the Teutonic Knights all went on the crusades to the Holy Land. This was an attempt by the papacy to grab the ancient land of Israel, dominate the Middle East, take over the Greek Orthodox Church, and to found a Christian kingdom in Jerusalem dominated by the Frankish knights.

The first crusade succeeded in taking the Holy Land, but later attempts to hold onto it failed. Eventually, after 150 years, the Arabs and Turks took it back and little remains of this great effort except for ruined crusader castles in the Middle East. Meanwhile, the actual word "crusade" will set Muslims off attacking Christians, since the Muslims "crusade" means genocide. Indeed, many of the crusader knights did commit mass murder (as did Mohammed) and the German knights went up to Lithuania, Poland and Prussia and exterminated thousands of people there, taking their land and founding their own Germanic kingdom called Prussia, the forerunner of imperial Germany.

1329-1490 AD - Forerunners of the Protestant Reformation: Wycliffe, Savonarola and Hus

Biblical reform was always close to erupting all through Church History. Missions were going on all through the dark ages. There were true Christians trying to preach the Gospel even while many of the crusaders were guilty of rape, pillage and murder. Saint Francis himself actually walked unarmed into the Arab-Turkish camp and preached the Gospel to Saladin, the Kurdish leader of the Muslims. He was almost persuaded, but challenged Francis "to go back and convert your crusaders. When they begin to live like your Jesus Christ, I will become a Christian." Unfortunately, sometimes the worst examples of Christianity are those who profess to live it. One wonders what would have happened if the crusaders had actually tried to live the Gospel instead of attacking and killing the Muslims. How different the Middle East would be today!

John Wycliffe

John was an Oxford university professor, born in 1329, who discovered the simple Gospel of Jesus Christ by actually translating the Latin New Testament into English. John had tried to reform the British Catholic church by encouraging the princes to get rid of evil clergy and taking the churches' considerable property away. As he read the New Testament, he realized that the Catholic Church had wandered far from its ancient roots. By 1382 he had translated the whole New Testament into understandable English (the King James Version in 1611 was influenced by Wycliffe's earlier version). He trained lay preachers to preach the simple message, often by singing the gospel in simple songs that their hearers could not only understand but learn by heart.

The Catholic Church had said that it was sole authority for the believer. Wycliffe said otherwise - the Bible was the sole authority and the church needed to return to the Bible and reform itself accordingly. Wycliffe demanded to know where it said in the New Testament that Christ had set up a papacy under the Apostle Peter. He had stumbled upon something quite fundamental. Put the Bible into the hands of the common people and they will believe in Christ and reform their own lives. The people will become freedom-loving and will not stand for tyranny. People who love God and the liberty of the sons of God will also demand true liberty. Wycliffe's movement was to lead to free speech, free voting in parliament, and the right to vote for all.

Bohemian (Czech) students studying in London carried Wycliffe's ideas back to their homeland when King Richard II of England married Princess Anne of Bohemia. Wycliffe's ideas also made their way to the University of Prague. John Hus, pastor of the chapel on Prague University campus, began to preach Wycliff's ideas from the pulpit. From 1402 to 1414, Hus carried forward his ideas of reforming the Czech Catholic Church. Tricked into traveling to the Catholic Council of Constance in 1415, where he thought he would get a hearing, he was arrested without being able to present the Gospel to the people there. He was ordered to reject his own preaching, but refused. Thereupon he was burned to death.

The blood of the martyrs is the seed of the church and three centuries later, a missionary movement was born in Bohemia

- Moravia in 1727. These men and women, known as Moravian Brethren, directly influenced John Wesley into starting the Wesleyan Methodist revival movement. Hus's doctrine was also well known later by Martin Luther, who started the Protestant churches in Germany one hundred years later.

Savonarola (1452-98), a Dominican Italian priest, tried to start a reform movement in the Italian church in Florence. His preaching stirred the common people to believe, much as Francis of Assisi had done 250 years earlier, but he made great enemies in Florence. He was arrested, strangled and burnt. Nevertheless, his name is well known as a reformer even today.

So confused had the Catholic Church become at the time of John Hus that there were actually three popes at the time, all claiming to be the true pope! A council (Constance, which killed Hus) was called, deposed all three and elected a new pope; whereupon all four popes claimed to be the real one! Not until all of the previous three claimants died was there to be one pope again. Reformation was inevitable. The papacy had proven itself incapable of self-reform. In fact, had become controlled by two Italian families, who shamelessly bought and sold high church offices with gold.

1517 AD - Luther and the Protestant Mission

Along came Luther! Born 1483 AD, Martin had decided to become a monk, to find salvation for himself through prayer. By now the previously spiritual Catholic orders of monks had fallen far from grace. Luther, unable to find spiritual peace, was ordered to study the Bible; what an order! In so doing, he had to learn Greek and Hebrew as well as Latin. While translating Romans chapter one, Luther discovered that the believer is justified by faith through grace alone, not by works. He was converted.

Preaching this, he began to get into trouble. Attempts were made to shut him up. Finally, he was called before the German parliament by the Emperor and ordered to stop on pain of death.

His answer has echoed down through history: "Unless by Scripture and reason you can persuade me otherwise, I cannot and will not recant my writings. I am bound by my conscience. Here I stand. I cannot do otherwise, so help me God."

It was a cannon shot heard across history! Luther was condemned to be burnt but escaped, was protected by sympathetic German princes and became the leader of the Protestant Reformation. He was ordered to go into hiding to preserve his life. While in hiding at Wartburg Castle, Luther translated the Bible into vernacular German, understandable to anyone who could read. Meanwhile, the reform spread all over Germany in weeks, helped by the invention of the modern printing press. Soon France, Switzerland, Poland, Britain, Hungary and Holland, and then all of Scandinavia were affected. The churches in most of these lands became Protestant, but Catholic armies managed to force Poland back under Catholicism. In spite of bitter opposition from Catholic armies from Spain, resulting in the loss of thousands of lives, the damage had been done permanently to the Catholic Church. It tried some reforms, but Protestantism was able to survive and flourish.

Out of Germany, Northern France, Holland, Denmark, England and Scotland came missionaries who later carried the gospel to the ends of the earth. The fruit of the Reformation was Protestant churches and eventually missions.

Unfortunately, right at the beginning differences over doctrine appeared among the Protestants and soon the Presbyterians split away from Luther under John Calvin. From the Lutherans, the Anabaptists and Mennonites split. From the Presbyterians, the Baptists split, and so on. This has been a tendency down through history until today.

Another unfortunate result of the Reformation was a tendency to reject all miracles as Catholic inventions. True miracles of the Holy Spirit had followed Francis of Assisi; he had cast out demons and healed the sick. Other so-called saints had done likewise, but when rejecting something, we have a tendency to overreact. These miracles were discounted as being inventions of Catholics trying to make their saints look like the apostles of the New Testament. John Calvin and Martin Luther tended to play down the miracles of the church. Calvin went so far as to say that miracles were no longer needed by the church! As a man thinks in his heart, so is he, or so does he believe!

It took another 200 years for the Protestants to begin to seek to practice the gifts of the Spirit. Another two hundred years went by for them to become considered "normal" in church life again. (Isn't it interesting how normal can become abnormal and abnormal become normal, just because some great person says that's how it should be?) Because of John Calvin's belief, millions of Bible-believing Christians have been deprived of the whole Gospel! Truly, "My people are destroyed for lack of knowledge" (Pro 29:18).

Great revival movements would begin, but for two hundred years, Calvin's influence would affect millions of Christians in the Presbyterian-Baptist churches. It would bring revival to change attitudes, but only in America, at least at first.

1700-1850 AD - Revival in America

There have been several major revival periods in American history. New England and the rest of the east coast down to Georgia saw the beginnings of revival in the 1730's. This revival exploded from 1739-1742 and became known as the Great Awakening. In the early 1800's, revival spread along the western frontier, especially in the Cane Ridge meetings in Kentucky. Others would add a fourth revival in 1859 in New York and a fifth with the Pentecostal Revival of 1901- 1914. But the two early ones were earth-changing in nature. The New York revival of 1859 was more local, while the Pentecostal one was not trans-denominational in flavor. The first two affected all of American life in the early years.

Oddly, the first New England revivals were started among

Presbyterians and other reformed groups, and then spread to other denominations. Jonathan Edwards' and the Tennant Brothers' preaching brought tremendous revivals in mid 1700's, changing New England's life for the better. Estimates are given that of three million persons in the colonies, over one million were converted!

In 1738, George Whitefield's and John Wesley's Methodist revivals joined up with the Presbyterian revivals until revival spread through all the thirteen colonies. The Methodist revivals affected Maryland, Virginia, the Carolinas and Georgia. Reformed churches, like the Presbyterians, dominated New England. These revivals, a generation before the American Revolution of the 1770's, molded the colonists' spirit so that they would be united and ready for that revolution. It is true to say that thirteen colonies would not have become one nation without the influence of the united revivals of the Presbyterians and John Wesley's Methodists in the eighteenth century.

From the beginnings of the Protestant reformation there was some discussion of missions and some missionaries crossed cultures to do missions work. Examples include Elliot in New England, who reached Indian tribes, two Danish missionaries who went to India in the 1730's, David Brainerd who reached Indians in the 1740's, and especially the Moravians who sent out 100 missionaries over several decades. Some Indian tribes were even evangelized in Canada by Huguenot fur traders. There was no concerted effort and no proper theology of missions, however.

This changed with the life of William Carey. He wrote in 1790 on the need to "use means" to reach the unreached people and soon went to India as a missionary himself. He spent almost 40 years in India. With him, a full theology of missions developed for Protestantism and a massive worldwide protestant missions movement began. Soon two major mission sending societies developed in England. One was with the Anglican Church and the other non-denominational. The first American missions societies would follow shortly. Many books list Adoniram Judson as the first American missionary to go outside the U.S. in about 1812, but there were actually three or four African American missionaries who left before him and went to various locations in the Caribbean to evangelize. The development 1) of a well developed Biblical theology of missions and 2) the organization of dedicated missions sending societies put teeth to the emerging worldwide Protestant mission's movement. Over time, through experience and many failures, the missions societies began to slowly accumulate understanding of other ethnic groups and learn do's and don'ts to be observed on the mission field.

From the beginnings of the Protestant Reformation, Bible translation into local languages was very important. People such as Luther and Tyndale left translations of the Bible in the local languages. When William Carey went to India, he put a major emphasis on translating the Bible into a number of local Indian languages. He established the pattern of Bible translation into local languages as an integral part of Protestant missionary work. To this day, Bible translation is an important part of spreading the Gospel among unreached people groups.

Protestant missionaries went from all the Protestant areas of Europe and North America. These would include Canadians, Finns, Norwegians and Swedish workers, those from Holland and Protestant parts of Germany and other regions. The missionaries were trying to go to the entire world. India was one of the first non-western targets as were the south Pacific and other developed British colonies. Eventually as regions in Africa were colonized, missionary work began there. China was opened by several people, but one of the most famous missionaries of all times, Hudson Taylor, founded the China Inland Mission in the 1860's; the mission's philosophy and prayer inspired generations of later missionaries.

Early missionaries went to some Muslim areas, including parts of India, Egypt and Turkey. There were Americans in eastern Turkey by the 1840's and British in Egypt at about the same time. However, there was discovered to be great resistance to the Gospel among the Muslims and most switched their focus to nominal Christian peoples in the area. The Americans, in Eastern Turkey focused on the Armenians and those working in Egypt on the Coptic Christians. Islamic missions were to remain a largely neglected area well into the 20th century. Protestant attempts to reach Muslims throughout the 19th century were scattered and often saw little success. At the beginning of the 20th century, Samuel Zwemer began a more focused interest in reaching Muslims. He devoted years of research to reaching Muslims. Slowly, more and more Protestant mission agencies began to emphasize Muslim missions.

Unfortunately, there were strongly paternalistic and colonialist ideas among some of the Protestant missionaries. Some tried to break this mold and see all groups as equal and to create a missions movement that recognized ability and giftedness more than ethnicity and culture. One great example was Henry Venn, an Englishman who worked in the latter part of the 19th century. He appointed Ajai Crowther, an African as Anglican bishop in part of Nigeria. Many of the English in Nigeria were opposed to this move because of racist ideas. White groups in America eventually stopped the sending of many African American missionaries from the U.S. after the civil war. Henry Venn also developed one of the most important missions concepts, called "three self". He said that emerging churches and denominations on the mission field should eventually be self-supporting, self-governing and self-propagating. This cardinal principle holds true to this day wherever indigenous church planting movements are being started. Henry Venn and British missionary Rolland Allen developed strong understandings and philosophies of how church planting movements are to be spawned and fostered.

There also developed a strong support system for missions in the sending countries. Churches would often have missions committees and prayer groups dedicated to missions. Certain pastors and evangelists became great supporters of missions, including George Mueller in England and Dwight L. Moody in the US. The Bible training schools, such as Moody Bible Institute, began training missionaries and courses were offered on missions in seminaries. The lives of famous missionaries, such as David Livingstone and Adoniram Judson, were read by many young Christians. Home based mission organizations began to proliferate. Some were denominationally based and others worked non-denominationally. By the year 1900 the idea of missions and giving to missions was deeply rooted throughout Protestantism in churches that were evangelical in nature. An excellent example is the American Southern Baptists who have been one of the greatest missionary sending and supporting organizations ever founded.

From time to time on the mission field there would occur what is called a "people movement," where a significant portion of an ethnic group or region would turn to Christ in a short period of time. Missionaries had to learn how to deal with this. Revivals would occur on the missions field throughout the 19th and 20th century, where the same characteristics of revivals found in the sending areas would occur on the field. These include a powerful outpouring of the Spirit with repentance, evangelistic fruit and unusual manifestations of the Spirit. Many of the worldwide denominations of Protestantism all over the non-Western world were birthed in revival.

One such development began in Germany in the late 1700's. Initiated by Don Schleiermacher, this was the rise of what is now called Protestant Liberalism. Slowly, more and more seminaries in Germany and other countries became liberal. Within two generations after seminaries would liberalize, the denominations would become liberal. This would eventually impact denominations in nations as far away as India. The movement had a devastating impact on Protestant missions. Missionaries, under the influence of Liberalism, no longer believed many of the core Christian doctrines, such as the need for new birth or the divine inspiration of scripture. As a result, the scriptural mandate toward missions was watered down greatly. Some mission organizations, such as the China Inland Missions, held to the inerrancy of scriptures, while others abandoned this core doctrine.

In the 20th century, missiology developed as its own field of study. Areas of interest, such as anthropology, world religions, history of missions and church planting, began developing and were incorporated into the training of some missionaries. Understanding of worldview and differences between Western and non-western cultural norms and patterns began to develop so that missions became more balanced and began to more clearly separate what is cultural from what is Biblical. The Western anti-supernatural world view was first challenged severely by the early Pentecostal pioneer missionaries who saw spectacular results partly because they understood the supernatural realm. Later even many evangelical missionaries would begin to adjust to a worldview that accommodated the supernatural.

There were many factors that lead up to the Pentecostal outbreak in Azusa Street in 1906, but this movement was to have massive effects on the non-Western portions of the world and the entire worldwide Protestant missions movement. Some of these precursors were revivalists, pre-Pentecostal people who operated in the spiritual gifts, and the increasing growth of a non-Western based Protestant church that was hungry for the supernatural and did not intrinsically believe in cessationism.

Endnotes

[1] Nation, in scripture, refers to an ethnic group of people or tribe, not a modern state.

[2] Hocus pocus is a corruption of the Latin saying "hoc est corpus meum", meaning, "This is my body", words spoken by the priest during Holy Communion.

[3] This tax is still paid in Egypt. In most other Muslim countries, this choice has been removed. Christianity is not allowed in most Islamic nations.

Chapter 6
SPIRIT-FILLED MISSIONS

" *Both the history and the theological understanding of missions have been radically affected by the Pentecostal movement, which launched many into Spirit-empowered ministry in diverse places all over the globe. As a result of this outpouring, much of the church around the world today is familiar with the power of the Holy Spirit in ways that were less common in previous centuries. The Pentecostal emphasis on the imminent return of Jesus created a fresh zeal for mission activity, and their expectation of God's supernatural involvement in the world allowed Christianity to flourish in cultures that did not share the western naturalistic worldview. An understanding of this movement will not only give us a clearer picture of the world church, but also remind us of the vital importance of the empowering work of the Holy Spirit in missions.* "

- Clifton Clarke

Introduction

"But you will receive power when the Holy Spirit comes on you; and you will be my witnesses in Jerusalem, and in all Judea and Samaria, and to the ends of the earth." (Acts1:8 NIV).

The Christian mission is implicitly connected with the infilling and power of the Holy Spirit. This notion, in spite of its biblical precedent, has been greatly neglected in the Protestant theology of mission. Paul Pomerville, the author of the book *The Third Force in Mission*, which was written in response to this pneumatological neglect in missions, maintains that "an inordinate 'silence on the Holy Spirit is part of the Protestant mission heritage."[1] With the exception of aspects of the Pietist movements and the Evangelical Awakenings of the seventeenth and eighteenth centuries, the Protestant church has reflected very little on the place and function of the Holy Spirit in the theology and practice of missions. Consequently, a Protestant theology of mission has been somewhat slow in its development. For many of the reformers, including Martin Luther and John Calvin, it was assumed that the Great Commission was actually completed during the time of the Apostles.[2] Gustav Warneck, the father of missiology as a theological discipline, was one of the first Protestant scholars to bring this to our attention. He notes, "we miss in the Reformers not only missionary action but even the idea of missions, in the sense in which we understand them today."[3]

If one is to agree with the traditionally held view that William Carey (1761-1834) is the "father of modern Protestant mission," it took a period of two hundred and seventy five years (from the time when Luther posted his Ninety-Five Theses (1517) to the publication of William Carey's treatise 'An Enquiry into the Obligations of Christians to Use Means for the Conversion of the Heathen' (1792)) for Protestant Christian missions to be officially launched.[4]

The Pietist and Evangelical movements, referred to above, called for a more "heart-felt" and biblically based spirituality against the barren orthodoxy and dead formalism of Protestant Europe. These movements were early signs of a Spirit-filled mission but fell short of articulating a full theology of mission from the perspective of the Holy Spirit. The advance of a Spirit-focused missiology was therefore even slower in its development. One of the contributing factors for the delay in a pneumatological focus on mission was the contextualization project in Christian mission. From this priority of 'context' emanated a number of innovative theologies which included: liberation theology, contextual theologies, black theologies, Asian theologies, Feminist theologies, and African theologies, to name a few. This, however, created a missiology from 'below' that resulted in neglecting a mission theology from 'above' which would have included a Spirit-focused missiology.

The alarm bells warning of the perils of this pneumatological neglect were sounded by a number of theologians and Christian leaders whose voices it appears went unheeded. Roland Allen, who served as a missionary to China with the Society for the Propagation of the Gospel in the late nineteenth century, was one of these voices. He argued passionately that missionary work was an expression of the Holy Spirit and that this Spirit-empowered perception was vital for believers. Yet this expression of mission in scripture was given such slight and casual attention that it may go unnoticed by the hasty reader.[5] Max Warren, a former Anglican Priest and General Secretary of the Church Missionary Society in the UK, argued that the growth of the Pentecostal and charismatic churches was a result of the dearth of the pneumatological witness of the Holy Spirit. He believed that Pentecostalism was a protest movement against the pneumatological vacuum that had engulfed the church and its mission.[6] Melvin Hodges, a former Assemblies of God missionary to Nicaragua and Pentecostal missiologist, described the silence on the Holy Spirit as a "neglect of an indispensable qualification for missions - the enduement of Pentecostal power."[7] Hodges, following Max Warren, also believed the rapid growth of the Pentecostal movement was due to the rightful place that the

Pentecostal movement had given to the Holy Spirit in line with the New Testament.[8] Paul Pomerville's book, mentioned above, is a compelling thesis which convincingly outlines the indispensible role of the Spirit as the power-for-mission. Pomerville confronts western Enlightenment attitudes which ignore the miraculous and numinous in its missionary theology.[9] The culmination of these various movements and pneumatological insights have contributed to what we now know as Pentecostal missiology.

Pentecostal Missiology

Pentecostals have been at the forefront of bringing to the attention of the Christian church the vital place of the Holy Spirit for our generation and dispensation. This effective effort has been demonstrated through praxis and not by producing theological treatise. Allan Anderson notes that among early Pentecostals little weight was given to intellectual ability as a means of articulating the Pentecostal understanding of mission. Historically it seems that Pentecostals have been expert practitioners of mission, not scholars. As a result of this practical focus, there has been a profound lack of theological or missiological articulations of the Pentecostal mission understanding.[10] The Pentecostal movement has recently celebrated its first century and over the last twenty years it has taken its place among other global theological traditions; yet in order to maintain its effectiveness in teaching and empowering believers in mission, Pentecostals must begin to clearly express their theology of mission.

This chapter seeks to make a contribution to the Pentecostal articulation of mission. My main thesis is one that places the Spirit-filled life and the goal of world evangelization as mutually compatible and inextricably linked. Therefore, the goal of this chapter is to articulate a Spirit-filled missiology that could inform Christian witness.

Who are the Pentecostals?

Any attempt to come up with a precise definition of the modern day Pentecostal movement is fraught with difficulties. This challenge of characterization is due to the fact that Pentecostalism, as a movement, did not have a distinct beginning in a geographical place or particular doctrine.[11] Broadly speaking one could describe Pentecostalism as a historically related movement where the emphasis is on the exercise of spiritual gifts.[12] Pentecostalism is therefore an umbrella term that includes a wide range of different theological and organizational perspectives. The term Pentecostal is derived from Pentecost, a Greek term describing the Jewish Feast of Weeks. This event commemorates the descent of the Holy Spirit upon the early disciples of Jesus Christ, as described in the Book of Acts, Chapter 2. Pentecostals see continuity between this early outpouring of the Holy Spirit and the later outpourings at Azusa Street and in other parts of the world. The three major streams that are traditionally recognized are: classical Pentecostalism, neo-Pentecostalism, and Catholic Charismatics.[13] Classical Pentecostals comprise churches which broke away from the historic churches of Protestantism in the early part of the 20th century.[14] The neo-Pentecostals (also known as the Charismatic Movement or Charismatic Renewal) refer to a movement of the Holy Spirit in the late 1950s within the historic Protestant churches which emphasized the baptism in the Spirit.[15] The designation "Catholic Charismatic" or "Catholic Charismatic Renewal" refers to a movement of the Holy Spirit within the Catholic Church which was Pentecostal in expression. This movement involved a "baptism in the Spirit" and a renewed emphasis on the manifestation of the gifts of the Spirit.[16]

In addition to this more western representation, there are Pentecostal renewal traditions that arose in other countries quite independently from the three movements stated above. For example, in the late 1900s, Pandita Sarasvati Ramabi led a powerful revival movement in India. Ramabai, a converted Brahmin, was instrumental in the origins of Pentecostalism and in the acceptance of its phenomena among the wider Indian Christian community.[17] In Africa, Pentecostalism has a unique historiography emanating from various indigenous movements which include African prophetism, African indigenous churches and African traditional religion.[18]

As a movement, Pentecostalism has truly come of age and is a dominant force within global Christianity. The factor of Pentecostalism's exponential growth and worldwide scope has led to it being referred to as the "Third Force" in Christianity following Catholicism and Protestantism. [19]

The Missionary Spirit

As I mentioned above, Pentecostalism is polycentric in origin and diverse in expression. However, one common and central theme among Pentecostals is the belief in the supernatural and dynamic work of the Holy Spirit. A personal encounter with the Holy Spirit, who enables and empowers the people of God for service, is a non-negotiable experience. According to Steven Land, 'the starting point for Pentecostal theology is its distinctive spirituality: the Holy Spirit which is God with us'.[20] For Pentecostals it is highly significant that at the opening of the Acts of the Apostle (perhaps better described as the Acts of the Holy Spirit), towards the end of Jesus' ministry on earth, Jesus admonishes His disciples not to leave Jerusalem but to wait for the promise of the Father.[21] This promise would result in three things which are all central to a Pentecostal theology of mission. First, they would receive the baptism of the Holy Spirit (Acts 1:4); secondly, they would receive power (Acts 1:8a); and thirdly, they would become Christ's witnesses in Jerusalem, Judea, and in Samaria and unto the uttermost part of the earth (Acts 1:8b). The relationship between receiving the power of the spirit and becoming Christ's witnesses is inextricably linked and goes to the heart of Pentecostal mission theology and praxis. It is this experience of the fullness of the Spirit that is at the very essence of Pentecostalism. For the early Pentecostals, being empowered by the Holy Spirit was not an option because becoming a witness was the natural corollary of receiving the infilling of the Holy Spirit. For them, the Holy Spirit was a missionary Spirit. As the Indianapolis Pentecostal leader and the first General Secretary of the Assemblies of God, J. Roswell Flowers, put it in 1908, "when the Holy Spirit comes into our hearts, the missionary Spirit comes in with it, they are inseparable."[22]

The Return of the Spirit's Power

For many of the early Pentecostals there was a feeling that the supernatural encounter with the Holy Spirit in mission was lost when the church turned away from this original source of power. This left a spiritual vacuum which gave rise to a prolonged history of state operated nominal religion devoid of spiritual vitality and power. This came to its zenith during the 18th and 19th centuries with the rise of liberalism, which was further precipitated by an enlightenment agenda which poured scorn on the supernatural. Apart from the flickering light burning within movements such as Pietism, Lutheranism and Methodism, Christianity was stripped of its supernatural prowess and reduced to a rubble of lifeless creeds and dogma based upon reason and rationality. This is a somewhat simplified and reductionistic summary of post-Constantinian Christianity; nonetheless this was the historiographical lens through which many early Pentecostals saw the Church. It was the rediscovery of this Holy Spirit power and spiritual vitality in the Church that gave impetus to the rise of the Pentecostal movement early in the 19th century. In the same way that the early disciples became aware that God's mission would take more than human effort and ability, the early Pentecostals recognized that the success of God's mission would require supernatural abilities. This supernatural ability came in the form of the baptism of the Holy Spirit which was evident in the experience of the early apostles. Therefore this experience of being baptized with the Holy Spirit was a very significant feature of the early Pentecostal missionary movement.

The Baptism of the Spirit for Mission

The early Pentecostals spoke universally of the central experience they called "baptism in the Spirit" or "filling with the Spirit" which was believed to be accompanied by speaking in tongues. The Baptism of the Spirit was understood as a gift of power upon a sanctified life. Once received, one is empowered with the supernatural power of God. However, during the early years of the

Pentecostal movement, there was great misunderstanding over the purpose of speaking with tongues. Many thought the ability to speak in tongues was the supernaturally-acquired ability to speak in foreign languages.[23] In fact, many Pentecostal missionaries were disillusioned when the foreign hearer did not understand their tongue. This theology of foreign tongues or xenolalia was later replaced with the term "unknown tongues" or glossolalia. Cecil Polhill of the Pentecostal Missionary Union wrote in 1909:

In spite of what seemed to be a disappointment when they found they could not preach in the language of the people, and in spite of mistakes made chiefly through their zeal, God has blessed, and now more than ever the Pentecostal movement is truly a Missionary Movement.[24]

Pentecostals have never agreed on the precise formulation of their theology of the Spirit. There is still much disagreement as to the meaning and function of the baptism in the Spirit and speaking with other tongues. The centrality of the Spirit in mission has however remained a consistent theme that unites Pentecostals the world over. Pentecostals are acutely aware that the missionary endeavor of proclaiming the gospel to the world could have never been achieved merely by the enthusiasm or obedience of the early disciples. Melvin Hodge underscored this truth when he maintained that the apostles and the early church needed an inward impulse, something which they received on the Day of Pentecost.[25] Roland Allan, an early advocate of a Holy Spirit (or pneumatological) approach to mission insists:

Acts does not end with "the Lord Jesus said go", but with "ye shall receive power and ye shall be my witnesses". St Luke fixes our attention not on an external voice but upon an internal Spirit.[26]

He further notes that the Spirit given to the apostles is thus seen as creating in them an internal necessity to preach the gospel.[27] This internal pneumatological necessity is something which has been pivotal to Pentecostal missions since the earliest period of the modern Pentecostal movement. The mission emphasis of early

Pentecostalism almost always saw the task of world evangelization as something that that could only be accomplished through the power of the Holy Spirit. The baptism of the Holy Spirit is then a sign that one is sent and empowered by the Spirit. For early Pentecostals, it was the Spirit who sends and supports the missionary, not the formal church structure or mission agency.

In compassion to the "Missio Dei" of the older Catholic Church and Protestant mission and to the "obedience to the Great Commission" of evangelical mission, Pentecostal mission is grounded first and foremost in the conviction that the Spirit is the motivating power behind mission activity.[28]

Signs and Wonders in Pentecostal Mission

Mark 16:17 states, "these signs shall follow them that believe." Miracles and supernatural signs are a regular feature of both the Old and the New Testament. Pentecostals believe that the miraculous power demonstrated in the ministry of Jesus and the apostles has been restored in the present day as a part of the mission strategy to win unbelievers to Christ. The role of signs and wonders, particularly healing and miracles, is important in Pentecostal mission praxis and worldview.[29] Healing testimonies permeated the writings and activities of early Pentecostal missionaries.[30] William Burton, an early Pentecostal missionary to the Congo, wrote that healing was "the very foundation of pioneering missionary work."[31] Signs and wonders fulfill four important functions in Pentecostal mission theology. Firstly, signs and wonders in Pentecostal mission praxis confirm that the gospel message is genuine, that truly God's Kingdom has come to earth in power. Signs and wonders authenticate that the living and risen Jesus is present with his people and working through them through the power of the Holy Spirit. Secondly, signs and wonders affirm that the power of the Holy Spirit received by the baptism in the Spirit is presently active in the life of the church and believers. It further connects the ministry of the latter day church with the ministry of Jesus and the apostles. Pentecostals firmly believe that signs and wonders are not restricted to the period of the first century church but should be normative in the life of the present day church and in the lives of spirit-filled Christians.

Thirdly, signs and wonders are indicative of the reality of believers engaging in spiritual warfare with the kingdom of darkness. From a Pentecostal worldview, the context of a Christian life is one of battle. For instance, John Wimber sees believers as "caught between two ages" and in the life of Jesus we see how the "future age, the kingdom of God, invaded the present age, the realm of Satan."[32] We are, according to Wimber: "Thrust into the middle of a battle with Satan: it's a tug-of-war, and the prize is the soul of men and women. Satan's captivity of men and women has many facets, but denying them final salvation is his primary goal… Our mission is to rescue those who have been taken captives as a result of Adam's fall."[33]

The pentecostal mission is therefore "power mission." It is a mission that recognizes the power of darkness at work within cultures and peoples. Pentecostal missionaries are not just to be equipped with mission theories and methods of cross-cultural communication but with power to confront the enemies of God. Fourthly, God performs miracles to meet the needs of His people.[34] Pentecostals believe that God demonstrates His favor towards His people through supernatural intervention. This is especially evident among Pentecostals in developing countries that are faced with abject poverty and economic misery. During my ten years of missionary service in Ghana, it was normal to see African Pentecostals praying for God's intervention through the sending of rain, quashing political unrest or sending a financial "breakthrough." For them, God's mission and God's power are complementarily working together to fulfill God's end-time purpose through the lives of His people.

Healing in Pentecostal Mission

An important practice of signs and wonders is demonstrated in the pervasiveness of the healing ministry in Pentecostal spirituality.

According to Allan Anderson, healing permeated the writings and activities of many early Pentecostal missionaries.[35] Anderson notes that "the numerous healing reports confirmed that God's Word was true, his power was evidently on the missionary efforts and the result was that many were persuaded to become Christians."[36] In many respects, the worldview in which early Pentecostals operated is contrary to the rationalist and cerebral thought, pervasive during the early 20th century.

In part it was this biblical and traditional worldview - in which demons and witchcraft are taken seriously - that was a major contributing factor to the prevalence of Pentecostalism in Africa and Asia. In Africa, for example, Pentecostal missionaries were able to appropriate the Gospel's message within an African worldview because they were armed with the ability to perform signs and wonders as a corollary of the Christian gospel. On the contrary, the missionary message of the older historic churches - premised upon an enlightenment outlook - failed to bring peace to the deep recesses of the African soul due to their inability to evoke the supernatural. In a context in which sickness, poverty, and death are ubiquitous, Africans are obsessed with healing and wholeness. Pentecostals orientate their quest for healing and wholeness towards Jesus Christ, as He is considered to be healer par excellence. In an African context, salvation is therefore essentially freedom from all kinds of sicknesses and afflictions and the agents that bear these curses. Allan Anderson aptly says: "They proclaim and celebrate a salvation (or healing) that encompasses all of life's experiences and afflictions. They offer power to provide a sense of dignity and coping mechanism for life."[37] Healing, deliverance and miracles are very importance features of African (and Asian) Pentecostalism to this day.[38]

Missions, Signs and Wonders and Demonology

Mark 17:17 states, "And these signs will accompany those who believe: In my name they will drive out demons…" For many Christians (and non-Christians) demons and evil spirits belong to the primordial age and worldview. Adopting this more rationalistic and scientific reading of scripture often leads to an enlightenment type of biblical interpretation which utilizes the historical critical method. According to this more liberal interpretation of Scripture, demons and evil spirits are understood in more symbolic and metaphoric terms. Pentecostals, however, share a pre-enlightenment worldview that was evidenced in the early church. For them, demons and evils spirits are real and God has given them the power of the Holy Spirit to exercise authority over them. Exorcism is derived from a Greek word meaning to adjure, or bind by oath. Although "exorcist" is only found once in the (King James Version) Bible, what exorcism represents, in terms of casting out demons, is found in the Scriptures in a surprisingly complex number of ways. Pentecostals observe that much of Christ's ministry of preaching the coming Kingdom of God involved "healing all that were oppressed of the devil." It is significant that it was done by the power of God, through the Holy Spirit that was within Him. Scriptural text, such as Acts 10:38, states: "How God anointed Jesus of Nazareth with the Holy Ghost and with power: who went about doing good, and healing all that were oppressed of the Devil; for God was with Him." The power to cast out demons was an important aspect of early Pentecostal missionary formation and this remains so up to the present time.

Pentecostal, Demons and Culture

The zeal of early Azusa Street missionaries, spurred on by the thought of an imminent parousia, left no room for studies of cross-cultural communication and of other cultures. The consequential lack of cross-cultural preparedness and cultural ignorance led to a pejorative posture towards other cultures. Like the Catholic and Protestant missionaries who preceded them, western Pentecostals went out to "foreign lands" with the idea that they were the light shining in the dark heathen, pagan, and satanic lands that they were conquering for Christ. In many cases, traditional cultural expressions such as dancing, funeral rites, traditional ceremonies, rites of passage, traditional healing practices and so forth were taken to be dark demonic and occult practices. This negative approach to other cultures, which still prevails among many Pentecostal missionaries, has been a hindrance to creatively indigenizing the Christian faith in other cultures.

On another level, the Pentecostal missionary worldview strongly resonated with the worldview of many of the traditional cultures that they visited, particularly in Asia and Africa. Their belief, in the supernatural and of a Christ that confronts traditional evil forces, allowed them to enter the worldview of indigenous cultures with the power to overcome and subdue traditional deities and spirits. One of the crucial areas that put the early missionaries on the wrong footing, from the very outset of their missionary enterprise, was their failure to grasp the fact that Africans and Asians operate in a frame of reference that is alien to the western rationalistic worldview.[39] This cerebral and discursive way of looking at the world was reflected in a cerebral religion, which poured scorn upon an understanding of the world which was teeming with spirits and beleaguered with powers.[40] Thus, the gospel of Christ was presented through a discourse that was instructional and not intuitive, by sermon and not by symbols, in a way that appealed to reason and not to the intuition, and often through literary means and not orality. By perceiving Christ from the vantage point of a western enlightenment understanding, the Christ the missionaries preached was not able to inhabit the spiritual universe of the indigenous people of Africa except as a complete stranger. Pentecostal spirituality on the other hand employed a Spirit Christology in which Christ was "at home" in the spiritual universe of non-western believers.

Signs and wonders in African Pentecostalism

A good example of how the Spirit-filled mission has been employed effectively can be seen in African Pentecostalism. The 19th century (otherwise known as the missionary century) was a time of great Protestant missionary activity in Africa. Even though the mode of Protestant mission was communicated through western cerebral approaches, African Christians soon employed a more "Spirit empowered" approach to the work of Christian mission. In his book, *African Pentecostalism*, Ogbu Kalu notes, "From the earliest contact with the gospel, Africans have tended to appropriate the charismatic dimensions, attracted to the extra power offered by the new religion, and stamped it with an African identity."[41] This predilection towards the power dynamic within Pentecostalism was first demonstrated by African prophets; many of whom posed like Old Testament prophets, donning flowing gowns, sporting luxurious beards, and carrying Moses-type staffs. The leaders of this early African Spirit-filled contextual approach to Christian mission included William Wade Harris, whose ministry started in 1910; Garrick Braide, who operated between 1914-1918; Joseph Babalola, who left his job as a driver in 1928 in West Africa; and Simon Kimbangu, whose ministry lasted one year, 1921, in the Congo, and many other less well know prophets. Each of these prophets utilized the signs, wonders and healings which became an important feature of African Pentecostalism and continues to be so. These Pentecostals evangelists often filled the space occupied by traditional healers and diviners.

This prophetic movement was behind the monumental rise of the African indigenous church that sprang up all across the continent. In fact, the African indigenous churches that emerged from this African prophetic movement are often called "Africa spiritual churches" or "Africa spirit churches" because of their strong emphasis on the work of the Holy Spirit in the life and mission of the church. Signs and wonders expressed primarily through spiritual healing were a central feature to this spirituality, along with a strong emphasis on the Holy Spirit.[42] African indigenous churches, and the subsequent African Pentecostal churches, well knew that in order for Christian mission to succeed it needed to confront the spiritual powers that were part and parcel of their worldview. The signs and wonders were the physical manifestation that the power of God was working in the lives of the believers. This power would therefore not only advance the cause of the gospel by confronting the evil powers that kept people in bondage and fear, but could also protect the believer from wicked and malevolent spirits at work in the world. It was the power to heal, to raise the dead, and to perform miracles that made Christianity a force within the African spirit world. For them the Kingdom of God had come in the power of the Holy Spirit and would crush all other powers holding people in captivity.

William Wade Harris, the African prophet I mentioned above, would enter into an African village across the West African coast where he preached, then confront and challenge the traditional fetish and Juju priest. He would first demonstrate that the power of God was greater than traditional African fetish powers in the midst of those kept under its spell. This African approach was influenced by a reading of scripture focused on the prevalent power encounters between God and evil spirits in both the Old and the New Testament.[43]

The belief in witchcraft, ancestral spirits, and curses creates real fear and a need for protection in the lives of African people. Protections often take the form of talismans, amulets and other symbols to ward off evil spirits. Unlike the earlier missionaries, African Pentecostal missionaries appropriated their message within this world beleaguered with spiritual powers. In the face of these powers, Pentecostals invoked the "blood of Jesus" and broke curses through the power of the Holy Spirit. Pentecostal Christology portrayed Jesus as a God who was "at home" in a universe permeated with evil spirits and magical powers. Pentecostalism as an African religious form is well suited to the African personality and worldview and may provide important insights for the Church in the global north.

Spirit-Filled Mission and Pre-millennial Eschatology

Soon and very soon we are going to see the King

Soon and very soon we are going to see the King

Soon and very soon we are going to see the King

The above song, well known in many Pentecostal circles, was written by songwriter Andre Crouch. This song reflects the futurist pre-millennial theology of most early Pentecostals and many "classical"

Pentecostals today. Pentecostals pride themselves on adhering to a balanced gospel in spite of a Holy Spirit focus. This balance theology is expressed by many as the "Full Gospel" or the "Four Square Gospel." The basis of this teaching is the theme of Christ as Savior, Healer, Baptizer (with the Holy Spirit) and Soon Coming King. The idea of Christ as the coming King was the motivation that provided urgency and fuel for Pentecostal mission endeavors.

This was the motivation for an emphasis on evangelism "before the end comes," while the more spectacular signs, like speaking in tongues, prophesy and healing, were subordinate to and confirmed this emphasis. Believing that Christ's return was imminent, early Pentecostals saw the baptism in the Holy Spirit and speaking in tongues as evidence that they were living in the last days. It was this pre-millennial and dispensational eschatology[44] that fuelled their mission urgency.[45] The church was, as Steven Land notes, "an eschatological community of universal mission in the power and demonstration of the Spirit."[46] According to Michael Pocock:

Pre-millennial eschatology has deeply influenced the missiology and praxis of evangelicals, particularly from North America, from the 19th century to the present. The eschatological orientation of missionaries and their sending churches affects their view of the Christian life, the direction of their work, their hopes for the future, and their relationship to the culture of nonbelievers around them.[47]

According to Pocock, the adherents of a Pre-millennialist eschatology stress the importance of Christ's followers living a holy life daily. This they do to witness to the regenerating power of the Gospel while they wait for Christ's return and work in the light of

Christ's command to disciple the nations (Matt. 24:1-51; 28:18-20).[48] It was this manner of living with the daily expectation of the coming of Christ that gave intensity and power to the lives of Pentecostals. This provided balance in respect to their attitude toward worldly possession and ambition and oriented them to the future hope that they had in Christ. Within a Pentecostal understanding of mission there is an important link between eschatology and the Holy Spirit. Eschatology for Pentecostals focuses on two particular beliefs: the eschatological Kingdom which has been inaugurated in the Holy Spirit and Jesus as

returning soon.[49] For Pentecostals, the reality of living in the "last hour" of history catapulted the need for evangelism to the top of the church's agenda. This often meant that other issues, such as social concern and matters of a more earthly nature, were put on the back burner. The urgent need for the harvest of souls around the world shaped their missiological outlook and theology. As Allan Anderson points out, this has further blurred the distinction and tension between the "already" and the "not yet" understanding of the Kingdom of God.[50] The case that the Kingdom of God was a present as well as future reality, and that this had to be kept in tension, was heard loud and clear. Biblical scholars such as Gordon Fee have contributed significantly to a more balanced Pentecostal eschatology.[51] In spite of this theological corrective on behalf of Pentecostal eschatology, it remains that Pentecostals have discerned the mission urgency of the Holy Spirit. It is this urgency that they have sought to demonstrate and one that they need to communicate to the wider church.

Eschatology and Social Responsibility

The futurist framework of Pentecostal eschatology tended to engender a fatalistic posture towards matters that pertained to social justice and political action. Their apparent emotional disconnection with earthly matters earned them the reputation of being "too heavenly minded and no earthly good." There appears to be some justification for the accusation that early Pentecostals were socially and politically quietist, although there is a danger in exaggerating this claim. As I mentioned in the previous section, the prevailing thought among early Pentecostals was "why waste time with such earthly endeavors when Christ's coming was imminent 'even at the door.'"

Later Pentecostals embraced a much more a realistic eschatology. As the belief in xenolalia (missionary tongues) and Pentecostal expectation of the Second Coming began to fade, eschatology was replaced by speaking in tongues as the 'initial evidence' for the baptism of the Holy Spirit. According to this understanding, adherents would speak in others tongues as "proof" that they had received the baptism of the Holy Spirit. This teaching is still very prevalent among many classical Pentecostal groups today, such as the Church of God (Cleveland, TN) and Church of God of Prophecy.[52] As Pentecostalism began to gain ground among the more affluent members of society and the world became a much more comfortable place to live in, the intense pre-millennial eschatology began to wane. Steve Land comments that "upward social mobility is clearly affecting the apocalyptic fervor and urgency as the world looks a little better to contemporary, more affluent North America Pentecostals."[53] The proliferation of the prosperity preaching today, with its emphasis on health and wealth has caused many to ponder whether Pentecostals have become too "earthly minded that they are no heavenly good." The upward mobility of Pentecostals in North America today coupled with an eschatology that is far more "this world" focused, has brought about a much more socially engaged movement. Among Pentecostal churches today, social responsibility and action play a more central role. Churches continue to have a very active mission agenda within the local church as well as within evangelistic ministries. It is not uncommon for Pentecostal churches to send food and clothing to people in developing countries, as well as build churches and schools as an extension of their church or ministry.

Spirit-filled Liberative Missiology

"The Spirit of the Lord is upon me, because he hath anointed me to preach the gospel to the poor; he hath sent me to heal the

broken hearted to preach deliverance to the captives and the recovering of sight to the blind, to set at liberty them that are bruised," - Lk 4:18

In spite of working to alleviate poverty, natural disasters, and economic crises, the Pentecostal movement lacks a prophetic voice. Pentecostalism, as a movement, needs to acquire a much louder prophetic voice and to not only work towards alleviating poverty but to become an antagonist against systems and political structures that cause poverty and injustice. The Luke 4 passage above is a popular text among Pentecostals. Its pneumatological thrust on the lips of Jesus provides a powerful basis for a Pentecostal theology. Perhaps this is the starting point where a Pentecostal vision of liberation can begin. In this passage, Jesus combines the Holy Spirit and the quest for liberation of the oppressed. He declared that the purpose of the Spirit being upon Him was so that He could be empowered for the task of liberation. Jesus explicitly and concretely targets the poor, the brokenhearted, the blind, and the bruised for liberation, while bringing the role of the Spirit in the cause of liberation to center-stage in the here and now. The power of the Holy Spirit baptizes the believer, both empowering and orienting each one, for mission and for the cause of liberation in the here and now.

The development of a Spirit-filled liberative missiology goes beyond this paper but is, however, a venture I will be researching as a future project.

Conclusion

In this Chapter, I have sought to explicate the contribution of a Spirit-filled Pentecostal mission theology. At the heart of what I want to put forward is the issue of the Holy Spirit's power and how this relates to mission. As I mentioned, the Holy Spirit is a missionary Spirit and one that prepares and empowers the church for mission. Through the baptism of the Holy Spirit, believers are empowered to confront the evil powers that operate in our world. Signs and wonders are the corollary of the Spirit's power which should be normative for every believer engaging in God's mission. Pentecostals remind us of the place of the Holy Spirit within the eschatological unfolding of salvation history. Whereas traditional evangelical theology has tended to articulate the relationship between the Father and Son in mutual love and sacrifice, Pentecostals remind us of the undergirding and synergistic work of the Holy Spirit. Pentecostal missiology insists on the pervasiveness of the Spirit's work in relation to the Father and the Son. The Spirit also empowers the believer, provides the mission impulse for the church, and truly ushers in a new eschatological future.

Endnotes

[1] Paul Pomerville, *The Third Force in Missions: A Pentecostal Contribution to Contemporary Mission Theology* (Peabody, MA: Hendrickson Publishers, 1985), 3.

[2] David Bosch, *Transforming Mission: Paradigm Shifts in Theology of Mission* (Maryknoll, NY: Orbis Books, 1991), 243-248.

[3] Gustav Warneck, *Outline of a History of Protestant Missions from the Reformation to the Present Time: A Contribution to Modern Church History* (Edinburgh and London: Oliphant, Anderson and Ferrier (3rd English ed., translated from the eight German ed.), 1901), 9.

[4] This position is held by Stephen Neill in: *A History of Christian Missions: Second Edition* (London: Penguin Books, 1964).

[5] Roland Allen, *The Ministry of the Spirit* (Grand Rapids, MI:, Wm. B. Eerdmans Publishing Company, 1960), 21.

[6] Max Warren, *I Believe in the Great Commission* (Grand Rapids, MI:, Wm. B. Eerdmans Publishing Company, 1976), 126.

[7] Melvin Hodges, *A Theology of the Church and its Mission: A Pentecostal Perspective* (Springfield, MO: Gospel Publishing House, 1977), 149.

[8] Ibid., 359

[9] Pomerville, *The Third Force in Mission*, Chapter 3.

[10] Anderson notes that the emphasis in early Pentecostal leadership was on spirituality of the leader rather than on his/her intellectual abilities. They therefore did not place

great weight on the merits of theological training, so most of the early missionaries had little or no training at all. See Allan Anderson, *Spreading Fire: The Missionary Nature of Early Pentecostalism* (Maryknoll, NY: Orbis, 2007), 260.

[11] Allan Anderson describes it as being a series of movements that took several years and several different formative ideas and events to emerge. He maintains that Pentecostalism is a poly-nucleated and variegated phenomenon. Anderson, *Spreading Fire*, 4.

[12] Anderson, *Spreading Fire*, 4.

[13] For a detailed explanation of Pentecostal traditions and teachings see: Allan Anderson, *An Introduction to Pentecostalism: Global Charismatic Christianity* (Cambridge, UK: Cambridge University Press 2004).

[14] These include churches such as the Assemblies of God, Church of God (Cleveland, TN), etc.

[15] Pomerville, *The Third Force*, 10.

[16] For a more comprehensive treatment of the Pentecostal movement see: Allan Anderson, *An Introduction to Pentecostalism: Global Charismatic Christianity* (Cambridge, UK: Cambridge University Press, 2004).

[17] Anderson, *Spreading Fire*, 77.

[18] Ogbu Kalu, *African Pentecostalism: An Introduction* (Oxford and New York: Oxford University Press, 2008).

[19] Pomerville, *The Third Force in Missions*, 20.

[20] Steven J. Land, *Pentecostal Spirituality: A Passion for the Kingdom* (Shefield, UK: Shefield Academic Press, 1993), 29 and 32-33.

[21] Emphasis mine.

22 Anderson, *Spreading Fire*, 65.

23 Anderson, *Spreading Fire*, 57.

24 Alexander A. Boddy, "Confidence: A Pentecostal Paper for Great Britain," *Confidence 2*, no. 8 (August 1909), 181.

25 Hodges, 34.

26 Allen, 5.

27 Ibid, 27.

28 Anderson, *Spreading Fire*, 207.

29 Anderson, *An Introduction to Pentecostalism*, 211.

30 Ibid, 216.

31 William F. P. Burton, *Missionary Pioneering in Congo Forests: A Narrative of the Labours of William F.P. Burton and his Companions in the Native Villages of Luba-land* (Preston, UK: R. Seed & Son, 1922).

32 John Wimber and Kevin Springer, *Power Evangelism* (San Francisco, CA: Harper and Row Publishers, 1986), 44.

33 Wimber and Springer, 33.

34 See: New International Version, Exodus 14:22; Exodus 16:4-31; Exodus 17:5, 7; I Kings 17:4-7; I Kings 17:10-16; Matthew 6:8-10; John 2:1-11; Acts 28:3-6.

35 Anderson, Spreading Fire, 216.

36 Ibid.

37 Allan Anderson, *African Reformation: African initiated Christianity in the 20th century* (Trenton, NJ: Africa World Press, 2001), 250.

38 Important texts that discusses African and Asian Pentecostalism are: Allan Anderson and Edmound

Tang (eds), *Asian and Pentecostal: The Charismatic face of Christianity in Asia* (Oxford: Regnum Books, 2005) and Ogbu Kalu, *Introduction to African Pentecostalism* (Oxford: Oxford University Press, 2008).

[39] S. K. Odamtten notes in reference to the Methodist mission in the Akan town of Akuapem that the mission approach of spreading the Christian faith was through religious instruction given in a classroom setting; he also noted that translating the message into the vernacular was initially difficult. See S. K. Odamtten, *The Missionary Factor in Ghana's Development up to the 1880s* (Accra: Waterville Publishing House, 1975), 30-65.

[40] Sydney G. Williamson observes that the primary task of the missionary among the Africans was, as he saw it, the destruction of the traditional and superstition and the implantation of the Christian faith. See Sydney G. Williamson, *Akan Religion and the Christian Faith: a comparative study of the impact of two religions* (Ghana: Ghana Universities Press, 1974), 54.

[41] Ogbu Kalu, 23.

[42] An early study of African indigenous churches was conducted by Bengt Sundkler in *Bantu Prophets in South Africa* (Cambridge, England: James Clarke & Co., 2004).

[43] A good example of this type of encounter is seen in Acts 8:9-24.

[44] Dispensational pre-millennialists believe that Christ will come before a seven-year period of intense tribulation to take His Bride (church) into heaven. After this period of fulfillment of divine wrath, He shall then return to rule from a holy city (i.e., the New Jerusalem) over the earthly nations for one thousand years. After these one thousand years, Satan, who was bound up during Christ's earthly reign, will be loosed to deceive the nations, gather an army of the deceived, and take them up to battle against the Lord. This battle will end in both the judgment of the wicked and Satan and the entrance

into the eternal state of glory by the righteous. This view is called pre-millenialism because it places the return of Christ before the millennium and it is called dispensational because it is founded in the doctrines of dispensationalism.

[45] Anderson, *An Introduction to Pentecostalism*, 218.

[46] Land, 59.

[47] Michael Pocock, "The Influence of Pre-millennial Eschatology on Evangelical Missionary Theory and Praxis from the Late Nineteenth Century to the Present," *The International Bulletin of Missionary Research* (July 2009), 1.

[48] Pocock, 2

[49] Andrew Lord, *Spirit-Shaped Mission: A Holistic Charismatic Missiology* (Milton Keynes UK: Paternoster, 2005), 38.

[50] Anderson, *An Introduction to Pentecostalism*, 219.

[51] Murray A. Dempster et al (eds), *Called and Empowered: Global Mission in Pentecostal Perspective* (Peabody, MA: Hendrickson Publishers, 2008), 7-21.

[52] Anderson, *An Introduction to Pentecostalism*, 219.

[53] Land, *Pentecostal Spirituality*, 71.

Chapter 7

PROPHECY & MISSIONS

" *Missions activity can be powerfully impacted by prophecy. God may give prophetic words to minister to unbelievers and open their hearts wide to the kingdom of heaven. Prophecy may also be instrumental in calling specific individuals into missions or in guiding the direction of upcoming ministry. When we earnestly desire spiritual gifts, especially the gift of prophecy, God equips us to do His work in increasingly effective ways.* "

- Rolland Baker

I like to make things as simple and obvious as possible. We need not rely on clever and unusual nuances, obscure interpretations and fresh insights that distract us from the faith once and for all delivered to the saints. The power of the Gospel lies in its fundamental, unassailable truth, comprehensible to a small child. The intelligent and sophisticated have trouble accepting the most basic elements of the Gospel, but the broken and humble receive easily.

It should not require great prophetic powers to perceive that in this life Christianity is missions. As long as others have less than we do, the love of God compels us to share what we have. As long as we possess the Presence and power of God that others do not, we have a mission to accomplish. Jesus came not to judge the world, but to save it, and if we want fellowship with Him, we must partake of His nature and have His purpose in common.

If what we have is of value, we cannot keep it to ourselves. We should not have to argue the primacy of missions before the church. If we know anything of the love of God, we know that the Good News applies to everyone on the planet, even in the farthest corners. If all people everywhere need what we possess, missions is logical, natural and morally obligatory for us who believe.

It is also simple and logical to understand that we need God's power and direction to carry out missions. Otherwise, when confronted by vast need and evil opposition, we reach the end of our resources quickly and our mission is over. The overwhelming challenges of missions take us to one place: faith to rely not on ourselves, but on God who raises the dead (2 Cor. 1:9). Rather than being defensive about our insistence on the miraculous intervention of God in all that we do in missions, we should just openly admit our total weakness and need of Him. The hungry and desperate will find and receive.

On the one hand, we agree that the plain words of Scripture should be enough to impel us to missions. It is amazing how powerfully the Holy Spirit can and does back up our simplest understanding of the Great Commission. Most remain relatively unmoved by the word "Go!" but those who are taken captive by it have already received a gift of decisive revelation.

This is a plea to take revelation from God seriously, whether by the written Word or by the gift of prophecy. Those who take it to heart may have their entire lives transformed by just a few urgent, insistent, unmistakable divine downloads early in life, or by simple, naïve, radical response to the words of Scripture. We have seen tremendous fruit flow from the lives of young believers in China, for example, who are saved and motivated to extreme heights of faith and sacrifice by exposure to small bits of the Bible. God honors them abundantly and angels watch in amazement as they believe and pour out so much in response to so little input. Truly God is thrilled with their magnificent faith, and they may be rewarded more than those who need all kinds of books, teachings and prophetic input to achieve the same result.

By contrast, some take revelation casually, almost for granted, and while they claim to hear from God daily about so many minor details, they hardly do much in radical obedience to the thrust of Scripture, and the fruit of their lives is held down to a minimum.

My aim to is understand and appreciate how Word and Spirit work together. We need to be utterly obedient and responsive to what the Spirit shows us in the Word, and through the encouragement of Scripture, also treasure more revelation by the Spirit that helps us with specific details in our lives. There should be no divide! We desperately need God's full provision for us. We love God by valuing every way in which He chooses to teach us, direct us, and manifest His Presence.

On the other hand, revelation and prophetic input in addition to Scripture are to be valued and sought after. The opposing argument is that prophecy is either in agreement with Scripture, and therefore redundant, or it is untrustworthy because it is not Scripture. Simple logic, however, tells us that God is perfectly able to speak to us however He likes and will make His will known as clearly as He pleases. We have no reason to believe that He cannot and will not communicate with us anymore. Still, He knows His own value, and wants to be wanted. Scripture tells us that we will seek Him and find Him when we search for Him diligently with all our hearts.

It is hard to comprehend missionary effort that expresses no need for God's power or supernatural direction. Jesus categorically states that we can do nothing without Him and our missionary experience is actually a long history of finding out how much more we need Him than we thought! Our attitude now is that no matter what disappointments we have had in the past or how limited the experience of others around us, we will accept no limits to the degree we can find, know and experience God. Because of the Cross, we are always bold to approach Him with confidence. We have no choice. Our hearts have been captured by His and we must get closer still. We cannot tolerate distance from Him.

Our experience in missionary work has been one of extracting absolutely everything possible from Scripture and experiencing everything we can in our relationship with Jesus. Our forerunner and example in this is my grandfather, H. A. Baker, whose life story helped establish in us the core values of Iris Ministries. His autobiography, "Under His Wings," is to me essential reading for our missionaries and hugely helpful to anyone seeking the fullness of God's Presence in their lives (available online at www.irismin.org as a .pdf file).

My grandfather boldly and resolutely responded to the Great Commission by determining to go to the uttermost part of the earth and get as far away from the nearest white man as possible. He finally ended up in Batang, Tibet, where he labored dutifully for seven years. Obeying the Scriptural command was not enough, though. He longed to experience living water from the throne of God, and taste the powers of the age to come. His time in Tibet was nearly fruitless. In frustration with his lifeless missionary organization, he returned to America broken and lost.

His desperation and hunger drove him to pursue the Baptism of the Holy Spirit in every way he knew how and Jesus rewarded him overwhelmingly. Beginning in Toronto, Canada, he experienced spectacular visitation and a rich variety of manifestations, including the intense, supernatural joy of heaven itself. Holy laughter, drunkenness in the Spirit, falling under the power, and fluent tongues all came to him in a flowing river of power. Equipped with such a Baptism, he was told by God to return to China with his wife, who was also beautifully filled, and depend on Him for everything. He experienced such a down payment on the life of heaven that the thought of dying and going there was purest joy!

Back in China, he didn't know what to expect. He was a poor preacher and never knew how to prepare a sermon. He was only effective when the Holy Spirit came upon him and gave him every word to say. He became dependent on the Holy Spirit's guidance and power in the small details of everyday life. He and my grandmother were led to begin an orphanage, taking in ragged beggar children off the streets of Kunming in southwest China where I was born. And so he learned to start at the bottom, with the "least of these."

This time around he saw revival, the tremendous outpouring of revelation recorded in his book, "Visions Beyond the Veil." Never in church history have I heard of such thorough revelation of heaven and hell, Bible events and the end-times. Visions were granted to the orphanage children around the clock for weeks and months, precisely detailing what God wanted to communicate.

This outpouring was a prophetic event of first magnitude. My grandfather searched the scriptures to assess all that was being revealed to the children. Without any prior knowledge of the Bible, they were shown visions of David and Goliath, the crucifixion and resurrection of Jesus, powerful miracles in the last days, bodies rising in the air to meet Jesus at His second coming, life in the New Jerusalem in all its glory and much more. It was an utterly faith-building prophetic confirmation of Scripture, and an extraordinary encouragement to me and other missionaries around the world two generations later.

I cannot overemphasize how valuable all this prophetic input has been to me all through our ministry in Asia and Africa. The chief themes of the Bible were unmistakably underscored in a way that removed all doubt. We are to go out into the world and rescue lost sheep as good shepherds, willing to lay down our lives for our sheep. We are to stand at the foot of the Cross where the highway divides into the narrow, difficult way that leads up to life and the broad, easy way that leads down to destruction. There we are to warn and persuade people to the limit of our ability. We are to tell people that destruction and judgement are coming, Jesus is coming back, and to repent and believe the Gospel. We are to rejoice in all our affliction, for we are obtaining the salvation of our souls.

After months of time in heaven, these children lost their love of this world. They became fearless preachers in the villages and towns of China, developing extremely powerful gifts of prophecy. In their guileless innocence, they would get up in front of large crowds of resistant unbelievers and suddenly, with strong adult voices and vocabulary, prophesy until the Holy Spirit brought heavy conviction. So overtaken were they by the Holy Spirit that they had to ask their friends later what they had said.

Heidi and I wanted to see a continuation of "Visions Beyond the Veil" in Africa, with the same values that my grandfather had. We wanted the living Presence of Jesus brought by the Holy Spirit. We wanted, and needed, the power of God for everything; we wanted to start at the bottom with the poor and "the least of these." We were willing to endure suffering and whatever it took to see such revival and we wanted an overflow of the joy of the Lord to sustain us through every trial and enable us to delight in the Lord always.

In the years following this outpouring in 1926, my grandfather continued to see revival in the remote mountains of the

Yunnan province among minority tribes. All through his ministry, prophecy and revelation were his guiding engine. Without the Presence and power of God, he would have been crushed. But in the Holy Spirit he was given life, strength and direction far beyond himself, and to this day he is still bearing fruit in Africa. Without his prophetic example, we would never have had the vision to begin with children and the poorest of the poor, counting on God to be with us sovereignly in power, love and joy all the way.

God also dealt with Heidi and me directly and prophetically as well. Heidi was decisively convicted and saved at age sixteen. Right after that she was filled with the Holy Spirit and graced with an extraordinary three-hour visitation by Jesus. In her vision, Jesus told her, among other things, that she would be married to Him and be a missionary and a minister to Asia, England and Africa. She was so filled with the Spirit that all she could do was laugh and speak in tongues for days. Unwelcome in most churches as a woman preacher, she took to the streets and began leading missions teams at every opportunity. From the beginning, she prophesied and called out incredible healings. She launched missions trips on detailed instructions from the Lord, always with supernatural financial provision.

Obviously she functioned on far more than she could gather from Scripture alone. When I met her, I knew immediately in the Lord that she was the first and only person I had met with whom I could live a life of faith on the mission field. We were joined supernaturally. Her heart had first been turned to missions by her sixth grade teacher, a retired missionary from China. That teacher turned out to be my mother! Heidi and I were both more hungry for the Spirit than for social life. We both had gravitated to a small charismatic church in Dana Point, California. We met and began spending time together, not dating, but sharing the things of God by the hour and leading ministry teams.

During Christmas of 1979, Heidi was on a missions trip to Mexico City when Jesus again spoke audibly to her and told her that she would be married to Rolland Baker, that we would go to Indonesia as missionaries by a certain date. She would get her master's degree by the age of twenty-five, and more. Jesus even told her the day I would ask her to marry me. All came to pass exactly as expected.

We asked for no wedding presents, only ticket money, and that added up to one-way tickets with thirty dollars left over. Two weeks after our wedding we were in Jakarta, seeing God heal the sick and sustain us with no support from America. We learned that we could not casually assume God's provision, but needed real faith and direction from Him. Others who tried to imitate us without input from the Holy Spirit soon met with disaster. For thirty years we have learned to lean heavily and totally on His guidance. We are lost without supernatural direction and cannot make any major decisions without Him.

At many critical points in my life I have been preserved, sustained and hugely inspired by specific prophecy. The most influential prophesies were given to me by people I never met before and have never met since. I never could have survived and be doing what I'm doing today as a minister and missionary without these touches from God through the gift of prophecy. In the years before I met Heidi, one very close friend was so prophetic that I rarely had to discuss anything with him, as he would so often know exactly what I was thinking. In many ways I learned more from him about God than I did in any of my classes in biblical studies at college. He was not called to public ministry in churches, but counseled people privately and prophetically only as the Holy Spirit led. Miracles were a daily occurrence for him and my faith soared by knowing him. I would not be here in Africa with Heidi without his influence in my life.

I learned, in part through the Jesus Movement and especially the Indonesian revival spoken of in Mel Tari's "Like a Mighty Wind," that real faith, knowing the voice of God, and working miracles is not a mechanical procedure, but a Song of Songs romance. We need to know Jesus well enough to know what He wants to do in a given situation. We need to know what His love feels like. We need to share His mood and outlook. We need His boundless joy.

We understand that He can and does speak loudly, specifically and directly without giving much understanding at the time, but that will follow. Surpresa Sithole, our Mozambican national director, was apprehended audibly at age fifteen as the son of witch doctor parents in a remote bush village. A voice, so loud it shook the bed he was on, said, "Get out of the house or you will be dead in a week!" He fled down a dirt trail and hid out in the bush during the civil war until he met a pastor in Malawi who led him to Jesus.

Others of our present leading pastors were sovereignly called by God like this before Heidi and I ever arrived in Mozambique. The Holy Spirit preserved some from danger by telling them where to avoid fighting and shooting each day. Even today our mature pastors are filled with testimonies of visions, visitations and prophesies that keep them going in power and fruitfulness. We cannot imagine missions without revelation and direction from God!

The Christian life is more than miracles and gifts of the Holy Spirit, of course; it is love and romance made possible by the Presence of God. Heidi's experience is that God most often speaks to her when she is in deep worship. She has a childlike love for God, a pure, emotional force that overrules all other passions in her life. God loves to reveal Himself to her. The visitations she has received have been critical guideposts for Iris Ministries at every turn. We could not have survived without them.

The prophecy Randy Clark gave her in Toronto in 1997 sent her back to Mozambique full of fiery, unquenchable vision that has sustained her ever since. God asked if she wanted the nation of Mozambique, and with every ounce of energy within her she screamed, "Yes!!" Without that, and all that God imparted to both of us at Toronto Airport Christian Fellowship, we would never have seen this people movement of a revival in southeast

Chapter 8
POWER & MUSLIM MISSIONS

" *Reaching out to Muslims is a crucial strategic task in missions today. Ministering with God's supernatural power, including using spiritual gifts such as words of knowledge, healing, or prophecy, has proven to be a key in opening doors that were thought by many to be closed. In the testimonies of Muslims encountering God through miracles, we see how the release of God's power is a vital force in Kingdom expansion.* "

- DJ

Even some of the most conservative Christians would concede that if there was place in the world that "needed" signs, wonders and miracles, it is the Muslim World. The wind of the Holy Spirit is blowing across Islamic nations and we are witnessing a season of the greatest breakthroughs in the history of missions to Muslims.

Just a generation ago, many heading to nations/areas controlled by the religion of Islam were told that they might serve a lifetime and see only a handful of disciples. This is what I was told, but due to two primary factors, this is simply no longer the case. More Muslims are abandoning Islam and embracing the Christian faith than at any other time in history. One of those factors has been the advent of Christian satellite television and the other one is an unprecedented increase in dreams, visions and healings. It is this second factor that we will investigate further.

"Why Didn't You Tell Me Christians Could Heal?"

Several years ago, in a country on the Arabian Peninsula, an Arab Bedouin Muslim named H. was invited to our weekly "Encounter God" meeting. He wanted to talk to me, so we found ourselves in the kitchen; I got a word of knowledge for a problem in H's lower abdomen. When I inquired, he looked to my friend who had brought him and asked if he had said anything to me about his condition, which he hadn't; the Lord was revealing a Muslim's need for a miracle. We prayed and H. was completely healed. He went on to explain that he had spent tens of thousands of dollars on Western medical treatment and had even gone to Islamic folk healers whose treatment included burning him. Nothing had worked. Having known my Christian friend for nearly two years, he then looked at him and asked, "Why didn't you tell me Christians could heal?"

God wasn't finished with him that night. After we rejoined the others, he received a number of accurate prophetic words from different members of our team. God seriously got H's attention!

This man's story didn't end that night in my home. Some months later, H's father was diagnosed with terminal cancer that was spread throughout his abdomen. A couple of us were brought into his hospital room and had the chance to discreetly lay hands on him, pray and release the Kingdom. We felt nothing, though often that doesn't seem to matter. He left the Middle East to pursue treatment in Europe and ultimately the United States. He didn't need to receive any further treatment because on two occasions when they opened him up, they found the tumors were shrinking. On the final surgery, they discovered the cancer was gone. Afterwards, I spoke with the American surgeon (a believer) who had overseen his case at the beginning. He told me that he would like to see all of the medical reports for, if true, they constituted a medically documented miracle!

One final miracle occurred when we were brought again to pray for one of H's relatives, a teenage Bedouin who was in a long-term coma after a near fatal car accident. After prayer, he came out of the coma the following day and fully recovered.

H. had seen God's power manifested through accurate prophetic revelation and miracles of healing. First, his condition was revealed through a word of knowledge and he was healed. He got his "mail read" as several prophesied over him. Finally, his father and a relative were dramatically healed. The result? H's and his wife gave their lives to Jesus – as far as we know, the very first believers in one of the largest unreached people groups on the Arabian Peninsula!

My Christian friend had been giving a "verbal witness" of the Gospel to H. for nearly two years. He had given H. a Bible, which he had read. He had lived a life of love before H., which obviously God had used. Ultimately, it took demonstrations of God's miraculous power to bring him and his wife to faith.

While stories like this are common throughout the Muslim world, most of the ministries who are attempting to reach the Islamic world for Christ are still not pursuing approaches that focus on signs, wonders and miracles. And it's not that we don't have solid evidence – both biblically and empirically - that the manifestation of supernatural power brings greater breakthroughs for the Gospel.

The biblical case has been made compellingly in a number of works, including Jack Deere's *Surprised by the Power of the Spirit*.[1] As for the further empirical evidence amongst Muslims, read on.

The Importance of the Supernatural in Bringing Muslims to Christ

As for the importance of supernatural ministry in the Muslim world, perhaps no better case has been made than by Islamic expert Dr. Dudley Woodberry of the Fuller Theological Seminary's School of Intercultural Studies. His landmark survey, which examined the factors that led to the conversion of 750 former Muslims from 30 different Islamic countries, revealed that signs, wonders and miracles were arguably the most critical factor that brought them to Christ. I personally interviewed two former Muslims, a Palestinian and an Egyptian, for Dr. Woodberry's survey.

The findings of this survey were summarized in Christianity Today's 2007 article "Why Muslims Follow Jesus". Woodberry states that the second most cited reason given by these 750 respondents that led them to Christ "was the power of God in answered prayers and healing."[2] In addition, the survey separately notes the importance that dreams and visions played in the lives of these converts. The study reveals that, "27 percent [of the former Muslims], noted dreams and visions before their decision for Christ, 40 percent at the time of conversion, and 45 percent afterward."[3] Dreams, visions and other demonstrations of God's power were critical factors in their coming to Christ and also in their remaining faithful when they faced persecution afterwards (which included imprisonment and assassination attempts).

When we combine these two factors, God's power demonstrated through healing and revelation in dreams/visions, I believe that the role of the supernatural in the lives of Muslims who come to Christ becomes the single most important factor.

These were things that we knew, at least intellectually, from the time we began our full-time ministry to Muslims in the late 1980's. Still, it wasn't something that we "pursued" until more than a decade later. Since the year 2000, we have witnessed hundreds and hundreds of miraculous demonstrations of God's power (healings, visions, trances, angelic visitations, deliverance from demons, prophetic words and/or other supernatural encounters) as we've ministered to Muslims.

In 20 years working among Muslims, there is simply no comparison between the first decade we ministered, when we saw very little of the Holy Spirit's supernatural activity and the last one, which has been characterized by regular manifestations of His power. The lives of thousands of Muslims have been touched miraculously by the Kingdom of God. Consequently, we have seen many more come to faith than before. Perhaps most significantly is the way God has been equipping hundreds of Christians throughout the Muslim world in power and prophetic evangelism, which will lead to a far greater harvest in the years to come.

I despise exaggeration and hype. Those of us who are contending for signs, wonders and miracles need to be far more careful in our reporting and also more honest about the times when we don't see breakthroughs. We try to document each and every healing or miracle we see and I have been careful to go back and re-read the accounts of each story I have included in this chapter.[4]

How We Were Trained as Missionaries

Like many Evangelical missionaries, I spent several years preparing to go to the Mission Field. I studied Cultural Anthropology, took courses in Bible and Theology, and even studied Missiology and Islamics in seminary. I joined a well-known missions organization that provided further training in Muslim evangelism and spent two years studying Arabic full-time in the Middle East. By most peoples' standards, I was considered fully prepared for a career as a missionary in the Arab World.

In my first few years, I experimented with a number of different approaches in reaching Muslims. I remember reading John Wimber's Power Evangelism, and even trying to pray for the sick more regularly.[5] Ultimately I got discouraged and abandoned this approach.

In hindsight, I'm not sure why I didn't see how important the supernatural was in ministering to Muslims early in our ministry. One of the Egyptian Muslims I prayed for in the wake of reading Wimber's book had been crippled after falling four stories off a building. He was told he would never walk normally again. I met him in the hospital, prayed for him, and was shocked to discover that he had become a Christian when I saw him again six months later.

How did that happen? A couple of days after I prayed for him, he was completely healed and could run normally. He knew it was Jesus who had healed him and since he couldn't find me, he found another Christian who helped him grow in his faith. I believe God was trying to get our attention, revealing to us the way He wanted to work amongst Muslims. Sadly, at that point I thought I was pursuing "better" strategies.

Even though we saw very few come to faith during the 1990's, we kept pursuing different approaches that, for the most part, did not emphasize the miraculous. It wasn't that we were opposed to supernatural ministry; we had simply never experienced "the real thing" – that was about change!

Our Supernatural Encounter – When a "Prophetess" Came to Town

In 2000, we were invited to a Church meeting in the Arab country we were living in to hear a "prophetess" minister. My wife and I went a bit reluctantly. I can honestly say that until that night neither of us had ever seen prophetic ministry. It changed everything in our lives and our ministry. After being called out and subjected to about 10 minutes of the most accurate prophetic words we have received to this day, we left that meeting saying, "whatever that was, we want it." That was all the hunger that God needed!

What followed was the quickest possible orientation we could put together while still living in the Middle East. We started dialoguing with men like Jack Deere, reading dozens of books, attending conferences and trying to familiarize ourselves with the Charismatic Christian landscape that was quite foreign to us. Thankfully, we seemed to find many who were able to help us grow by both demonstrating God's power and imparting gifts through the laying on of hands and prophetic utterance.

A Disturbing Realization – Christians with "Islamic" Ideas

I need to emphasize at this point how important it is that we develop a theology that emphasizes God's goodness and His willingness to heal if we want to see miracles. When we began to wade into the waters of the miraculous, there were a number of theological barriers that needed to be overcome. Being that this chapter is focusing on signs and wonders in the Muslim world, it seemed appropriate to share how Islamic theology actually helped me to overcome some of the "bad doctrine" that we Protestants received from the neo-Platonic ideas of Augustine and John Calvin and currently popularized by authors like R.C. Sproul and John Piper.

I began to notice that my Muslim friends basically shared the same theology as my own Protestant Evangelical background when it came to sickness and God's willingness to heal. Muslims believe that God can and does heal. They also believe that sickness is "allowed" by God's permission to teach people things and therefore it isn't normally His will to heal. In other words, God could do something about the problem of sickness, but He simply doesn't want to. It isn't His will. This was a disturbing realization! Muslims basically believed the same things about God's will and sickness that my Evangelical background had taught me. To think that the God and Father of our Lord Jesus Christ is somehow "allowing" all the horrible cancer that has tortured and taken the lives of a number of close friends should disturb any follower of Christ. I knew He was in no way behind the rapes and violence. I also needed to get to the place where I also "knew" that God wasn't behind the sickness, disease and associated pain.

Thanks to Islamic theology, my theology was "delivered" from exaggerated notions of God's sovereignty, control and His unwillingness to heal. I realized for the first time in my Christian life that it was always God's will to heal sickness and disease. When it comes to healing, His will is often not being done! Similarly, it's always God's will for people to be saved, but many are not – His will is not done.

But isn't God in control? It sounds almost heretical to consider that there are many things that are not, but how can it be otherwise? I live and work in a Muslim country, where a false religion dominates every facet of society. Five times a day the name of their false prophet is broadcast from loudspeakers on the minarets of the mosques. Is this what God being "in control" looks like? Add to these things famines, wars, crime, all types of abuse, etc. God has *nothing* to do with any of these things.

What is the "last word" on the topic in the New Testament? The Apostle John, Jesus' closest disciple said it this way, "We know...that the whole world is under the control of the evil one" (1 Jn 5:19 NIV).

Sicknesses and diseases are not God "in control" – our mandate is to bring His control into situations that are currently out of His control. That is at least one of the things that Divine Healing is all about. When we heal the sick, deliver the demonized, or prophesy God's destiny to an unbeliever, we are bringing God's control (His Kingdom) into a depraved world. Greg Boyd's book *Is God to Blame?* is the most user-friendly work I know, exploring the problem of evil, God's control and how to reconcile these with His matchless love.[6]

How We Train People Now
(Hopefully like Jesus Trained His Disciples)

For years we had no idea that we had the mandate to preach the Gospel of the Kingdom, a message that biblically was demonstrated with supernatural manifestations of God's power – healing, deliverance, prophetic revelation, etc. I thought the keys to breakthrough in the Muslim world included fluent Arabic and sound missiological methods. Even to this day, I have friends who are still pursuing some kind of "magic formula" – the right Bible translation, the proper "Apostolic government" or some other technique/theology/emphasis that will somehow "unlock" the Islamic world for the Gospel. I was there. I tried all the newest techniques. But why had I neglected the ministry model of Jesus Himself?

I had never seen it demonstrated, but that night when the prophetess demonstrated a supernatural prophetic gift we were immediately convinced. I had "played around" with praying for the sick, but I had seen so little real breakthrough that I honestly thought there was nothing there.

One of the main ways that we now train people is simply to invite "unbelieving believers," a term coined by Bill Johnson, to come and witness healings. I don't think it was all that different in Jesus' day – I think many came initially "to watch" (i.e. Luke 9:11). Often after somebody has seen a miracle, their unbelief begins to go and their journey into the miraculous begins. That was what happened to my Christian friend who had invited his Bedouin friend H. to my house – he had begun to "see" miracles, and like us, got hooked.

I'll never forget one particularly definitive night for him, while on a ministry trip in Yemen. We had invited a well-known healing revivalist to join us as we partnered with missionaries who lived in the country. One night a Yemeni came who had one arm about half the width of his other arm. As my friend prayed with the revivalist, he saw the arm grow out to its normal length right before his eyes – a creative miracle! To this day, my friend is marked by that experience (and many subsequent ones).

When people ask me how they can prepare to servce God on the mission field, I tell them something like this. Learn how to hear God's voice (prophetic ministry training), how to heal the sick and cast out demons. Sure, we'll help you get the language and teach you about the culture, but in the end it is most important that missionaries today can actually emulate the ministry of Jesus. That is exactly what Jesus trained His disciples to do – how have we moved so far away from the main and plain teaching of the Gospels? I hadn't learned any of those things in Bible school, seminary or from the training I received in my missions organization. Our home church hadn't taught me about these things either (we have since found another home church, as you might have suspected!).

It's not that we don't want those with flawless language skills, and sound cultural and theological training. We do. I work today with many native speakers of Arabic in our outreach to Muslims. What we emphasize now more than anything is what we call "Filling & Spilling." We need regular encounters with God – we love the highlights, the milestones, but many Charismatics are not connected to life-giving communities whose singular pursuit is the presence of God. That has become our overall focus in the past 10 years. We have nothing to give away if we aren't filled ourselves.

Charismatics also tend to get filled up and often never to give away what we have. This is our secondary focus – "to spill." When we are filled with God's power and presence, we have something supernatural to release on those around us. This has become a lifestyle for our growing community in the Arab Muslim country where we live and the fact that we live in the Muslim world means that the recipients of our "spilling" are often Muslims.

Some "Spilling" Stories

A couple of months ago, I was taking out a Western couple that wanted to see healing for the first time. Coming upon a group of Lebanese Muslims, I got a word of knowledge for a back problem and one was healed. Then we saw one of the most "visible" miracles we'd ever seen. A Lebanese man's arm was 2 inches shorter than the other as a result of a serious shoulder/elbow injury from a car accident. It grew out in front of our very eyes! It gave us the chance to talk about the Kingdom and exchange numbers.

One night back in 2007, while taking out some Ethiopian believers to release the Kingdom, we were driving by an undeveloped desert area. A strong word of knowledge slammed into my left ear and I told the driver, "Turn out into the darkness, there is someone out there who is deaf." Reluctantly, he agreed and we found ourselves driving out into nowhere. After a few minutes, we saw a Land Cruiser (surely belonging to a wealthy Gulf Arab Muslim) parked with its lights off. I approached the car, found two men sitting there, and asked them if one of them was deaf in his left ear.

At that point, you would have thought the man had seen a ghost. He was completely deaf in his left ear and insisted I tell him how I knew. When he saw the Africans with us, he thought, "He's got practitioners of black magic" - you've got to love stereotypes. He began to try and search us to see if we had some type of "device that revealed his deafness to us" (his words). We assured him that no such device existed.

Interestingly, he wasn't healed. He came to visit us at one of our homes a few nights later and still no healing. God had gotten his attention (as He did ours!) and he heard the Gospel, but was unwilling to repent. I've never gotten a stranger word of knowledge in my life.

We also had a demonized Qatari Muslim woman begin to manifest demonically as we were ministering in the Spirit's power in Qatar in 2004. She herself was an Islamic "healer" and admitted to healing through the jinn (an Islamic concept for spirits that they believe can be either good or bad). She was not interested in being set free when we offered to pray for her. We learned later that she was institutionalized.

Some other remarkable deliverance stories occurred in Yemen in late 2006. While in a village, our team was taken to two homes where in one place the man was literally "naked and in chains." One man was completely set free after prayer and some time later a missionary in Yemen sent a picture of the second man "clothed and in his right mind." As strange as casting out demons is for many Christians today, it was not only one of the predominant signs of the Kingdom coming in Jesus' ministry, but was one of the dominant ways that the our faith spread in the second and third world centuries.

In April 2010, we saw two Palestinian Muslim women come to Christ in the center of mall. One of our team members got a word of knowledge for headaches but dismissed it thinking that these two women were "too conservative" (dressed entirely in black). They finally approached them (a mother and her adult daughter) and it turned out to be an accurate word. After praying for the headaches, the mother eagerly asked for prayer for her shoulder. The shoulder was instantly healed and then the mother opens her wallet to reveal numerous pictures of Jesus! Another team member began to prophesy over this woman's daughter, specifically about her son. Tears welled up in her eyes as she is "hit" by the accuracy of the words coming forth. They discover that the mother had been ministered to years previously by some Filipino Christians and had had a visitation from Jesus Himself at that time. These women had been prepared and were both ready to become followers of Jesus. They prayed right their to invite Him into their lives, surrounded by people at this Middle Eastern mall!

One final "spilling" illustration comes from a ministry trip I took with my good friend "Isaac" when we went to Damascus, Syria in 2007 for a four day Holy Spirit adventure. A Syrian Bedouin friend decided to join us. This Muslim man had no idea what he would witness over the next few days. What followed was arguably the most healings we had ever seen in such a short span of time. Everywhere we went, we just offered to heal the sick, give people prophetic words and try to be obedient to whatever we felt the Lord was saying. We probably prayed for more than 100 people on this short trip and saw God touch the lives of Muslims and Christians both. At one point, Muslims were coming to our hotel room (our Pool of Bethesda) for healing and one man had an encounter with an angel.

Our conviction is that we should first demonstrate God's power and then speak. I believe we must "earn the right" to be heard and miracles seem to be the quickest way to get that hearing. Often, Muslims ask us to tell them more about what just happened and why we prayed in "Jesus' name." Having debated with Muslims for years, I can say that things go much better when they want to hear about Jesus!

At the end of our ministry trip in Syria, as we were literally walking back to our hotel to go to the airport, our Bedouin friend said to me, "I've never seen anybody who loves like you guys do!" That affirmation was quite possibly the greatest compliment I've ever received by a Muslim friend.

No Purer Demonstration of Love than Healing

If there is a single criticism that I seem to be responding to again and again from well-meaning Evangelical friends it is this: "What good are all these people getting healed if they aren't then coming to Christ"?

Admittedly, I initially assumed that many more would come to faith soon after encountering miracles. As I've said, we've seen literally hundreds of Muslims healed of many different conditions. However, we've probably only seen a few dozen make commitments to Christ in the different countries we've ministered in this past decade.

So how do I respond? First of all, whereas we have only seen some of the fruit, we have no idea how many others have put their faith in Christ in the wake of their supernatural encounters. I am reminded of the crippled Egyptian man that I mentioned earlier, who gave his life to Christ six months after he was healed. It was only by God's grace that I found out about it. I do remember asking him when he was in the midst of being persecuted by his family how he held onto his faith and he simply said, "I was crippled, and now I can walk." Sounds a lot like the blind man who was healed in John 9:25, doesn't it? Miracles always "point to" someone – they point Muslims to Jesus!

I remember an elderly Yemeni Muslim man who came to me for healing prayer. His daughter and son-in-law were followers of Christ, but he wasn't. He limped into the room with a knee swollen the size of a small soccer ball. I prayed and saw nothing happen at the time. Two days later, while ministering in a village in the north of the country, we received a phone call. The man was dancing around, completely healed and testifying to all of his Muslim friends and neighbors that Jesus had healed his knee." Did he personally come to faith? Not that I know of. Will I ever know the impact of that healing on all the other Yemenis who heard about his healing (and saw him healed)? Not till the Age to Come! I'll come back to this man's daughter in a minute.

The real issue when it comes to healing is that it isn't some "optional" extra for some Christians to pursue. Healing is at the very center of the ministry of Jesus. To put it more bluntly, if we aren't healing the sick, we are disobeying Jesus (Matt. 10:8)! I am completely unapologetic about pursuing healing ministry with a vengeance. Many saw Jesus' miracles, yet were unconvinced. For the most part, the Pharisees rejected Him, even having seen and heard about countless healings.

We sow the Kingdom as widely as we can, demonstrating a Gospel of power and leaving the results up to God. One thing I believe is that an undeniable miracle of healing communicates far more deeply than the Arabic Gospel tracts I used to distribute.

Nothing against literature – it's just that I'll take the supernatural touch of the Living Word of God, Jesus over the handing out of the Written Word in the life of a Muslim any day. After that encounter with the Living Word, the Muslim is hungry to read the Written Word of God and is far less likely to throw it in the trash, as I witnessed endlessly when I was primarily distributing Arabic Gospels and tracts.

"Preach the Gospel at all times and when necessary use words," said Francis of Assisi. I am convinced that Francis was onto something (note: Francis did believe in preaching with words too and interestingly enough did so amongst Muslims). He lived in a day and an age when the Gospel lacked serious credibility due to the nominalism and corruption that characterized much of the Medieval Christian Church. We too live in a day when nominal Christianity and powerless expressions of a "Gospel of words" are found all over the world. Our witness is often not credible to an unbelieving world. There is no greater desire in our hearts than to see the followers of Islam come into a relationship with Christ. When I approach a Muslim stranger, armed with the Love of God and perhaps a word of knowledge revealing a painful condition they have, and they are healed in Jesus' name, I know that they have just "heard" perhaps the clearest preaching of the Gospel imaginable. Healing is one of the purest demonstrations of God's love, and I am convinced that is why Jesus was so focused on healing the sick.

When I walk away, not having tried to "sell them anything" and expecting nothing from them, when all Islamic healers charge money, I know their world has been shaken. They will never be the same. I don't have to be the one who tries to "close the dea.l" There is a massive comfort in believing in a supernatural Gospel, in believing that God is more than able to work drawing them to Himself. I do try to leave them a phone number or tell them where I work, so that when they are ready, they can find their way back to at least one Christ follower.

Training & Equipping Former Muslims for the End Time Harvest

There is perhaps no more important ministry that God has given us than the privilege of seeing former Muslims walking in the supernatural themselves. We are seeing a growing number of former Muslims join us who are hungry to see God's healing power flow through them. The testimonies they are hearing are hard for them to ignore and they want to get in on some of the "fun" they keep hearing about.

As was documented earlier, most of them came to Christ through some type of supernatural encounter. However, many were not then discipled with the expectation that they would see healings and other miracles following their lives as a normal expression of Christianity. Our desire has been to do all we can to address this deficiency. If God is pouring out His Spirit in supernatural ways, then it is critical that former Muslims are discipled not only to know God's Word, but to know how to release His power as well.

To illustrate, I want to return to the story of the Yemeni woman whose father danced and told his village after Jesus healed his knee. She and her husband are leaders in an emerging Arab Yemeni Church made up entirely of former Muslims. My wife and I had less than an hour to share some of our stories and cast a vision for them to move in more of the Holy Spirit's power. They got to "see" us pray for her father. Perhaps most significantly, we had the opportunity to lay hands on them and ask God to impart gifts of the Holy Spirit to them (Rom. 1:11). We had no idea what God was about to do. Shortly after our meeting, this Yemeni woman led a group of Yemeni Christian women in prayer for a five year-old child who had never walked before.

The Arab women gathered around this little girl, and not really knowing what to do, wept over her as they prayed. And the child got up and began to walk!

These Yemeni believers' first healing was someone who had never walked before. Not a bad introduction to life in the power of the Holy Spirit! God knew that it was important for them to see that they carried something by themselves, without the aid of a missionary standing by.

We are seeing former Muslims receiving gifts of the Spirit and growing in the use of those gifts on a regular basis. Equipped, Spirit-filled former Muslims will truly be the way that God brings in the great End Time Harvest in the Islamic World in the years to come.

An Apology Letter to a Muslim who was not Healed

I am so persuaded that healing is one of the predominant ways that we are to represent Jesus to the world. When we fail to see the breakthrough in healing, we need to apologize for misrepresenting Christ.

How many people did Jesus walk away from and leave unhealed that he prayed for? None, and then He had the audacity to describe our commission in this way, "[Just] as the Father has sent Me forth, so I am sending you" (Jn 20:21 AMP). This he reiterates in John 14:12 where He fully expects us to do the same works (works here referring to the miracles) that He did.

So what are we to do when we don't get the same results that Jesus got?

We don't start to answer the "why not" questions that God isn't answering. We shouldn't say, "I guess it's not God's will" because Jesus said it was (Matt 8:3) or give yet another common excuse telling them that "It's not His timing" because "NOW is the day of salvation" (2 Cor 6:2 NIV).

I believe we simply humble ourselves and apologize for not accurately representing Jesus to the person who wasn't healed. The following is a letter I wrote in 2006 for an Iraqi Muslim man who we never saw healed of his deafness. This is a summary of what I told him verbally in Arabic:

Dear Friend,

I want to apologize to you from the bottom of my heart. As Christians we are actually called to represent Jesus wherever we go and to whomever we meet - we are to be His representatives. For years I really had a very limited idea what it meant to "represent" Jesus. To be His representative means we must "RE-present" Him. What He would say, we should say. How He would act, we should act. How He would treat a person, we should treat a person. And, the real critical one, "What He would do, we should do." If you study the life of Jesus, you immediately notice it was full of the miraculous. As He announced the message of the Kingdom, He healed the sick, and He cast out demons wherever He went. In fact, whereas He obviously passed by people who didn't ask Him for healing, the Gospels tell us He never once refused to heal a person who came to Him asking for it.

Here is why I must apologize. I told you that we, as followers of Jesus, heal the sick. I told you many testimonies of God healing people through my life and the life of my friends. I told you that God has never changed and that what He did before, He also does today. As a man who is nearly deaf in both ears, you came to me/us for healing. You came because I told you that Jesus heals deafness. You came because I told you about deaf people that I had personally seen healed. You believed me and came with some expectation that God would perform a miracle.

The night you came we gathered around you and prayed. We prayed several times and yet nothing happened. We can come up with many different excuses and search for reasons "why" the healing didn't come, but that is actually not at all helpful.

The bottom line, my Muslim friend, is that on that night we did not accurately represent Jesus. Had Jesus been with us that night in the flesh, you would have walked out of my home without your deafness. You would have discovered what everyone who ever came to Jesus for healing when He walked the earth discovered - they were healed.

I have gone many times before the Lord since the night you came. I have cried out to Him that I would be able to more accurately represent Jesus. I know that the Scriptures teach me to be just like Jesus in every way:

John 14:12 - "...the works (miracles) that I (Jesus) do, you (Christians) will do also..." (interesting is doesn't say "might" do or "could" do but rather will do).

1 John 2:6 - "the one (i.e. Christian) who claims he belongs to Him (Jesus), must live in the same way that Jesus lived." I want you to come back soon. By God's grace, I (we) will be ready to "do the works" that Jesus did. There is no deafness in His Kingdom - He hates deafness. He wants to show you His love and give you your hearing back. He has never changed.

Please accept my humble apology,

Your Christian friend

The Gospel of the Kingdom in the Muslim World - The Word & The Spirit Together

I started by mentioning the two factors that are the main reasons that Muslims are coming to Christ. When I personally met with the world's most effective televangelist to the Arab the Muslim world, he was thrilled to know that there were a growing number of people "on the ground" who were confirming the Word with signs, wonders and miracles. He acknowledged that "words alone" are insufficient and ultimately an incomplete witness of the Gospel. The humility of this man astounded me. He was honestly more interested in hearing the few miracle testimonies that I had the privilege of sharing with him than telling me how he has become the tool that God is using to literally leads hundreds of thousands of Arab Muslims into Christ's Kingdom.

One of the last things he said really caught my attention. "God is destroying the religion of Islam from the inside". He is doing this by both the preaching of His Word amd demonstrations of the power of His Spirit.

The greatest chapters in Church History are about to be written. Many of these chapters will be stories coming out of the heart of the Muslim world as the Gospel of the Kingdom is preached with undeniable "demonstrations of the Spirit's Power" (1 Cor 2:4). One day soon, one of Jesus' most incredible (and disbelieved) prophecies will also begin to be fulfilled; the time when we will begin to see the "greater works" (Jn 14:12b) being performed. In the coming years, millions of Muslims will be swept into God's Kingdom. My prayer is that the Church and the missionary force of tomorrow will be prepared for their finest hour!

Endnotes

In gratitude: the ministries of Jack Deere, Randy Clark, Bill Johnson, Heidi Baker, Mike Bickle, Rick Joyner, Greg Boyd, Patricia King and Todd White have shaped our ministry in the Muslim world.

[1] Deere, Jack, *Surprised by the Power of the Spirit* (Grand Rapids, MI: Zondervan, 1993).

[2] Woodberry, J. Dudley, G. Marks and Russell G. Shubin. "Why Muslims Follow Jesus." *Christianity Today*. October, 2007   http://www.christianitytoday.com/ct/2007/october/42.80.html?start=2 (24 APR 2010).

[3] Ibid.

[4] *Joel 2 Generation Blog*, http://joel2generation.blogspot.com.

[5] Wimber, John, *Power Evangelism: Equipping the Saints* (San Francisco, CA: HarperCollins, 1985).

[6] Boyd, Gregory, *Is God to Blame? Beyond Pat Answers to the Problem of Suffering* (Downers Grove, IL: InterVarsity Press, 2003).

Chapter 9
THE PROPHETIC DESTINY OF
ISRAEL AND THE JEWISH PEOPLE

"

One exciting way in which prophecy enlivens missions is by revealing God's heart for specific nations or people groups. Israel is one such people group, and scripture is replete with evidence of what God is planning to do among them in these last days. By recognizing God's overarching plan for these people, we are better able to participate in their prophetic destiny through prayer and action.

"

- Jonathan Bernis

"And this gospel of the kingdom will be preached in the whole world as a testimony to all nations, and then the end will come." (Mt 24:14 NIV)

What remarkable times we are living in today! Less than 50 years ago, when God was gathering arm loads of Jewish people into His kingdom through the Jesus Movement of the sixties, few could imagine we would see the day when more than just a handful of His chosen people came to faith in Messiah at one time.

Yet, I am privileged to witness a great event that is taking place right now! Just as the Bible predicted, the Jewish people are being restored to their land and to their Messiah in numbers not seen since the first century. We are seeing biblical prophecy unfold before our very eyes - prophecy that promises a return of the "exiled of Israel" in the last days.

Is this a sign that the end is near? Does prophecy - both ancient and more recent - impact 21st century missions endeavors? The answer to these questions is a resounding and unequivocal, "Yes!" We are surrounded on all sides by "the mission field." The end is near. Satan knows it. I know it. And when you finish reading this, I am sure you will know it is true.

In recent years, many have become obsessed with trying to unravel the Bible's mysterious prophecies, especially concerning the last days. They analyze every word in the newspaper and on television in an attempt to find some connection to the end times. This is especially true if that news has to do with Israel or the Middle East. Yet, while we focus on such esoteric matters, we don't seem to notice other more obvious signs that the Bible prophecies of the end times are happening right in front of our eyes.

Over the last several years, Jews all over the world have continued to return to Yeshua in record numbers. Not since the days of the Book of Acts have so many of Abraham's children opened their hearts to receive the Messiah. Through the ministry of Jewish Voice alone, where I am privileged to serve as President and CEO, some 75,000 Jewish people have responded to altar calls in the past seven years! That's less than a decade. Our efforts to reach the Jewish people with the truth of the Gospel include Festivals of Jewish Music & Dance from Russia to Argentina, as well as humanitarian and medical outreaches from India to the so-called "Lost Tribes of Ethiopia." We are able to touch thousands of Jewish people there who are awaiting Aliyah, the return of the Jews to their biblical homeland.

Signs of Yeshua's imminent return are all around us! At issue is this: Do we have eyes to recognize the signs? What if much of what we've believed about the end times is wrong, or at the very least off target? What if we have looked for the signs of Messiah's return in all the wrong places? Please don't misunderstand me, there is absolutely nothing wrong with seeking to understand Bible prophecy and live in the light of that understanding. This is precisely what God expects us to do. I just think perhaps our focus can be misdirected. I believe we run the risk of missing out on the marvelous thing God is doing right now to prepare the world for Messiah's return when we focus on things like red heifers and saber-rattling in the Middle East.

Isaiah 2 reveals Jerusalem's destiny as the center of peace and government for the nations of the earth. The nations will send representatives to her and learn of God and take His Word to their lands. War will end, peace will reign. It is difficult to envision in the current climate of strife, terrorism, anti-Semitism and impending war. Yet this is clearly a land of miracles for His Name's sake. Zechariah further promises:

> *"I will return to Zion [Messiah's return], and dwell in the midst of Jerusalem. Jerusalem shall be called the City of Truth, the Mountain of the Lord of hosts, the Holy Mountain." (Zec 8:3 NASB)*

The Psalmist asks, "Why do the nations rage?" (Ps 2:1). Jerusalem is obviously more than a geographic city. It is the heart of a Nation called and chosen by and for the Creator, a city within a nation of destiny. From Jerusalem will flow righteousness and salvation to the ends of the earth as the eternal overtakes the temporal and the Glory of the Lord blurs earthly boundaries. Jerusalem offends those fending off eternity's rule, while those who are called by His Name love this city where He has placed His Name.

The Gospel to the Jews First and then to the Nations

The word "nations" brings to mind landmasses set apart by geo-political boundaries and established by man. Yet the word used in Matthew 24:14 is actually the Greek term "ethnos," which means a race, a tribe, or, as we more commonly speak of them today, a people group.

In almost every country in the world today, there are a wide variety of people groups - including the Jews. This is a people group that has been scattered all over the world. They live in almost every country, yet only a very small number of ministries are reaching out to them. This is a great tragedy, not only because the Jewish people need to hear the Good News that Messiah has come, but also because God placed a high priority on reaching the children of Israel with the Gospel. The apostle Paul, writing to Gentile believers in Rome, declared:

> I am not ashamed of the Gospel, because it is the power of God for the salvation of everyone who believes: First for the Jew, then for the Gentile. (Rom 1:16 NASB)

God's intention is to bring the Gospel to the Jew in every nation where they are scattered. Only then will the Messiah return! The call to evangelism, which simply means sharing the Good News as the Messiah instructed, is central to the essence of Messianic Judaism.

Some object to this. When they see Messianic Jews declaring the Gospel to other Jews and to Gentiles, they say, "Why are you doing that? That's not Jewish. We Jews are not a proselytizing faith." That may be a popular notion to many people, but it isn't true. Let's take another look in The Book:

*"Woe to you, teachers of the Law and Pharisees. You hypocrites!
You travel over land and sea to win a single convert and, when
he becomes one, you make him twice as much a son of hell as
you are." (Mt 23:15 NIV)*

Clearly, the Jewish leaders of Jesus' day were proselytizing.
They were telling people about God and they were winning
converts, Yeshua says. Sharing our faith is definitely Jewish. Not
only was it true in the First Century, and before Messiah came, but
it is also true today. It began in 1948, when Israel was restored as a
nation with a homeland after nearly 2000 years. Now that's news,
but not the kind that warrants the extended worldwide coverage
that this nation has received since it was reestablished. The extent
to which the eye of the world is riveted on Israel goes far beyond
what one would expect in the natural. Israel is, after all, just a little
sliver of land, barely more than a dot on the world map. Why
would all the earth give it so much attention?

Israel's restoration to the map in 1948 and Jerusalem's in
1967 was a prophetic statement to the world. God was fulfilling
His promises to Israel made thousands of years ago, predicting the
restoration of His people to their land. The physical presence of a
land named "Israel" is a bold declaration made by God, on public
display for all to see and which cannot be ignored: "Sit up, world,
and take notice! I promised to restore the land of Israel and I have
done it! I'm faithful to my promises. They will all be fulfilled."

In the same way, the Messianic Movement is also a sign,
made visible through Messianic Jewish congregations, that God is
restoring His people to Himself. Paul writes:

*I ask then: Did God reject his people? By no means! I am an
Israelite myself, a descendant of Abraham, from the tribe of
Benjamin. God did not reject his people, whom he foreknew.
(Rom 11:1-3 NASB)*

Paul was saying, "Hey, you can't say God has rejected His people.
I'm Jewish! I'm living proof that God has not rejected us. I'm a
physical sign, ministering before you today, that God is faithful to
His promises. He will fulfill them."

In the same way, our Messianic congregations, with their physical buildings and their signs, are a visible testament to our covenant-keeping God, a prophetic statement that what God has promised concerning the spiritual restoration of the Jewish people is being fulfilled. Our existence alone boldly declares it in a way that cannot be ignored.

Some years ago, a woman I knew was walking outside her offices in New York City when a person approached her and handed her a tract. She wasn't a believer yet, but she had been raised in a church. She glanced down at the pamphlet in her hand and saw the words, "Jews for Jesus." Her eyes got really big and this excited shock wave ran through her body. She did a little hop right there on that New York City sidewalk. "Jews for Jesus" she exclaimed. "Jesus, You're coming soon!"

You see, that woman had been told that one day, the eyes of the Jewish people would be opened and that would mean Jesus' return was soon. That Jewish tract was a sign to her that God was doing what He said He would and that the Messiah's return was near. A few weeks later, she became a believer - and it all started with a little tract distributed by a Jewish believer, giving evidence that prophecy was being fulfilled!

As I consider the impact just one Jewish believer had on one Gentile lady, I can't help but think about the impact entire Messianic congregations on fire for Yeshua can have - locally, nationally and internationally. That's why I'm so committed to seeing Messianic Jewish congregations established all over the world. When one person is sent proclaiming Jewish faith in Yeshua, perhaps a few people will hear. As Jewish believers draw together, unified through community, soon whole communities are hearing the proclamation: "Look! God is restoring His people. He is fulfilling prophecy written by the prophets centuries ago."

Messianic Judaism is a Revival Movement

"This is what the Lord Almighty says: 'In a little while I will once more shake the heavens and the earth, the sea and the dry land.

I will shake all nations, and the desired of all nations will come, and I will fill this house with glory,' says the Lord Almighty. 'The silver is mine and the gold is mine,' declares the Lord Almighty. The glory of this present house will be greater than the glory of the former house,' says the Lord Almighty. 'And in this place I will grant peace,' declares the Lord Almighty." (Hag 2:6-9 NASB)

I am fully dedicated to the idea that the Messianic Jewish Movement has been raised up to be a vehicle for revival, for the Jewish people and all the nations of the world. Here in Haggai, as well as many other portions of the Old and New Testaments, God talks about a latter day outpouring upon the Jewish people, and ultimately the nations will be greater than at any other time in history. The Spirit of the living God is moving and I believe we are living in those days!

Messianic Judaism is not someone's "good idea." It is the first fruits of the latter day rain upon Israel. God in His Word declares it, and nothing will stand in the way of Him ultimately bringing revival and restoration to the nations. What we have witnessed over the past 40 years is marvelous indeed - more than we ever expected - but I believe this is just the beginning. The "latter house" - the assembly of all believers, both Jewish and non-Jewish - is definitely going to be greater than the former one, greater in size, in scope, in depth of understanding and relationship.

The Messianic Movement is charged with a great purpose: to bring this revival, which the Gospel boldly proclaims, to the entire earth. It is going to take prayer, hard work, finances, time and energy, but we must be willing to invest all of these things in the revival of the lost sheep of the house of Israel. There is no better or wiser investment we can make. We are called to invest in nothing less.

Messianic Judaism is a Restoration Movement

In Acts, we read the familiar story about Peter, John and the healing of the lame beggar at the gate called Beautiful. The crowds of people who witness this miraculous healing are understandably amazed. Noticing this, Peter tells them what God has provided for them through the death of Yeshua haMashiach. Then he said:

> *"Repent, then, and turn to God, so that your sins may be wiped out, that times of refreshing may come from the Lord, and that he may send the Messiah, who has been appointed for you— even Yeshua. He must remain in heaven until the time comes for God to restore everything as he promised long ago through his prophets." (Acts 3:19-21 NASB)*

Who is Peter talking to in the temple? Jewish people! He's telling the Jews to repent for two reasons: first, that their sins might be "wiped out," but also that "times of refreshing may come from the Lord." My understanding of what this verse declares is, as the Jewish people repent and their sins are forgiven, it will release upon the entire world "times of refreshing." Many authors have used this statement as a definition for revival, but there is so much more!

In Acts 3:10, we see that these "times of refreshing" are connected with Yeshua's return. So, even though revival of people is a great thing in itself, the best thing is that this refreshing and "restoration of all things," as I understand these Scriptures, will mean Yeshua's physical return to earth. Through the salvation of the Jewish people, Peter was saying, "times of refreshing" would come, according to the original Greek text, not only for them, but also for the entire world. When that happens, God can send Yeshua back.

> *"Again, I ask: Did (the Jewish People) stumble so as to fall beyond recovery? Not at all! Rather, because of their transgression, salvation has come to the Gentiles to make Israel envious. But if their transgression means riches for the world, and their loss means riches for the Gentiles, how much greater riches will their fullness bring... For if their rejection is the reconciliation of the world, what will their acceptance be but life from the dead?" (Rom11:11-12, 15 NASB)*

What is this "life from the dead" that Paul is writing about? It's the same thing that Peter was referring to back in Acts 3. It's part of "the restoration of all things." But we won't experience this "life from the dead" until the Jewish people repent and are restored to their God, nor will we see the return of our Messiah to earth! The very fact that the natural branches of the olive tree are being restored declares that God is in the process of "the restoration of all things" and that Yeshua's return is near. This is an inseparable connection between the Jewish people getting saved and the restoration of the nations. The Jewish people are not just another people group. They're the gauge of God's biblical timetable.

Mark Twain was once asked why he believed in God. Immediately, he replied: "The Jew, my friend. The Jew!" How do we know that we're living in Israel's biblical prophetic destiny, earth's final days, that Yeshua is about to return and that we're in the process of "the restoration of all things?" The Messianic Jew, my friend. The Messianic Jew!

Chapter 10

POWER EVANGELISM IN SHORT-TERM MISSION TRIPS

"

What is the place of short-term missions in the big picture of world evangelization? It is not meant to replace long-term mission efforts, but to be in cooperation with them. Those who go on short term mission trips and minister in the power of the Spirit often return home with a new passion for what God is doing on the earth. Such trips can also benefit the ongoing work in the field, impacting large groups of people through evangelistic meetings, bringing impartation and refreshment to the host pastors and churches. By seeing what God does through short-term missions, we may engage in His overall plan in a strategic way.

"

- Randy Clark

How Can We Bring Lasting Impact From Short-term Mission Trips?

In the first chapter, I tried not to use personal illustrations regarding the importance of power to missions. Instead, I mostly drew upon the Bible and other peoples' stories that I was told directly, along with illustrations from Church history. In this chapter I am choosing only to draw upon experiences from my own short-term ministry trips. The stories below are those experienced and witnessed by ministry team members and others blessed by our ministry. For more of my own stories and experiences, check out *Lighting Fires* and *There is More*.

The Affect of Short-Term Mission Trips on Team Members

1.) The "Vicious Downward Spiral" is reversed

Several years ago I ministered at a large Vineyard Church in Champaign, Illinois. I had known the pastor for many years and was shocked at the change of atmosphere in his church from the last time I had ministered there some years before. The church had continued to grow numerically, but there was a noticeable difference in the people's expectation for God to move in their midst. I felt such a spirit of grief that I found it hard to speak.

Later, when I met with the Pastor Happy Leman and his staff, the executive pastor asked me a very important question. This question changed the way I looked at inviting people to come with me to minister in other countries. Prior to that time, I felt somewhat awkward inviting people to go with me, as if what I was doing was self-serving. But after this question I have never felt that inviting someone to go with me to the nations was self-serving. The question was, "What do you do to keep your expectation for healing high?" The executive pastor continued, "Our doctrinal belief hasn't changed since you first met us years ago. Then, what we believed doctrinally we expected to happen in our midst. However, since then, though our beliefs have not changed, our experience has not matched our beliefs. Our expectation has dropped. With the dropping of our expectation, our experience dropped, and we see less than before. We are caught in a vicious cycle. Each year it seems like our experience is less and our expectation drops even more." Then he asked the question, "What do you do to not get caught in this vicious cycle?"

I responded, "I have to go somewhere where there is an open heaven, where there are apostolic leaders who are getting a break through, and minister in that context for a couple of weeks twice a year. In that time I will see more healings than most pastors will see in a lifetime. This builds up my experience and causes my expectation for healing to remain high." This is what I have been doing for 17 years, and it not only works for me, but also the people who come with me as well. Their experience seeing so many people get healed and seeing God use them to bring healing to people raises their faith.

I have had several pastors from various denominations come with me to the nations who were so discouraged that they were looking at the want ads in the paper. They felt like they couldn't continue in ministry unless God refreshed them and touched them. They were "burned out," discouraged and depressed. I watched the Holy Spirit touch these men and saw them experience a whole new zeal and energy for ministry. Depression was broken off. Hopelessness was replaced with faith that God would use them. One of these pastors was 60 years old at the time. The years since then have been the most productive, most exciting and most fruitful of his entire 40+ years in ministry.

On the trip I am describing, the team is the ministry team. They gives words of knowledge and pray for the sick to be healed for hours every day. This is important for the creation of faith that God will use the team members. "This experience changed my life" is one of the most common responses we get on our evaluation forms.

2.) Full-time missions service

Two pastors who have taken more people with me to the nations are Tom Jones and Tom Hauser. When they first started going with me on short-term ministry trips to the nations, Tom Jones was pastoring one of the largest Church of God Cleveland, Tennessee churches in Florida. Tom Hauser was on staff as the Executive Pastor of a large Vineyard church in North Carolina. Their churches developed not only a strong openness to the Holy Spirit, but also a strong commitment to missions. Both of their churches would have several people leave their secular jobs and become missionaries after going with us on short-term ministry trips. Tom Jones had a total of six people become missionaries in ten years. Tom Hauser had a total of eight people become missionaries in six years. He has seen around 160 go on short-term mission trips and his church helped establish two orphanages and plant 73 churches in Nepal, India, Costa Rica and the US. It is true that there could be other factors contributing to this outcome, especially considering that both churches were deeply committed to renewal and the outpouring of the Spirit in Toronto. But when you compare the percentage who went on trips to the percentage who didn't go on trips in relationship to going into missions or other mercy type ministries, I believe the variable is sufficiently removed to give us a better indication of the effects of the trips.

This is not just true for my ministry trips. I have a spiritual father, Cleddie Keith, who was for many years in the Assemblies of God denomination and who took people from his church on ministry trips with him. These trips were very similar to mine in that the people were expected to be the ministry team and pray for the people. He has taken several hundred on short-term mission trips. During the last 17 years since the beginning of the renewal, which he was very committed to, over 30 people have gone into missions or full-time ministry from his church.

3.) Connections are created between local churches and the host country leaders or churches

People we took on our first few trips to Mozambique to work with Heidi and Rolland Baker of Iris Ministries became a great blessing to their ministry. Many of these pastors and businessmen continued to provide support to their ministry. Terry Inman's Assembly of God church in California has been supportive with finances and with people going to serve. Alan Hawkins, pastor of a charismatic church in New Mexico, has made several trips to minister with Iris Ministries. Tom Hauser has made many trips and has sent several couples and individuals to work with Iris since his first trip to Mozambique. On our first trip, we had people from Australia and the United States with us. Two of the people came back as full time missionaries within one year of that first trip.

What I hadn't expected, though I should not have been surprised, was how my own interns and the students from our school would be sent to help Heidi and Rolland. Will Hart and his wife Musy were recently married when they led the trip for me to Mozambique. I received an email from Heidi: "Randy, will you give Will and Musy to me? I am in need of them!" I told her of course I would and if they wanted to go, I would bless them. The Harts went and spent three years serving Rolland and Heidi after Will had already spent three years serving me. In Mozambique, they had their first two children, born at home without a doctor or midwife. They only had a book to read. Then Jean Nicole, another of my interns, went and became a missionary with Heidi. He married another Iris missionary named Teisa. Today, they are working with Iris South Africa. On my last trip to Mozambique, I took Timothy, a young intern of mine. He is very bright and graduated first in his high school class. He loved our time in Mozambique and wants to move back there with his new wife. The two plan to help Heidi and Rolland as Timothy continues his theological studies.

One of the most exciting short-term ministry trips we do is in Brazil every July. Called the Youth Power Invasion, this trip draws 125-200 youth from all over the world. Young adults, ages

13-29, join with several hundred youths from Brazil. We spend a week teaching the youth how to preach, heal the sick, receive words of knowledge, and lead ministry teams. At night the youth divide into four groups and go with me and other key leaders to conduct services for healing and impartation in the local churches. The second week our key speakers go home and the youth lead the teams. They often see up to 8,000 healings during those two weeks! Many of the young people are so impacted that they quit their careers or schooling to take two years to be trained at our Global School of Supernatural Ministry in Mechanicsburg, PA.

From my trips to Brazil, I know families that have continued to go to minister on their own in the country. Several couples and individuals from Tom Hauser's church and from Tom Jones' church have gone as longer-term missionaries. We have people from our Global School of Supernatural Ministry who first went to Brazil with us that are now going back long term. Five students started a Global School of Supernatural Ministry in southern Brazil and hope to have 5-10 other classmates join them next year. A 74 year old student went to be a missionary with an Indian tribe that is in revival as a result of our team going to minister near the reservation where the Baileys, mentioned in chapter 1, work. This tribe continues to reach out to the other tribes of the same dialect in the region.

Our ministry works with apostolic leaders around the world. When we first started the Global School of Supernatural Ministry, we sent out a letter to ask the apostolic leaders what they needed most. Their response was a school similar to ours that could be conducted in their country. Presently, many of our students desire to go and start ministry schools in Brazil, South Africa, Thailand, England and India. Others who went with us to Brazil have gone back to begin orphanages and to work in the favelas (slums) with the poor. Several others are now taking their own teams into Brazil and other Latin American countries.

On one trip to the Ukraine we took with us veterinarian Frank Pack and his wife Robbie. When I wasn't able to continue going into the country on a regular basis, the Pack's picked up where I left off. They have made multiple trips to serve the church, including medical trips, trips to work with drug addicts and trips to strengthen the pastors and churches. They lead their own teams from the church they attend.

I led my first team to Russia in 1996 and continued to take large teams there for about three years. Russ Purcello, pastor of a large independent church in Tennessee, went with me. He had been involved in taking mission trips to Honduras, but had never felt a burden for Russia. When I shared about the trip, however, he felt he should go. Since his first trip, he has continued to replicate my meetings in almost every political region in Russia. God touched him so profoundly that for more than a decade, he and his church have been going into Russia to strengthen the young pastors and leaders. He has invested hundreds of thousands of dollars into his efforts to strengthen the churches in Russia. After my initial three-year commitment to Russia, the door was opened wide for me to work more in Brazil. It was such a relief to see Pastor Purcello continue the much needed training and impartation to the leaders and pastors of Russia that I could no longer reach.

These stories are just some of the fruit from connetions between the local churches and the host church or leaders. Some of these missionaries have received substantial help including hundreds of thousands, if not millions of dollars, that came through their continued connection with the pastors and wealthy business men that went with us. When they saw what was being done, their hearts and wallets were opened.

4.) Vision is created for International Ministry

Almost all of the people mentioned in the above paragraphs had no vision for international ministry or mission work when they first went with us to the nations. But, for the majority, their first trip touched them so profoundly that they made several trips as finances could be raised, and some ended up either starting ministries that reached out to the world or to a local country. Most began these in the country they visited first or the one they visited most on short-term trips with us.

The Effects of Short Term Mission Trips upon the

Receiving /Hosting Group

1. Apostolic Impartation for Pastors

Most of our International Ministry Trips are focused on equipping and imparting to pastors and leaders who are related to national indigenous apostolic leaders. The exception is Mozambique, where Rolland and Heidi Baker are not indigenous, although they are apostolic. I say "ministry trips" rather than "mission trips" because the implications of mission traditionally seem more paternal, when in reality, some of the places we work are far ahead of much of the Western Church. I will be sharing what some of these leaders have told us regarding the value of our ministry trips to their leadership.

A. Brazil

Most of our international ministry trips have been conducted in Brazil. We have averaged about five trips each year, with about 70 days a year in Brazil. No other nation has received so much of our time and resources.

When I first went to Brazil, I had already made several trips to Argentina where I worked with Dr. Pablo Deiros and Dr. Carlos Mrarida of the Baptist denomination. I also worked with Omar Cabrera Sr. in his denomination, Vision de Futuro. When I made my first trip to Brazil I told a friend, "I feel like the revival in Argentina has peaked and is diminishing in power. I feel like we are catching the beginning of the wave of revival in Brazil and I want to ride it to its end."

I believe Brazil will be the number one missionary sending country in the world in this century. A few years ago, I heard C. Peter Wagner remark that Brazil is the country most in revival. I believe that wherever revival is the strongest is where you will see the most missionaries sent out. I wanted to have a part in this revival, equipping and focusing the revival upon the nations with an emphasis of sending forth missionaries.

Around 1999 I was in Toronto, just after traveling to Sydney, Australia. While there I worked with Pastor Frank Huston who was a great apostolic and prophetic leader, especially for the Pacific area. I was in a season of trying to determine from God what was next. I wanted to know if there was anything God wanted me to know. I asked God to give Frank a prophecy for me in Sydney, but he did not have one. When I was in Toronto, however, Frank called me out and gave me this prophecy: "As God has used you in Toronto, God is going to use you to birth revival in six nations in the near future. Four of those nations your feet have not touched yet." A few hours later, I met with delegations from Korea and Brazil, inviting me to come to their countries. I definitely believe Brazil is one of those six nations.

As I mentioned earlier, Brazil seems to be the land of my anointing. It is definitely the land of my greatest favor. I went there without knowing how to speak a word of Portuguese, without being part of a denominational heritage connected with the country, and not knowing a soul in Brazil. Now, 11 years later, I have spoken in more churches in Brazil than in the United States, including some of the largest in the nation: Pentecostal – Assemblies of God, Quadrangular Four Square, new denominations that are Pentecostal/Charismatic in nature, Methodist, Baptist, and Nazarene. Most of these churches have over 1,000 in average attendance and some have 8,000, 12,000, 30,000 or 60,000 in just one local church. What follows are some of the stories from these trips.

1. Belem – Quadrangular

In Belem, located near the mouth of the Amazon in Northeast Brazil, we worked primarily with the Quadrangular denomination. I was invited by Pastor Josue Bengtson, who is over the Quadrangular Church in that region. They have over 30,000 members among many churches in the city of Belem. His son Paulo told me, "You are the first American that my father has invited back." When I asked why, he told me that most Americans his father had invited were proud and boastful, but our teams were humble. Paulo also told me that he believed their churches had grown rapidly recently due to two main reasons: their commitment to cell groups and the impact of our trips upon their leaders. He told us that our teams really encouraged their pastors and leadership with not only the teachings on equipping, but also the experiences of impartation that their leaders received through the Holy Spirit in our ministry.

2. Maua – Baptist

Pastor Silvio Galli is the pastor of the Living Waters Baptist Church in Maua, Brazil. When we first came to his church, it was a small 300 memeber church down a dirt road. It was a traditional Baptist Church, but Pastor Galli was open and desperate for the power of the Holy Spirit. When we first ministered in his church, the Holy Spirit fell powerfully and there were many healings, including some of the members of the staff. The church building was too small for the crowd. People were outside listening through the windows, in the hallways and were packed in beyond capacity. Pastor Galli was very excited about what God was doing in his church.

Three years later we revisited this church. I was surprised when we pulled up to the church. It was not down a dirt road. It wasn't the same little building that could barely seat 300. Instead, it was right on a main street in the city in a building that could seat about 1,500. They had multiple services to accommodate the 3,000 weekly attendance. He told me that the rapid growth had come for two main reasons: 1) the implementation of the cell system and 2) the impact of the Holy Spirit upon the congregation. This congregation had experienced a significant corporate impartation during our meetings and there were many healings and more continued after we left. They truly received an impartation to move in the gifts of the Holy Spirit.

Six years later we returned to the church. The church had again relocated to a building that would seat over 2,000 people.

The church had grown to over 14,000 in six locations with 9,000 at the main congregation. Again, the power of God came mightily. Pastor Galli told me that our last two visits to his church were significant in the rapid growth of the church. This time only one fourth of his church could come on each of the four nights due to the limitations of the building. On the third night, we had a noticeable increase in the miraculous; blind eyes saw, deaf ears opened and tumors disappeared. One paralyzed person walked and talked after a stroke had taken both abilities away. A cast was cut off the arm of a woman who had been in excruciating pain. All the pain had left her after she heard a word of knowledge about her condition. Knees with no cartilage were healed, and pain from childhood polio left. Movement was restored to an ankle and much more. The following night, a man who was paralyzed from the neck down and couldn't even move a finger because of MS got out of the wheel chair and walked. There were so many healings.

3. Joinville – Quadrangular

We visited Joinville in the south of Brazil, where we ministered to the Quadrangular denominational leaders. The main overseer was so discouraged that he was going to resign his post if the Holy Spirit didn't come powerfully upon the other pastors during our meeting. He didn't resign - we had a wonderful visitation of the Holy Spirit. On one of the nights, a man came with such horrible neuropathy that he couldn't lift his feet from the floor but could only shuffle his feet with the aid of a walker. As he began to walk that night, his doctor, who was also present, told me, "I am his doctor. He can't do that. He hasn't been able to walk without a walker or pick up his feet in years!" Another man was healed of a substantial heart problem. Deaf ears were opened and blind eyes were healed.

Just as importantly, the pastors and leaders experienced a powerful impartation and left the meetings encouraged by this fresh visitation of the Holy Spirit. Some received gifts of healing and greater faith for operating in the gifts of the Holy Spirit.

4. Manaus

Manaus is a city in northern Brazil located 1,000 miles into the rainforest. We first ministered there in September 2001 with Pastor Rene Terre Nova. He was one of Cesar Castellanos' original 12 in the G-12 movement. Outside of our ministry and the ministry of Heidi Baker, he does not allow anyone to speak that is not in the G-12 movement. We have made three or four visits to his church over the last 11 years. As I mentioned earlier, his church was disfellowshiped by the Baptist denomination after the Holy Spirit visited it with healing and manifestations. When the church left the Baptist denomination, it had an average attendance of 700. As of our first visit, it had grown to 25,000 in only seven years.

I will never forget that first visit about a decade ago. At the time, I had only seen a few deaf people healed in my whole lifetime. However, in one night we experienced an amazing outpouring of the Holy Spirit connected with a manifestation of nature. The building did not have walls yet and we began to see rain falling and wind blowing inside the building even though it was not happening outside! Within a few minutes, we had eight deaf people hearing. On our second visit we had over 40 deaf people healed. The church had grown to 40,000 in one congregation. This time the walls were built, but the main doors had not been installed. Once again the rain and the wind only occurring inside the building were supernatural signs of the visitation of God. Wind blew chairs down in the building when there was no wind outside the building. On our last trip, we had a lot of angelic activity. We saw about 9,000 people healed the last night. The church had grown to 60,000.

The associate pastor, Aaron, told us that the people of the church had nicknamed our teams, "The Wonderworkers." They could not believe the people who traveled with me were not professional healers who traveled with me everywhere we went, even after I had specifically told them that only about one tenth of the ministry team were ministers. The other nine tenths were people just like them who had paid to come and pray for the sick and minister in Jesus' name.

5. Sao Paulo

I want to end this section with the first place we went in Brazil. It was a meeting for about 1,200 pastors and pastoras (female pastors) in the state of Sao Paulo. I taught for three days. Our team of 11 was small in comparison to what they would later become (30-200 with an average of around 70). No one on my team was a pastor. The meetings were so powerful that on the second day, I lost control of the meetings. So many people were being healed during the sermon on healing that the noise from the crowd was drowning out my voice. Even with proper sound amplification, people were unable to hear me.

The last day, I emphasized that we were passing the baton to the Brazilians to do the ministry during ministry time and that they would be the ones to give words of knowledge; my team would only be coaching. After a time of impartation, they were released to minister themselves the things our team had been doing.

During that trip Pastor Dirceu had been overseeing setting up special meetings for the Quadrangular denomination. The next time I visited, he told me that the few days with our team were the most impacting on the Quadrangular denomination that he had seen in his life. He told me, "Your ministry has impacted our pastors more than anyone else's we have brought to Brazil." I asked him, "Why? How were we different?" He responded, "It isn't that you are more anointed than others. We have brought some of the most famous ministers in the world to minister to our pastors. They are powerful men of God who preach powerfully. But when they left, we were the same. When you came, you told us how you moved in the gifts of the Spirit. You explained to us how to receive words of knowledge. You told us we would be able to do so. You told us God would impart these gifts to us, and when you prayed for us, He did." Pastor Dirceu also told me that he had heard of many testimonies of pastors who had gone back to their respective churches and had seen many healings, where before they had seen few, if any, when they prayed. He said, "When you and your team left, we were different."

B. Mozambique – Pastors' Conferences

Next to Brazil, there probably isn't another country that I have been so committed to serving as Mozambique. For many years we sent two teams a year to Mozambique. I knew that my job description, given to me by God in Toronto, was to be a "fire lighter, vision caster, and a bridge builder." When I was leaving Mozambique after my first visit and was about to make my first visit to Brazil, Heidi said to me. "Randy, when you get to Brazil, don't forget us. Tell the Brazilians about us. They already speak the language and it is easier for them to adjust to the culture than westerners. Tell them this is not the Macedonian Call- this is the Mozambican call." I was faithful and during my first years of visits to Brazil, I often used illustrations about Rolland and Heidi. God used this to open the door for them to visit some of the greatest churches in Brazil.

Short-term ministry trips are one way of cross-pollinating between different streams in the revival. Casting a vision for Mozambique and building a bridge between Mozambique and Brazil has been one of my primary goals on these ministry trips. It isn't enough for me to be used by God to light the fire of revival in countries. I am to cast vision for God's purposes and build a bridge between networks, denominations, countries, mission sending and mission receiving countries. I am to communicate the truth that missions follows revival and that missions is one of the greatest evidences of true revival.

1. Beira – Heidi and key leaders "thousands of churches and millions of people."

During my first visit to Mozambique, I preached at three pastors' meetings arranged by Rolland and Heidi Baker in Maputo, Beira and Chimoio. I do not like ministering in Mozambique, primarily because I don't feel needed there and feel intimidated by my translators who have often raised the dead. Rolland and Heidi have encouraged me to continue coming because of the importance of the connection between our ministries. When Heidi visited

Toronto for her second time, I was also there ministering. As I was preaching, she ran to the front and knelt to pray in response to the message. I knew her name and said, "Heidi, God wants to know- do you want the nation of Mozambique?" To which she responded, "Yes!" I said to her, "God is going to give you the nation of Mozambique. You will see the blind see, the deaf hear, the lame walk, and the dead be raised." The Spirit of God hit her very powerfully immediately following the prophecy. Then she heard God speak to her, "Hundreds of churches and thousands of people." She replied, "How, God? How can this be? My husband Rolland and I have started four churches in seventeen years and it has almost killed us."

God spoke to Heidi a few other things during those seven days and nights as the experience continued. He told her to gather 12 men together and prophesy over them everything that I had prophesied to her, which she did. In just a couple of years, they started over 200 hundred churches.

When I visited her for the first time at their Beira base, the Spirit once again fell upon Heidi, Rolland and the main leaders who were present. I could tell by the look on the people's faces that this was not normal for Heidi in Mozambique, though it was normal for her when she visited the Church in the Western world. This time she went into a vision and saw ships coming with food and supplies and heard the Lord say, "Thousands of churches and millions of people." She told me that this was easier to believe than the first word of hundreds of churches and thousands of people, because God had fulfilled the first word. Now Heidi had faith for Him to fulfill the second word.

These types of experiences are of great value to apostolic leaders in other countries. It helps establish them in the purposes of God and gives them faith to attempt what was given to them in a prophecy or vision.

2. Chimoio – Mountain Vision

We left Beira and went to Chimoio, where Heidi preached the first message. Her message was powerful. Everyone was lying prostrate on the ground in prayer. I could find no room to lie down; the floor was covered with the bodies of the saints in prayer. I leaned up against a wall and began to pray. I was very much aware of the fact that I was going to be translated from English into Portuguese and from Portuguese to the local dialect. I began to pray, "Oh Lord, I have not come half way around the world to give a teaching. God, I must hear from you. What do you want to say to these people? Oh God, I want to see. I want to see into the spiritual realm. I want to see!" Suddenly, I thought I might have seen something. I said, "God, what was that? Did I just see something?" I had had a brief mental picture in my mind's eye, like a daydream. I thought I had seen a man standing on a mountain looking over a great amount of land. He was asking the Lord, "Lord, do you want me to go into this land?" I had an impression that the answer was "yes."

I have never been a seer and mental pictures were not something I had much experience with. After the meeting I asked Supresa Sithole, one of the key leaders of Iris Ministries, to translate as I interviewed Johnny, who had raised the dead. Not long after this encounter, Supresa began to raise the dead and has since raised several. On the way I asked Supresa if he had open visions, where he wouldn't see anything except what God was showing him. He told me he did. This intimidated me more.

That night while I was preaching, I gave an invitation for men who had been on a mountain asking God if they were to go into this land to come forward for prayer. About seven men came forward. A few of them were key leaders in the movement and another two had actually been on a mountain a few days earlier fasting and praying. These two men had seen a vision of a ball of fire moving through the sky and hovering over Chimoio. They heard God tell them to go to this building (the one we were meeting in) and there they would find their overseers. These men eventually became powerful leaders in Iris' ministry.

Heidi told me later that she had been praying for months asking God who was to go into the Muslim northern provinces of Mozambique. God gave her the answer that night. Sometime later, I found out that this story was on the webpage of the Toronto Airport Christian Fellowship. It was called, "The Mountain Vision." How funny! What started out as a very weak, "I thought I might have seen something," was now called the "Mountain Vision."

3. Pemba – Mrs. Tanuecki

During another trip to minister in Mozambique with Heidi, she invited me to a pastors' conference. After preaching and ministering I was once again very much troubled by what felt like my own inadequacy. I went to Heidi and told her that I didn't want to come back to Mozambique. I said, "You don't need me here. These people are more powerful than I am. They pray better and they can communicate the gospel to their fellow Mozambicans better than I can. They are raising the dead; what can I do for them?

Heidi stopped me and pointed to a woman in the crowd named Mrs. Tanuecki. She told me, "That woman over there has been involved in raising several people from the dead, but when you touched her and prayed for her, God took her into a trance. She is still in the trance. We do need you to come with your teams to Mozambique. You carry a special grace, a special anointing."

Later that day, Heidi had four people pray for me, all of whom had raised the dead, and a few of them who had raised three or four from the dead. It was a humbling experience, but one for which I was very grateful. I want to receive an impartation for raising the dead.

4. Maputo

As with the section on Brazil, I want to end this one on Mozambique with my very first night in Mozambique and the fruit of that meeting. I was exhausted by the time I arrived. Heidi said,

"You might want to rest for a bit. Tonight, I want to take you to the dump where we minister to people and then into the city, and I want you to lead devotions with my staff before we leave."

I was exhausted and didn't feel like leading devotions for the staff. When we met I asked them, "Why are you here? Tell me your story." I was shocked to hear that every one of them had been touched either in Toronto or by someone from Toronto who was carrying the anointing. They were from Israel, England, Canada, the United States, and Australia. I began to realize how impacting the Toronto Blessing was upon missions, at least in Mozambique.

I interviewed many people while in Maputo. I remember interviewing the only nurse on the base. At that time there weren't any doctors on the base and this nurse was working long hours. She was a pretty blond from England, but she was exhausted. She was planning to go back to England in the near future after having fulfilled her commitment. A few days later, I preached a message called "Spend and Be Spent" from 2 Corinthians 12:11. At the conclusion I saw this nurse come forward weeping, touched by the Holy Spirit. She committed to stay longer in Mozambique that day.

I learned quite some time later that on that same day there was a person on our team from Nebraska named Betty. She too had heard God speak to her about coming back and helping Heidi. She would later return and serve as Heidi's personal assistant and in other positions for some time. She had no special training or cross-cultural education. She did, however, have a heart that had been touched by the Holy Spirit. Our short-term ministry team had not only impacted the missionaries working in Maputo; the missionaries, in turn, had impacted our team. Those who came to "refresh others" had themselves "been refreshed."

On my next trip to Mozambique, I was surprised to see several of the people who had been visiting for the first time during my initial trip. They had returned to become part of the crucial leadership team. One man, Steve Lazar, was an educator from

Australia. He began a school for Iris that would become the #1 rated primary school in Mozambique. Several couples from my team also went back as full time missionaries to work with Rolland and Heidi.

I would like to conclude with a strategy God gave me to help Rolland and Heidi. I believed that I was to take the pastors of the largest churches I had relationship with to Mozambique with me. I knew that I was to not only invite pastors, but also very successful businessmen. I wouldn't have to say anything about helping Rolland and Heidi, and I knew that Rolland and Heidi wouldn't either. I knew that when these pastors and businessmen saw what God was doing through Rolland and Heidi and saw their hearts, they would begin to help them. I had heard God correctly. These people would become some of the strongest financial supporters of Iris Ministries.

C. Russia – Moscow – Pastor's Conferences

I was attending a conference in Kansas City years ago when I heard Terry Law share about his experiences in Russia. At this meeting an offering was taken up for Bibles for China. In this one offering, $1,000,000 was raised. I had an impression that one day I would lead my worship team to Russia and they would sing in Russian. My church was just getting started and had less than 100 people in it at the time. A few years later, I had an impression from the Lord: "Ask me for $100,000." I knew it wasn't for me personally, but I did not know what it was for. I didn't need to know to obey. Around 1994 I began asking the Lord for $100,000 dollars.

On January 1, 1995, I was preaching and told my church, "We are to go to Russia." I told them that we were to take to Russia the anointing that had fallen in our church in 1993 and in Toronto in 1994. I said, "I need the worship team to go with me. I now know what the $100,000 is for. We are going to do a Catch the Fire conference in Russia. Begin raising the money and if you can't raise enough, I will help you. Oh, another thing- you can't sing in English. You have to learn Russian and I don't have a clue how this will happen!"

About a week later I was conducting meetings in Melbourne, Florida where another revival broke out after I preached. This one lasted six nights a week for about eight months. While there, a young man in his early 20's named Keith Major asked me to pray for him. I asked him, "For what?" He said, "About going back to Russia. My wife and I were among the leaders of one of the first churches started after the wall came down. That is where we met and got married. I want to go back, but don't know what to do." I said, "I will pray for you, but could you and your wife eat with me after the meeting?" He said they could.

During our 3:00 a.m. meal, I asked his wife, Iwona, "What did you do in Russia?" She replied, "I taught English speakers how to speak Russian." Long story short, I asked them to move into the parsonage of my church, train my team how to sing in Russian, and to translate our songs into Russian. This took about a year, but eventually the team and I made it to Moscow, ready to do the first Catch The Fire – Moscow.

1. Models for new forms of worship

The Berlin Wall hadn't been down for long when we first went in the fall of 1995 for our "spying out the land" meetings. We returned in the spring of 1996 with a full team of musicians. I hadn't any idea how far behind the Russian Protestant churches were at this time. It was like stepping back into what I imagined the American church worship experience looked like in the 1920's and 1930's. Many of the songs were American songs that had been translated into Russian. The worship was led by someone who was more of a "song leader" than a worship leader. The instruments consisted of a piano and nothing else.

On our "spy out the land" trip, a Russian leader told me, "We Russians are not like you Americans. We will not fall down, we will not laugh, nor will we become drunk in the Spirit."

The time had come for our meeting and the musicians were on stage. The Izmaillovo Hotel Civic Center was filled to capacity-1,000 pastors, church planters and worship leaders had come. The $100,000 required had grown to $130,000 due to inflation. My worship leaders, Bob and Kathleen Balassi, my associate worship leader Gary Shelton, the whole worship team and some special musicians from Nashville had all come to help us. In addition to the keyboards, two acoustic guitars, an electric guitar, a bass guitar, a saxophone, a flute, a harmonica and drums were the wonderful vocals of people who once sang in bars with their own bands. We also had a voice major who was so good that she had received a college scholarship and even sang for the Pope in the Sistine Chapel.

During the first song, the Russians sat there as the team sang the song once through in English. The Russians had no expression and showed no joy. But when the team switched to Russian the second time through, the place exploded. The Russians got to their feet, shouting, twirling, waving, falling down and getting drunk as they learned new worship songs. They were not like us Americans. They were more abandoned to this new instrument-filled experience of worship!

You could see people taking their video cameras, looking up at the words, and then down to the guitar necks to get the chord progressions. A year later we went back to do a larger event. We had worked on getting the music onto a CD recording to give to them, but it was already too late. We were told that those songs had gone all over the country. Another fruit of this event relating to worship was what happened to one famous Russian rock and roll singer who was newly saved. He had laid his guitar down, not seeing a way it could be used in church. When he saw our team worship, God called him to become a worship leader. He was immediately catapulted into being one of the most famous worship leaders in the former Soviet Union. He would later work with a church in Ukraine.

2. Models for small groups

We also taught about small groups at this meeting. We encouraged them to consider small groups as a way of discipling the new converts. This was an important part of the fruitfulness of our ministry there.

3. Models for philosophy of ministry

While there, we emphasized a new kind of leadership - servant leadership - which exemplified humility rather than an authoritarian model. I was very much aware of the typical image many people had of American evangelists who were loud, braggadocios and proud. I have tried to offer a different model wherever we have gone in the world.

4. Impartation – Boris and Oleg and the South African Church Planter

The most important thing that happened at the Catch the Fire – Moscow was the experience of impartation that so many of the pastors experienced. Later, I learned of two close friends from Ukraine that had come to this meeting: Boris, the Rabbi of the largest messianic Jewish congregation in the world in Kiev, Ukraine, and Oleg, who had become the bishop of the protestant churches in Nikolaev, Ukraine. Both men had been overwhelmed by the mighty presence of the Holy Spirit and had returned in the "power of the Spirit" to their cities. I met them later to hear their stories, visit their congregations and minister with them many times.

A year after Catch the Fire – Moscow, I met many young pastors who had received gifts of healing at our meeting. They told me many testimonies of healings, miracles, blind eyes that saw and deaf ears that heard. They were very excited and very grateful.

Almost 14 years later, I was ministering for a South African apostle, Nevel Norton. While in his church ministering to his network of pastors, I met a South African pastor, Hugo V. Niekerk, who was touched at the Catch the Fire – Moscow 1996 while he was a missionary. He had since planted over 200 churches in Russia. He told me how powerfully he had been touched in that meeting and how it had impacted his ministry and his faith. Only heaven really knows the fruit of such meetings.

This was also the meeting during which Russ Purcello was touched. Through him, we have been able to continue to impact churches across Russia. As I shared earlier, he continued to go back every year offering other cities what he had seen us do in Moscow. This American pastor has been used to powerfully affect the Protestant Church in Russia.

D. India – Pastor's Conferences

In January-February of 2010, I led a team to Bangalore and Krishnagiri, India. Bangalore is predominantly Hindu, but Krishnagiri has a strong Muslim presence. A young apostolic leader named Ravi invited us to come. The focus of the first meeting was to equip about 2,000 pastors. The second meeting had about 600 pastors, but also had a small crusade with 5,000-9,000 people. We decided to spend most of our money on the pastors' meetings rather than on a larger crusade. There were many spectacular healings, miracles and salvations.

No one had ever conducted a healing crusade in this city. A Hindu school with 700 students and teachers were curious and sent a delegate to the meeting asking if we would send someone from our team to tell them about Christianity. A small team was sent, and they prayed for many who were healed. All the students, teachers, and administrators prayed the sinner's prayer to receive Jesus and some were filled with the Holy Spirit. Afterwards, they were concerned about how they would be persecuted by family for accepting Jesus.

The same day, three Muslim women came to the pastors' meeting, which was held in a public hall. They sat outside the hall, but because the doors were open for ventilation, they could hear everything. At the lunch break, the mother and her sister came and asked to be set free from demonic problems. The daughter, who looked to be in her 20's and wearing a Berka allowing only her eyes to be seen, had leg problems. The mother was set free from the demonic attack and the daughter's legs were healed. That night the husband/father came with them to the healing meeting. He was one of the first healed through a word of knowledge. When the invitation for salvation was given, this Muslim family was among the very first to come forward to confess their sins and commit their lives to Jesus Christ. I have since heard that they are on fire for God, telling others about the great healing power in God's Son, Jesus Christ. God is using them to heal many, including key leaders in the Muslim community.

One pastor at our meetings went straight from the impartation service to a woman in another city who had been in a coma for about a year. When he laid hands on her and prayed, she came out of the coma. Another pastor that week had promised a Hindu teenager who was crippled in his legs that if he would go to the meeting, he would be healed. The boy went with the pastor, but was not healed at the crusade. The pastor was beside himself, since he had promised healing and did not want to be a poor testimony to the Gospel. He didn't know how to explain the lack of healing to the family. However, when the boy woke up the next day, he could walk. During those four days in Krishnagiri, the blind saw, the deaf heard, the lame walked, the terminally ill were healed. The pastors were greatly encouraged.

A few months after these meetings, the apostolic leader from Bangalore and Krishnagiri came to our headquarters and told us about the fruit that continued to happen. The pastors were not seeing many healings before the event, but now they were occurring regularly. Two people had been raised from the dead and over 90 Muslims, including several leaders, had been saved after being healed. Greater prosperity had come to the city in the form of job opportunities offered by the government. Even the land was impacted, as mangos began to grow once again after many years of little to no growth.

Ongole – James Rebbavarapu

James Rebbavarapu is an apostolic leader that we work with in the Ongole area in southeast India. He received his Masters of Divinity from Oral Roberts University in Tulsa, Oklahoma. He was sent out by a small Vineyard Church of about 80 members with enough money to live on for one year. He stretched this into three years. When I met him, he was already overseeing about 200 pastors and had a powerful ministry to the social and spiritual needs of the community. During the next five years, the 200 pastors grew over 2,000 pastors. We worked with him in about five other cities and saw thousands of Indians coming to Christ and even more being healed. Mass worship events and healing crusades were instrumental to the growth of James' churches.

We had a healing crusade in Ongole, where about 85,000 people were healed in three days. About 45,000 accepted Jesus. The healings drew the masses to the meetings and convinced many of them of the truth of the gospel. About half of the people were healed and a little less than a third were saved. The largest crowd for one night was about 100,000.

While there, I was taken to the highest place in the city, to the exact place where Baptist missionary Lyman Jewett had been praying in 1853 for the salvation of that region. He had labored long and hard with little fruit and very few salvations. The mission board began advising people to move to Burma because so few had been reached with the gospel in India, but in Burma, many more were responding. Several years later, however, the Lord began to answer his prayer for the region by directing another missionary couple, John and Harriet Clough, to turn their attention to the poor. God did this by independently highlighting 1 Corinthians 1:26 to the husband and wife: "Brothers, think of what you were when you were called. Not many of you were wise by human standards; not many were influential; not many were of noble birth." When the Cloughs began ministering to the poor, a great revival broke out with thousands led to the Lord. The key was hearing God and obeying His commands.

After our first trip to India, the infamous tsunami of 2004 hit the coast where much of James' work was done. As a result of the bond James and I formed on our mission trip, he called me to see if we could help with relief. We ended up sending containers worth millions of dollars in medical supplies and other necessities. Since then, we have continued to take teams to work with Apostle James, and the same percentage of healings and salvations among the crowds have continued. The pastors continue to be encouraged and they report a significant increase in the people being healed through their own ministries.

E. Cambodia

We have made two short-term mission trips to Phenom Phen, Cambodia. Both were to pray for the pastors and leaders that apostolic leader Sophal Ung had gathered together from all over Cambodia. The second trip also included pastors from Vietnam. There were many who were healed and who received impartations that equipped them to see more healings and more success in their own ministries. Sophal and his wife Debra are very excited about the work God is doing in Cambodia and they continue to see the fruit of our visits.

F. Norway

In 1995, I prayed and prophesied over a Baptist pastor in Norway named Leif Hetland. During the prayer, I told him, "I see you in a dark place. All around you is darkness, but behind you is light. I see a multitude of people following you out of the darkness into the light." The power of the Holy Spirit knocked him to the floor where he shook for 2 ½ to 3 hours. He got up and by the next week was operating in many gifts he never had before. Every person he prayed for was healed. Still, he didn't yet understand the prophecy I gave him. The next year he had his neck and back broken. While recuperating from the injury in traction, he was meditating on the prophecy and realized he was not to remain a Baptist pastor but was to go to unreached people groups.

Since then he has led 850,000 people to the Lord in Islamic countries as of March, 2010. By conducting healing meetings, many Muslims believe in Jesus because of the healings they saw. Leif has also started over 2,000 Lighthouses of Love in these countries, which focus on healing, deliverance and restoration of lives. God is using him throughout the Western Hemisphere, Africa, Asia, the Middle East and Europe. Great healing miracles take place in his ministry even as he endures serious pain from his own injuries. The anointing that led him to the nations has resulted in him being away from his wife and four children for up to 200+ days a year. He has even had threats against his life, including several from the Taliban. However, nothing has prevented him from continuing to preach the Gospel and heal the sick.

G. Mexico

Juan Aguilar is an apostolic leader in Mexico City. I took two short-term missions teams with me to minister to his leaders. On each trip the power of God came upon the pastors and leaders. During the first trip, several key leaders in the Baptist denomination were powerfully touched and began to see much more of the power of God in their ministries. Many other pastors from diverse denominations and apostolic streams were empowered, as well.

In 2009, I took a very small team to Queretaro, Mexico to minister in another apostolic network of pastors. We taught them how to receive words of knowledge and how to pray for the sick out of a place of dependence on the Holy Spirit. We had a special time of impartation for over 1,000 pastors and leaders. Then we had a service where we prayed specifically for the terminally ill, blind, deaf and/or crippled. The day after I left, they did it again and saw many healings, miracles and 11 blind people healed. The pastors were so excited because there had previously been very little healing in their ministries. They exclaimed, "We received an impartation!"

One of the miracles that occurred at this event was the healing of a woman who had cancer, resulting in a urostomy bag for her urine. She was accompanied by her daughter, who had cancer in her breast. Both women were healed of their cancer and the woman no longer needed a urostomy; her organ was reconstructed and was working normally. She was able to go to the bathroom normally before she left the building instead of the urine flowing into the bag.

During this meeting a Baptist pastor came up to me at the end of the meeting and asked to be prayed for by the laying on of hands. I prayed for him and his wife. They fell down, but there did not initially appear to be a strong anointing. They were resting quietly on the floor without much trembling or shaking. However, the longer he was on the floor the stronger the anointing became. About an hour later, I saw him being helped from the building by two men, unable to walk. He shook the whole next day and it was quite noticeable to all who were there. The following day, now two days after the impartation, he ministered in his 10,000 member Baptist Church. He was helped to the pulpit by two deacons. As they tried to help him, the Holy Spirit knocked all three of them to the floor. He was going to pray for the church to receive an anointing, but before he could say, "anointing," the Spirit came upon him and his church. Over 3/4 of the 8,000 people in attendance fell to the floor or shook under the power of God and many other manifestations of the Holy Spirit occurred that day in his church. The early service didn't end until about 4:30 p.m.

H. Argentina - Story of Baptist Church Planter out of Del Centro Baptist Church, Marcello Diaz

About 15 years ago, I went to Buenos Aires, Argentina where I ministered at a large pastors' meeting in a Baptist Church - La Iglesia Evangélica Bautista del Centro. This church was the first Baptist Church in Argentina. At this conference one young pastor, Marcelo Diaz, had been prayed for several times. Near midnight he came to me and asked for one more prayer. When I prayed for him, the power of God knocked him to the floor. I sensed an urgency to tell him to pray for everyone in his new church that he was starting in the area. When he did this the next day, everyone he prayed for was healed, including a woman dying of cancer. The community named this new church plant the Healing Church. Today, it is one of the largest churches in that area of the city.

Summary

The most important aspect of the short-term mission trips that our ministry has is the impartation pastors receive, the encouragement that God can and will use them for healing, and the activation of the gifts of the Spirit in their lives and ministries. This reality is represented by the following two letters from an itinerate minister who has ministered in India for 22 years. I will let the emails speak for themselves regarding the importance of these types of short-term ministry trips.

Dear Randy,

This morning during prayer the Lord laid it VERY STRONGLY on both our hearts that a minister's conference by you, Randy, in north India would ignite a fire and accelerate what is already happening there. God has made you a modern day general and we need you to come to north India to give the marching orders and impartation to leaders. We could work to bring in 3,000 to 5,000 pastors and leaders form all over North India. Leaders from states like Himachal Pradesh, (the state the Hindus believe their gods originate from) where the anti-conversion law is in effect and Christians are consistently persecuted, leaders from Rajasthan, a state that has always had a militant Hindu government and has had very little or no Christian expression because of Hindu militancy would attend. Many, if not most, of these men and women have had little or no Bible training, but are pastoring because of the tremendous need there.

Most of India's population lives in north India. Only 1/5th of 1% are considered Christian! The door is wide open for you to come. Peter Youngren, Rienhard Bonnke, myself and others have been holding many open air campaigns all over north India winning 100's of thousands to Christ. But take it from one who has labored in north India for 21 years now. I believe that an event like this can have a greater impact on the nation than the open-air campaigns because of what God has put in you. This kind of event alone needs to be the focus in order for the open-air campaigns to have the impact in north India. Who knows? More Leif Hetlands and Heidi Bakers could come out of this event and help turn India upside down for Jesus Christ. Cities and villages you and I will never have a chance to go to will be impacted for Jesus with a strong impartation from this training conference.

All we ask is one conference conducted by you in north India as the Lord leads. The fire of evangelism could spread all over north India once you come and use the gifting God has put in you to ignite the fire. Waiting to hear from you!

Blessings my friend!

For the unreached & untold,

Mark & Sharmila Anderson, February 6, 2010

Randy,

I am back from a great trip to India & Nepal. There is great excitement about your possible coming to North India. Our ministry held a luncheon for pastors in Delhi and Agra to visit about this. The pastors were very encouraged to think somebody like you would come and impart to them. I also by chance/divine appointment met (after 11 years) with Pastor Robert Karthak (84 years old), the pastor of the largest church in Nepal and that entire region. I shared about you, and he was greatly encouraged by our meeting. He has extended his invitation to you to come to Kathmandu, Nepal and conduct a conference if possible. I think this would have tremendous impact on that nation. Maybe even more than north India, because of where this country is sitting right now politically. Pastor Robert's church ran 600 people in the early 90's when we first held leadership training conferences at his church. It now runs over 3,000 and they have planted over 70 more churches in that nation. Pastor Robert is a very, very humble man of God. Humility is very important to him as well. I was refreshed just being around him.

After hearing and seeing what is happening there, I feel if you did a conference in Kathmandu with Pastor Robert and other pastors, we would see tremendous fruit. We held many annual conferences for leaders in that nation in the 1990's. The effect of impartation and miracles greatly affected the Gospel going forth from 1992 to 1999. It went from 1/5 of 1% Christian to 3% Christian, because of the miracles, signs, and wonders that took place. We focused strictly on leadership training at that time period. It greatly affected evangelism efforts.

Now that Nepal has become a democratic country, but still unstable, it is the greatest time to impact this nation. That is why Pastor Robert really felt our time together last Sunday was from God, who ordered our steps.

Looking forward to visiting further on this. Blessings!

Mark Anderson, March 30, 2010

Conclusion

I am grateful to know that I am not only leading short-term ministry trips into many countries. There are many other pastors who first traveled with me and are now taking teams themselves into many countries. Our network, the Apostolic Network of Global Awakening, is only four years old, yet already our pastors and ministry leaders are impacting one third of the countries in the world. Not only are pastors who traveled with me taking teams into the world, but so are itinerate ministers. There has been a real multiplication of effect and a multiplication of countries we are reaching every year. We, or someone in our apostolic network, are taking short-term ministry trips to almost 50 countries a year, where people are healed, delivered and empowered to more effectively reach their communities in the power of the Holy Spirit.

Chapter 11
PRIMACY OF LOVE IN MISSIONS
WITH POWER

" *1 Corinthians 13 serves as a significant reminder of what is most important in missions. If we speak the local language fluently, operate in signs and wonders and willingly sacrifice our possessions - even our lives for the gospel - it is still worth absolutely nothing without love. When we are deeply rooted in the Father's love for us, our love for Him and for people will overflow in Spirit-empowered ministry that brings transformation to individuals and nations.* "

- Heidi Baker

The Primacy of Love

"If I speak in the tongues of men and of angels, but have not love, I am only a resounding gong or a clanging cymbal. If I have the gift of prophecy and can fathom all mysteries and all knowledge, and if I have a faith that can move mountains, but have not love, I am nothing. If I give all I possess to the poor and surrender my body to the flames, but have not love, I gain nothing."

—I Cor 13:1-3 NIV

Love is not a concept or theory, or even an important part of missions, but the center of everything we do and why we do it. It is the very heartbeat of our movement. Love has a face. It looks like something. It looks like someone. When we are motivated by love and are confident that "the God of the impossible" lives inside of us, we can do anything, go anywhere, and nothing will be too difficult. This is the great mystery: that God has chosen to inhabit and possess little jars of clay with His lavish love so that we can spread His fragrance to the darkest ends of the earth, and to every person we meet each day. When we know how extravagantly loved we are by the Father, we are able to lay down our lives in obedience with great joy. As ministers and missionaries, this is the life of joy to which we have been called.

The Father's Delight

"There is no fear in love. But perfect love drives out fear."

—1 Jn 4:18 NIV

As a missionary I have been beaten up, stoned, shot at, shipwrecked, had knives to my throat, been thrown in jail, slandered, mocked and ridiculed many times over, but I'm not afraid. I am not ashamed of the Gospel. I have known persecution and suffering, and counted it all joy! I have walked into the middle of gangs armed with guns and knives and told them to stop what they were doing, in the name of Jesus, and they dropped their knives and apologized! They were surprised to see that I wasn't afraid of them. Where does that kind of confidence come from?

One day I had a vision of the Father and He was smiling at me. I saw that He took great delight in me and His smile undid me. He picked me up and danced with me all around a field. He loved the dance. We pirouetted. We leaped across the field. He danced and smiled at me. I was completely undone by His love for me! I know that I am totally loved by my Father. This is the place from which my confidence flows. My fearlessness comes from knowing Him and knowing His delight in me. When the Father tells you that He thinks you're awesome, you'll go to the ends of the earth without hesitation. We are also willing to hear His discipline because we know He loves us. Likewise, a wife who is in love will obey her husband; it's hard for a wife to obey a mean, grouchy husband, but when a woman is in love, she doesn't have to be told to submit. She will do anything to please the one with whom she is in love. Obedience comes out of knowing you're loved. When you know you're loved, you will go anywhere He sends you and do anything with joy.

Happy Missionary

People often say to me that it must be a huge sacrifice to work with the poor, to spend time in the slums and be exposed to malaria, cholera and dysentery. My response is to laugh. To me, there is no sacrifice at all! It is a joy because I have given my life for the One I love. I find joy in being a missionary and doing what I am called to do. I am a happy missionary! To me, the poorest villages where I minister are simply wonderful! They are the most glorious place on earth because Jesus is there. When you get a revelation of the Father's heart for you, you love whatever He tells you to do and obedience is joyful. He rips away your fear and you are able to do things that you wouldn't normally do. Things that would usually bother you no longer do, because you're moving out of love.

I Will Not Leave You as Orphans

As a ministry, God has called us to take care of orphans and widows, but we never call our centers orphanages because the

Father never leaves us as orphans (Jn 14:18 NIV). He adopts us into His family and we become sons and daughters. Sometimes people come to visit us and they expect to see ragged misery, but instead meet hundreds of happy children. They wonder how an orphan can carry so much joy. Our children know that they have been adopted and are no longer alone. They are in a family and live lives full of love and joy, knowing that they are sons and daughters. In fact, they get to minister the Father-heart to our visitors. These are kids that the world says are cast-off orphans, yet they are generally a delight to be around. Jesus pours His extravagant love through them.

Access to Heaven

Every weekend some of our children come over to our house for a sleepover. One day I was watching them as they ran into our house, opened up the fridge and dumped the ice trays out all over the kitchen! We don't always have electricity, so when it's on it's very exciting because that means we all have ice. It is such a delight for the children to have ice and they get very excited about it. My children didn't come in and ask politely if they could have some ice. They simply knew that they had access to the fridge! They weren't even that sweet or tidy about getting it; they made a huge mess! As I watched them eat the ice, I was thrilled because I knew that they were confident that this was their home and that they had access to the things in our house. The Spirit of adoption had healed their orphan hearts.

Like them, I am starting to understand that we have access to heaven's resources. Whenever I preach the Gospel in the bush of Mozambique, I always ask if there is anybody deaf or mute in the village. When they bring the deaf mutes to us for prayer, we are always confident that we have access to their healing because we know that we are co-heirs with Christ and that we are seated with Him in heavenly places. We want to take that which God says is ours and release it in this world. As I lay my hands on them, they begin to hear and speak, and the village starts to come to Jesus.

When you understand who you are, then you will start taking risks, but if you have an orphan spirit, you will be too afraid to try in case you fail. Sons and daughters are able to flow in great humility and great authority at the same time. They are confident that they have access to the Father's house. They know that they are His so they are able to suffer without fear. I have watched our children preach the Gospel when they were being stoned, while visitors locked themselves in a truck! They are mostly unafraid because they know they are children of the Most High God, loved and accepted. They often fearlessly lay their hands on the blind and their eyes open up. They take hold of crippled legs and the cripples start to run! We cheer them on as we watch them move in Kingdom power. We even cheer them on when they fall short of the Kingdom.

The Father wants to embrace each one of us and tell us who we are until we believe Him and begin to move in unstoppable boldness. Ministry and missions have to flow out of this place of confidence because we can only change the world when we understand who we are and who He is in us. When we really understand that we are sent out as sons and daughters and not just servants and workers, it will change the way we minister and do missions. We will flow out of radical love and fearless confidence. We will move out of a place of rest rather than striving and we will go long-term, without burning out. We will finish well.

Abiding in Love

"I am the vine, you are the branches; he who abides in Me and I in him, he bears much fruit, for apart from Me you can do nothing."

—Jn 15:5 NAS

How do we bear abundant fruit? How do we birth revival and see whole cultures transformed, and nations bow at the feet of Jesus? We can't make revival happen. We cannot create it. We cannot force fruit to grow, just as a branch cannot bear fruit by itself (John 15:4). The only way it's able to bear fruit is by remaining on the vine. We cannot bear fruit that lasts unless we learn how to abide in Jesus. It's as we worship Him and enjoy His love that He creates the fruit. We cannot create fruit, but we can live in intimacy! A tree produces fruit by simply abiding, not striving. Many of those who come to visit our ministry ask about our method and strategy for growing thousands of churches within a few years. My husband Rolland and I start laughing because we know that we cannot produce anything ourselves. We do not have a ten-point plan on how to bear fruit. Fruit only comes from the One who is altogether perfect! Our desire in life is to live inside of the heart of Jesus and to love Him. We don't love Him to get fruit, but fruit always flows when there is intimacy. When we abide in Jesus, the true vine, it just happens (Jn 15:1). Our goal is not to be the leading church growth movement on the planet. Our one desire is to be in love with Jesus, to love Him well and to abide in that love until it flows from us and touches every man, woman and child we meet each day. We are on the mission field primarily to learn how to love. That's it. It's so simple that it scares people. We don't have anything else. We didn't just come here as teachers, but as students of love, desperate to know how to reveal the heartbeat of Jesus to this dying world. We are just starting to learn. My daily cry to God is, "More love, Lord!" Our national brothers and sisters often lead the way. They teach us what love and generosity look like.

Pruning the Vine

> "Every branch in Me that does not bear fruit, He takes away; and every branch that bears fruit, He prunes it so that it may bear more fruit."

> —Jn 15:2 NAS

Abiding in Jesus also means we allow Him to cut off every branch in us that bears no fruit. Out of His great love the Father cuts away everything that isn't fruitful in our lives. Sometimes it hurts, but the pruning is so that we will bear even more fruit. Once, when I was in Toronto, I was on the floor seven days and seven nights under the power of the Holy Spirit. I was unable to move in my own strength. I couldn't even lift my head and I had to be carried everywhere, even to the restroom! I couldn't eat or drink by myself. It was almost like being a quadriplegic. The Body of Christ had to take complete care of me. When I was thirsty, the Lord had to speak to someone to come and pour water down my throat. This was really difficult for someone as active as me, and I felt like I was going to die. The Lord told me that's exactly how He wanted me! Dead. Then He would raise me from the dead. During this time God was wooing me deeper into His heart and showing me how I could do nothing without Him and I could do nothing without His Body. I was learning about dependence on Him and inter-dependence in His beloved Bride. We were all created to be in family and can do nothing without each other.

On day three, as I was lying on the floor at church, I felt a hand on my chest and liquid love pulsated through me. I was completely undone; I had never felt love like this before. It was like a rolling river going through me, over and over again. I thought that the person who had his hand on me was the most anointed person on the planet. Later Rolland told me that no one had been anywhere near me during that time. The hand on my chest had been the hand of the Lord Jesus Himself! He was teaching me about His burning heart of passion.

Fruit Flows from Intimacy

At that time we only had three churches. One of them was for our children and staff, so attendance was mandatory. After being stuck to the floor for seven days under the heavy, weighty glory of God, when I got up and went out, revival happened! A team grew up around us. After that experience of intimate love, fruit just started happening through our little lives and through our Mozambican and missionary family. I began to see every miracle I had ever dreamed of. Then the Lord spoke to me and told me He wanted more of my time. He had to chop away the things that were not important to Him. Where I minister in Africa, we face many pressures and long queues every day. The needs seem overwhelming at times, so we have to contend for time in the secret place. Without the Presence none of it means anything. His Presence is what we live for and ministry only makes sense when it flows out of this place of abiding. I was determined to give Jesus even more of my time and not give in to the constant pressures around me. I am learning that in the anointing we can produce more fruit in a day than a lifetime of striving and trying. This is a place I must contend for daily.

Hearts Full of Passion and Compassion

Even though I had been a diligent missionary for twenty-nine years and preached the Gospel for thirty-three years, He still had to prune many things in my life to take me deeper into the secret place of His heart. Some of my favorite times are walking and snorkeling with Jesus. Just Him and me. Fruit comes out of a laid-down love affair with Jesus. God is not just concerned about how much we can sacrifice for Him by being on the mission field. He is not impressed by how miserable we can be. It doesn't earn us brownie points in heaven! He is concerned that our hearts are full of passion for Him and full of compassionate love for our neighbor. A heart that is full of passion will do anything, go anywhere and withhold nothing. This is how Jesus wants to send us out into His harvest field: full of passion and compassion. He wants to captivate our hearts with love until they burn with holy fire and we walk the earth as the fragrance of Jesus. I won't go for any reason other than love.

What Does Love Look Like?

To be the love of Christ to those around us, we have to ask ourselves this question: what does love look like? What does it look like, specifically, in the culture we are called to reach? In my nation, Mozambique, where there is much suffering due to clean water shortage, loving a village looks like drilling a fresh water well so that people don't have to walk for hours in the blazing heat to get a cup of clean water. Loving those who are hungry and dressed in rags looks like food and new clothes. This wouldn't be a good demonstration of love to those living in London or Seoul, where there is clean water running out of taps constantly and most have wonderful clothing. Most people in the first-world don't lack severely in a material way. They're not malnourished, barefooted and dressed in rags. We need to ask Jesus to give us eyes to see what their needs are and reach out to them with His heart in their poverty. Even though they may not be literally hungry, they may be starved of love and acceptance. To the lonely and rejected, love looks like acceptance and friendship. It may look like a hug or a word of encouragement. In the busy cities of the world, like Hong Kong, love may look like taking the time to sit with someone long enough to hear their story so that they know they matter. Love may look like you sharing a meal with them in the middle of a busy day. This should be our daily question: what does it look like to manifest the love of Christ to those that I meet today?

Teach Me How To Love!

"This is how we know what love is: Jesus Christ laid down His life for us. And we ought to lay our lives down for our brothers."

—1Jn 3:16 NIV

When we lived in London, we spent a lot of time on the streets ministering to the homeless. During this time, I met a dying alcoholic named Patrick. Nearly every day for two years I would tell him that I loved him and that Jesus loved him. And nearly every day he would get really close to my face, look straight into my eyes and tell me to go to hell. I kept bringing him food and telling him that I loved him and I kept crying out to Jesus to teach me how to communicate His love to this man. One of my constant prayers is for the Lord to teach me to love. I don't want any other thing but to live inside the heart of Jesus and to manifest His love to a dying world. Nearly every day for two years, I would visit Patrick and tell him about love. Often he would spit at me. Sometimes he would take my food and sometimes he would throw it away.

Reduced to Love

"Let us not love with word or with tongue, but in deed and truth."

—1 Jn 3:18 NIV

One day as I was out on the streets again, a woman I was ministering to began to beat me. She was a very angry and broken person. She had been raped sixteen times and had spent a year in the hospital with a broken pelvis. She was a lesbian and dressed like a man. I often told her that I loved her and that Jesus loved her as I held her, fed her and ministered to her. One day she was stoned and very drunk. She was beating me and pushing me, but all I could feel was overwhelming love for her. When I looked at her, she was beautiful. Jean had a broken bottle and she said she was going to rip open my face and throw me in the river Thames. I told her how amazingly beautiful she was! I knew that she too was called to adoption and was predestined to be a daughter of God. As she told me that she was going to kill me, all I could see in her was beauty. I told her I loved her. After some time I began to feel very tired and thought I would either faint or die. I told God that whatever happened I wanted His love to be known in that place. Patrick was watching all this happen and eventually he said he was calling the police. I told him not to because I didn't want Jean to go to jail yet again. Then that man, who for two years had told me to go to hell, came and rescued me from her! For two whole years I had loved him, but he couldn't see, understand or feel that love because there was too much pain in his own heart. Patrick grabbed me away from Jean, started sobbing on that street, and said, "For years you told me Jesus loved me. Now I've seen His love and I want Him." We just held each other as he fell apart. He held me and I held him. In his dirty clothes and his scabies, lice and alcoholic state, I just held him. He met Jesus that day because He saw love.

I believe we have complicated the Gospel. Jesus wants to reduce us to the simplicity of love. My cry is to be hidden inside God's heart so fully that I manifest His glory and never touch it. I want to be wholly hidden inside Him and love like Him, manifesting His love tangibly to the lost, the dying and the broken. I want to be His fragrance everywhere I go and love, not just with words, but in action and truth. A week after Jean tried to kill me, she came to my house with a dozen roses and said, "I'm sorry I tried to kill you. I want Jesus." What a wonderful day! She got set free from all her anger and pain. That day she came home to the Father's house.

Tenacious Love

Often we want plans and strategies to reach the multitudes, but love looks like something and revival has a face. Sometimes it looks like stopping for the same person, every day, for years, even if they keep telling you to go to hell. Love looks like laying down our lives for our friends and believing that they are lovely even when they don't seem lovely. Jesus tells us that there is no greater love than to lay our life down for our friends. In love, He stretched out His hands on the cross and gave Himself freely. He longs to fill His church with this same kind of love. Love that compels us to lay our lives down for our friends, so that we love them, even when they spit on us, reject us and persecute us. We love them when they are nice to us and when they are mean to us. And we keep loving them, whatever it costs, and never give up! If we love, we cannot lose! This is how we reveal God's heart to this broken world. Jesus wants to transform His Bride until she so radiates His tenacious love that no one can resist it! I will not say that this is not difficult. There are many days I don't feel like loving at all. I have failed many times, but He keeps on showing me the point. He keeps on forgiving my shortcomings and drawing me to His heart.

We often hear about revival in terms of multitudes, but I believe that the face of revival is stopping for the one that God puts in front of us every day. If each one of us stopped long enough to see the brokenness of the one in front of us, and ministered the love of Christ to them, it would look like the revival of love and power we are praying for and longing to see.

The Church That Loves

"This is my commandment, that you love one another, just as I have loved you. Greater love has no one than this, that one lay down his life for his friends"

—Jn 15:12-13 NAS

One of our pastors in Mozambique, Pastor Sithole, ministered the love of Jesus tirelessly in many villages day after day. He would walk and pray and pour out his life for love. This angered some people of another faith. They hated him for spreading the Good News, so one day they came to his house and told him that he would no longer spread the name of Jesus. They chopped off his tongue and cut off his lips so that he would no longer speak of His name. They chopped off his feet and told him that he would no longer walk and preach this message. They chopped off his hands and told him that he would no longer feed people. His wife and six children watched as this terrible thing was happening. Then they chopped off his head. In our movement, hundreds of people have been raised from the dead, but Pastor Sithole wasn't. His cousin, Pastor Surpresa Sithole, one of our international Iris directors, called us. The two of them had been very close. Together we cried and prayed on the phone. As we wept, we asked God what love looked like in this situation. Afterwards, Pastor Surpresa got in his truck and drove with a huge sound system all day and all night to the village where his cousin had been martyred. The police had caught one of the murderers, so when he got there he asked for the murderer to be released. Next he called the whole village together and said, "You may cut off our tongues, but you will never stop us from speaking about this message of love. You may cut off our feet, but hundreds will run behind us. You may cut off our hands, but we will still cry, 'We love you, we love you, we love you!' Because Jesus reached out His hands and He died for love." Pastor Surpresa shared this radical, ceaseless, endless love with the whole village and with the very man that had tortured and murdered his own cousin. The police said we were a crazy church and a crazy movement, but they also said that we were the church that loves. Thousands of people from another faith bowed their knee to Jesus that day because of love.

Radical fruit can only flow out of a radical life of obedient love and intimacy with Jesus. What would you do for love? Where would you go for love? What would you give for love's sake? Wholehearted lovers will do anything and pay any price. Nothing is too difficult for them because they are totally abandoned. Not all of us are called to die for Jesus, but all of us are called to live for Him. Even if just one person reading this really understands what I am communicating, they would become a nation shaker. I am only a baby on this journey, but I know where I want to go. If we would really live a life that is so radically obedient for love's sake that there is no "No" left in us, there would be so much fruit that whole cities would be turned upside down.

Possessed by Love

As missionaries, our primary job is to love. I always tell our staff that it doesn't matter what we do or how much we achieve in a day; what matters is how we went about it. Did we go through the day loving those we met? Did we treat the beggar asking for money with dignity? Did we take the time to hear what he had to say? Did we treat the children with patience when they misbehaved? Did we stop long enough in our busy day to see those in front of us and look into their eyes? If missions is just about programs and projects, then we need to stop, because what we do will be like a resounding gong or a clanging cymbal. If missions is about anything other than love, we need to stop and have more time in the secret place with Jesus.

Many of you may wonder who you are and what your purpose and calling is. My prayer for you is that you move deeper inside God's heart and become fully inhabited by love, because love is our highest calling and our greatest gift. We can spend ourselves in service to the poor and give our lives to missions, but if we have not loved we have gained nothing. If each one of us stops to love the one in front of us, each day, we will see the revival of power we long for spread to the ends of the earth.

Chapter 12

HOLISTIC
TRANSFORMATIONAL
MISSIONS AT THE MARGINS

"
Mission activity has sometimes swung between the two extremes of purely social work and solely evangelistic preaching. God created us as whole persons, however, and wants spirits, souls, and bodies to be brought into wholeness. Practical projects addressing physical needs are not incompatible with supernatural ministry; rather, they are an outlet for God's love and power to bring transformation to people's hearts and lives.
"

- Bob Ekblad

For over 28 years I have pursued a Gospel with power to change lives and mobilize people as agents of transformation. I long to see transformation from below as the good news of Jesus Christ impacts the poorest of the poor in every area of their lives and society. I have ministered among peasants in rural Honduras, Mexican immigrant farm workers in migrant labor camps in Washington State and with inmates in Skagit County Jail. I find that men and women trapped in addictions, violence, penal systems, poverty and the like are often desperate enough to open themselves to help from God. However, negative images of God and self constantly threaten the conversion process. These must be identified and countered in a holistic way as the basis for empowerment and transformation. Our mission to people caught up in places of greatest spiritual darkness requires a vast array of approaches, greater unity and collaboration within the body of Christ, strategic engagement with social-service, business, other players and advocacy before civil authorities.

Confronting oppressive images of God begins as trust is built through authentic relationships. Negative perceptions about God and self come from abusive parenting, unjust social structures, experiencing poverty, calamities, and other suffering, traditional religious interpretations, spiritual oppression and other sources. The origins of oppressive theology must be identified and addressed in a holistic way that includes proclamation and teaching backed up by signs and wonders, advocacy, accompaniment, counseling, inner healing and deliverance, sustainable development, preventative health care and many other approaches. A constantly evolving biblical theology informed by Jesus' teaching, the Holy Spirit's guidance, intercession and worship and fruitful engagement with the larger body of Christ and the world must ground our efforts.

God's respectful, saving Presence and high view of humans launches the Bible's story of redemption. The Spirit hovers over the chaos and darkness and God speaks light into existence, ordering time and space (Gen 1:1ff). God makes humans in His image and likeness, commanding them to "be fruitful and multiply, and fill the earth and subdue it; and rule over the fish of the sea and over the birds of the sky, and over every living thing that moves on the earth" (Gen 1:28). This reflects God's mission to bless, send out and multiply His image-bearers to fill the earth with His glory. This is nothing less than a vision of the Kingdom of heaven invading earth. Humans in right relationship with God are given authority to subdue and rule over an earth under the power of the ruler of this world. This authority is lost when we let the creation define God, "did God say…?" Letting creation itself or competing voices reveal God rather than God's very words and acts erodes our confidence in God's total goodness and grace, causing us to live by grasping, by the sweat of our brow instead of by gift.

Restoration is only possible when we find ourselves in some way met by a God who reveals Himself as one who pursues us, meeting, confronting, and yet loving us in the midst of our sin.

Cain is the first human God pursues - and we see that God's ministry priority from day one outside the garden is to deal with this violent, resistant humankind embodied in Cain. Persistent pursuit of notorious sinners through acts of love and holistic witness must be one of the church's highest ministry priorities.

Even for God this mission is not easy. The Lord does not succeed in stopping Cain from killing his brother Abel, even after His timely intervention in the heat of Cain's anger with one-on-one counseling, "why are you angry…"; personal mentoring, "if you do well…"; and discipling, "sin is crouching at the door, and it's desire is for you, but you must master it." Cain kills his brother anyway, but God does not give up on him or on anyone following in his footsteps.

The Lord confronts Cain for his murder, advocating for the voiceless victim Abel by directly questioning the powerful: "Cain, where is your brother?" God confronts the perpetrator with the secret sins, the hidden crime as the One who sees and hears the cries of the oppressed, and knows every clandestine burial site: "the voice of your brother's blood is crying to me from the ground"

(Gen 4:10). God reveals Himself as an advocate for the oppressed who is totally committed to justice on behalf of the voiceless victims, caring for orphans, widows, the unborn, the disabled, all oppressed minority groups, victims of human trafficking. Others must be high priority for missions today.

The Lord describes hard consequences coming to perpetrator Cain as a result of his killing - not as direct punishments, but natural consequences of his violence. "And now you are cursed from the ground, which has opened its mouth to receive your brother's blood from your hand. When you cultivate the ground, it shall no longer yield its strength to you; you shall be a vagrant and a wanderer on the earth" (Gen 4:11-12). Judgment leads Cain to cry out to God:

> "My punishment is too great to bear! Behold, thou hast driven me this day from the face of the ground; and from thy face I shall be hidden, and I shall be a vagrant and a wanderer on the earth, and it will come about that whoever finds me will kill me" (Gen 4:13-14).

God's response shows amazing mercy to undeserving sinners and illustrates the later word: "where sin abounds, grace abounds all the more" (Rom 5:20). God's stern warning of hard consequences is announced to all who decide to use violence against the violent, even in the name of justice: "Whoever kills Cain, vengeance will be taken on him sevenfold" (Gen 4:15).

God puts a sign of protection on Cain to keep people from killing him, showing special interest in violent perpetrators. This continues throughout Scripture and must inform our mission priorities today. Christians must die daily in the waters of baptism, emerging cleansed from allegiances to nation, laws, policies, attitudes and practices that would disqualify them from bearing good news to enemies and sinners. While Cain goes away from the presence of God in spite of God's best efforts, like the prodigal son he is coming back, and the Father pursues him with open arms. Will the prodigals find themselves desiring to return to us? Are we joining the Father in running towards and embracing the broken, returning ones?

We see that God's preferential option for sinners continues through Scripture. God chooses many key biblical characters who were violent men or criminals: Moses, Samson, Jacob, Judah, David, Matthew the tax-collector, Simon the zealot and the Apostle Paul. He cares for violent perpetrators for many reasons, longing to see an end to violence of every kind and pursuing would-be violators and seasoned killers to help them face their sin and receive healing for their deepest wounds - before they do more damage to others and themselves. Since the violent are those who remain alive, and who "win" against the weak, God pursues these survivors, winning them over through the only effective violence, the violence of love, the kindness that leads to repentance.

God's mission continues throughout Scripture, and is ultimately successful in Jesus. He undoes the entire system of vengeance by letting Himself be delivered over into the hands of violent men for our (and their) salvation. Should this not be one of our highest priorities today?

Violent men continue to be marked with the sign of the cross. Followers of Jesus must pray for the protection and peace God afforded Cain to be on contemporary equivalents of Cain (whether they be local criminals, Al Queda or Taliban combatants) and for the seventy times seven forgiveness that Jesus taught and embodied to overcome the 77 vengeance curses of Cain's descendant Lamech that menaces in places where violence is on the rise (Gen 4:24; Mt 18:22). Jesus accomplished this as He died at the hands of violent men, between two criminals, and we worship Him for this unfathomable love that saves.

We must pray for people caught up in violence, for safety so they will grow up into their highest callings in Christ. We must also pray for God's powerful presence of love to stop in their tracks people currently engaged in violence or plotting acts of vengeance or terror, as the resurrected Jesus stopped Saul on the road to Damascus. We long to hear all these gang members testify with Paul:

"I thank Christ Jesus our Lord, who has strengthened me, because he considered me faithful, putting me into service; even though I was formerly a blasphemer and a persecutor and a violent aggressor. And yet I was shown mercy, because I acted ignorantly in unbelief; and the grace of our Lord was more than abundant with the faith and love which are found in Christ Jesus. It is a trustworthy statement, deserving full acceptance, that Christ Jesus came into the world to save sinners, among whom I am foremost of all. And yet for this reason I found mercy, in order that in me as the foremost, Jesus Christ might demonstrate His perfect patience, as an example for those who could believe in Him for eternal life. Now to the King eternal, immortal, invisible, the only God, be honor and glory forever and ever. Amen" (1 Tim 1:12-17 NASB).

Facilitating Transformation through Confronting Negative Images of God

Facilitating transformation of individuals oppressed by negative images of God involves us first identifying and breaking agreement with false notions of God and self that demobilize us from becoming free subjects in God's Kingdom. The process of conversion involves progressive differentiation of images of God and self from false notions of God's and our own identity to increasingly truer perceptions. This happens through deliberate confrontation of negative theology and, most importantly, through experiences of the fullest, most authentic encounter with God in Jesus Christ. This frees humans to be the subject of their desire.

Many people on the margins of society have negative images of God that hold them back from any positive benefit or any spiritual attraction whatsoever. For many, "god" has already been defined by core experiences of a human father or authority figures who abandoned or rejected them, punished or abused them, was impossible to please and controlling or permissive and negligent. Negative images of God also come through people's assumptions that calamities, injustice, sickness and other forms of oppression are willed by God or sent as punishments.

When my Honduran colleague Fernando and I first began asking impoverished peasants why their corn and bean harvest were so dismal, I was startled by their near unanimous responses: "It's God's will." We launched our ministry, Tierra Nueva, by starting a demonstration farm, cultivating steep, eroded mountainsides using contoured terraces, rock or pasture grass barriers to prevent further erosion and soil building strategies like compost and cover crops. We planted corn, beans, vegetables and fruit trees to the curve of the land. We experimented with fish ponds, fuel efficient mud stoves and other appropriate technologies.

Our first year's harvest was ten times better than people were accustomed to seeing, drawing the attention of peasants from the surrounding area. We helped those interested in attempting our approach to establish an experimental plot on their own land, discipling them in these organic-intensive farming methods. When they saw for themselves that protecting and rebuilding soil led to dramatically improved harvests, God was "off the hook" and no longer to blame - a space was opened for them to hear about a good God who does not will crop failures and poverty.

My wife Gracie and our Guatemalan colleague Catalina taught vegetable gardening, nutritious recipes, hygiene and other preventative health measures, and the people found their health improving. As people learned that amaebas and bacteria could be eradicated by boiling their water, once again God was no longer to blame for the premature death of their children through malnutrition and dysentery. Health education brought a needed corrective to traditional explanations that attributed most common health problems to witchcraft or curses from enemy neighbors. While deliverance continued to be important in combating other kinds of oppression, subsistence farming and health education were also critical for community wellbeing, easing tensions from false accusations and taking away power from local curanderos (witch doctors).

While negative images of God can be removed by helping people see natural causes for common afflictions and social problems, the good news of God's self-revelation as Jesus is essential. We find that getting people to read and study the Bible, though very important, does not automatically bring clarity. We need to clearly present Jesus as the full embodiment of the Old Testament God and interpreter of the Hebrew Scriptures - law and prophets. When Jesus is transfigured before His disciples, the Father makes it clear that listening to Jesus trumps Moses and Elijah. Without this continual clarification, people get tripped up in legalistic and excluding appropriations of Old Testament laws or justifications of violence based on Joshua. Reading the Bible for good news begins with clear New Testament teachings about Jesus. In these last days, God has spoken to us in His Son, "and He is the radiance of His glory and the exact representation of His nature" (Heb 1:2-3).

"For He delivered us from the domain of darkness, and transferred us to the kingdom of this beloved Son, in whom we have redemption, the forgiveness of sins. And He is the image of the invisible God, the first-born of all creation" (Col 1:13-15 NKJV).

In the Gospel of John there is a clear articulation of God's unexpected otherness/holiness revealed in Jesus. In the prologue, the logos is identified as present with God at the beginning and as actually being God. To avoid any confusion, the writer emphasizes that this logos-God created all things, is the life and light shining on people and cannot be overcome by darkness. The writer of John emphasizes that this word/life/light enlightens every human (Jn 1:9).

Yet in a surprising twist the prologue states that the world does not recognize the word who becomes flesh, nor do His own people receive him! This is because a God "full of grace and truth" is completely different than the familiar, dominant images of God as an all-powerful, imposing, aggressive and conquering Sovereign (Jn 1:14). This word/life/light represents a God who is powerful. Yet at the same time there is a foreignness and holiness to this kind of power. It can go unperceived. It can be resisted.

Receiving/believing in this very different God leads to being born of God, a filial event called adoption. When this one is received and believed, people share in God's "other" power, which is called exousia, "authority": "But a many as received Him, who believe in His name, to them He gave the authority to become children of God" (Jn 1:12 ESV).[1]

Does being born of God shift people away from the limitations of their human identities as addicted, bound, imprisoned, unemployed, and oppressed? People on the margins are desperate to experience authority over longstanding habits and powers that oppress. John's Gospel describes with great subtlety the process of becoming such an empowered child of God. It all has to do with communion with Jesus. Human witnesses point to Jesus as the fullest revelation of God: "No one has ever seen God. The only God, who is at the Father's side, He has made Him known" (Jn 1:18 ESV).

John the Baptist articulates the role of all missionary announcers of Jesus as the "voice of one crying in the wilderness, 'make straight the way of the Lord'" (Jn 1:23 NKJV). He points people prophetically to Jesus, who Himself invites potential disciples to come and see where He stays. His team grows as he exercises authority by means of his prophetic gifting: naming Simon "Cephas/Peter", seeing Nathaniel where only God could see him and affirming his true identity, "behold an Israelite in whom is no guile!" (Jn 1:47 KJV). The role of prophetic ministry is to directly challenge negative views of self, inviting people into their highest callings.

Often my colleagues and I find ourselves sharing spontaneous impressions that people recognize as bringing to light details that only God could know. While praying for a Mexican farm worker in his late thirties, a faint picture flashed across my mind of an adult throwing rocks at a young boy who was shepherding animals. I asked him if his father ever lost his temper and threw rocks at him when he was a boy, causing him to run away terrified. The man began to cry and grabbed his leg where

273

he had been hit. That day he forgave his father for this offense, which was one of many others that contributed to this man's fear of displeasing employers and others in authority.

The Apostle Paul writes that the one who prophesies "speaks to people for their strengthening, encouragement, and comfort" (1 Cor 14:3 NIV) and makes God real to a person who do not yet believe when "the secrets of his heart are disclosed" (1 Cor 14:25 ESV).

A close look at Jesus' prophetic ministry as depicted in the Gospels overturns alienating traditional images of God. Jesus' revelation to the astounded Samaritan woman about her multiple marriages as He offered her living water in John 4 is one of many examples that subverts contemporary readers assumptions. Jesus' witness regularly challenges common beliefs that God favors the righteous over sinners, law-abiding people over criminals, the rich over the poor, the beautiful over the ugly, the intelligent over the ignorant, offering flashes of a very different sort of God.

People assume that God is like a rigorous admissions officer at an exclusive University or a demanding, scrupulous employer examining resumes, choosing only the most deserving into His ranks, especially if they are to be ministry workers or any kind of leader. Yet right from the beginning of the Bible, we see that God pursues the most unlikely candidates.

I recently led a Bible study on 1 Corinthians 1:26-2:5 to a group of 12-14 bedraggled Caucasian and Hispanic inmates in the jail. Most of the men, in their 20s and 30s, were addicted to drugs and alcohol and had not completed high school. They would be hard pressed to qualify for anything but low-wage jobs. Before reading the text, I asked the men what sort of people they think God would chose to be pastors or missionaries. "People from higher social classes," said one man. "People who were smart and educated, who had their shit together." "I think he'd chose people who'd been through lots of big troubles," said an older man. "He'd want people who could relate to ordinary people like us."

"Do you think they'd have to be educated, able to explain things well, be good public speakers and all?" I asked. I could see that the men were unsure how to answer, divided between the what they assumed to be the conventional answer, that God chooses strong, smart, righteous people, and the wisdom of the older man that included them. I invited someone to read the texts and watched their eyes brighten as the words witnessed to a God very unlike normal human authorities.

> *"Consider your calling, brethren, that there were not many wise according to the flesh, not many mighty, not many noble; but God has chosen the foolish things of the world to shame the wise, and God has chosen the weak things of the world to shame the things which are strong, and the base things of the world and the despised, God has chosen, the things that are not, that He might nullify the things that are..." (1 Cor 1:26-28 NASB).*

A God who purposely chooses those not mighty, noble, brilliant but rather those who are despised and nothing is a God that gives them hope. What kind of God reveals through being crucified, through speaking through the weak and inconsequential? The next reading brought even more hope to the inarticulate ones there in the circle. "Brethern I did not come with superiority of speech or of wisdom, proclaiming to you the testimony of God... And I was with you in weakness and in fear and in much trembling. And my message and my preaching were not in persuasive words of wisdom, but in demonstration of the Spirit and of power, that your faith should not rest on the wisdom of men, but on the power of God" (1 Cor 2:-5).

I often invite people to read the account of Jesus' calling of the fishermen in Matthew 4:18-22, asking questions like "where were Jesus' first recruits and what were they looking for when Jesus called them? Inmates are sometimes visibly afraid to state the obvious as the "correct" answer, as it directly counters the dominant theology. "At the sea looking for fish" is contextualized to "at work looking for money." People are invited to include their actual places of work, even if they are drug houses, bars, factories or fields.

When I ask people what Jesus' call of the disciples in Matthew tells us about God, people begin to perceive the refreshing otherness revealed in Jesus. God comes to where we are, wherever we are. God calls people who are not visibly seeking God, righteous, or religious in any way to join Him. The description in Luke 15:1 of all the tax collectors and sinners drawing near to Jesus confounds confounds people expecting God to be a law-enforcement agent type. There must have been something about Jesus that attracted the bad guys. What was it?

Frequently I invite people to look at the immediate aftermath of the first disciples' following of Jesus. In response to the question "where did they go and what did they do?" the text offers a compelling picture of an adventurous life that positively impacts hurting people, far more attractive than minimum-wage jobs, drugs and alcohol or a life of crime.

Jesus was going about in all Galilee, teaching in their synagogues, and proclaiming the gospel of the Kingdom, and healing every kind of disease and every kind of sickness among the people and they brought to him all who were ill, taken with various diseases and pains, demoniacs, epileptics, paralytics; and he healed them (Mt 4:23-24).

In our weekly jail Bible studies, visits to migrant camps and rural villages in Central America and everywhere we regularly lead Bible studies, we pray for suffering people and witness God's power to heal. Healing often happens before people come to faith. This undermines the dominant image of God that sees sickness and a sanction for bad behavior and healing or any sort of benefit as a reward for good behavior.

Once I offered to pray for a man suffering from shoulder and lower back pain after the police had violently pulled his arms behind his back, nearly dislocating his shoulders to handcuff him. They had thrown him in the back of the police car and the handcuffs had dug into his back. Before praying for him, I asked if he felt he needed to forgive the police for their excessive use of force. "No," he said. "I was drunk and resisting arrest. I'm a big dude and was pretty out of control. They were just doing their job."

I prayed that Jesus would undo the damage done by the police and show the man how much He loved him regardless of his violence. I stepped away and asked him if he felt any improvement. He said he felt the pain leave his lower back but said he was sure that if he drew his arms back behind his back the pain would be intolerable. He began to gingerly move his arms behind his back and amazement came over his face. "I'll grant it to you. I'll grant it to you. The pain is completely gone," he said, dropping to his chair and crying with his head in his hands. Like in the Gospel accounts, we regularly see God's healing presence overturn people's negative expectations as the one full of grace and truth makes Himself known concretely.

Healing is one important dimension of an important Greek verb *sotzo*, which literally means "to save," but is often used in the Gospels as a synonym for "to heal." There are two other Greek verbs used in miracles of healing, *therapueo* "to cure" and *iaomai* "to heal," so Gospel writers seem to be making a special point in using the highly theological *sotzo*, which is used in Paul's writings to refer almost exclusively to Jesus' saving work on the cross for eternal life (see Rom 5:9-10; 8:24; 9:22; 10:9-10,13; 11:14, 26; 1 Cor 1:18, 21; 1 Cor 3:15; 5:5; 7:16; 9:22; 10:33; 15:2; Eph 2:5, 8; 1 Tim 1:15). This meaning of salvation for eternal life is also present in the Gospels (Mt 10:22; 16:25; 24:12-13; 19:16, 25; Jn 3:17; 5:34; 10:9; 12:47). However, there are many occurrences of *sotzo* that are rendered in English translations as "heal" in miracle stories where people experience physical healing (Mt 9:21, 22; Mk 3:4; 5:23, 28, 34; 6:56; 10:52; Lk 6:9; 8:48, 50; 17:19; 18:42; Acts 4:9; 14:9). In addition, we see many other occurrences of *sotzo* in the Gospels and Acts that refer to being saved or rescued from danger in the lifetime of the beneficiary (Mt 8:25; 14:30; 27:40, 42; 27:49; Mk 8:35, 35; Lk 9:55-56; 23:35, 37, 39; Acts 27:20,

31). This rich verb and the related noun *soteria* "salvation" present a holistic notion of saving/salvation that includes salvation for eternal life, supernatural healing and deliverance, but also physical acts of helping, rescuing and liberation. Mission must take into account this rich diversity of actions that communicate God's love to our hurting world.

I traveled to Guatemala in September 2008, to train pastors working with gang members. We visited one of Central America's most infamous prisons to visit the gang member inmates of perhaps the most notorious street gang in the Western Hemisphere. A week before leaving for Guatemala City, I dreamed of a heavily-tattooed man with a hole in his right side. I met this man in the second prison-- a big intimidating guy with tattoos and a myriad of scars from stab wounds and bullets all over his body—including a big indentation on his right side from a near-death shootout with the police.

This man, a gang leader serving a 135-year sentence, ended up taking me back into the heart of the prison to find a bathroom and then invited me into his cell. I shared with him my dream and he was visibly moved, welcoming my offer to pray for him. He told me about his worries about his son and shared his longing for God's peace and love in his heart. I prayed for him and anointed him with oil.

He led me back into the yard where we succeeded in gathering many inmates for a Bible study on Jesus' call on Matthew the tax collector. I described how Matthew was a tax-collector, a member of a notorious class of people that nearly everyone hated.

"Who might fit the description of tax-collectors today?" I asked.

Gangs in Guatemala force businesses in their territories to pay "protection taxes" [from themselves] and taxi drivers to pay "circulation taxes" - the men smiled and looked at each other, acknowledging that they fit the description.

"So what was Matthew doing when Jesus called him?" I asked.

The men looked surprised when they realize that he wasn't following any rules, seeking God or doing anything religious. He was practicing his despised trade when Jesus showed up on the street and chose him.

"So let's see if Jesus made Matthew leave his gang to be a Christian," I suggested, and the men looked closely at the next verse.

There Jesus is eating at Matthew's house with other tax-collectors and sinners and the disciples.

"So who followed whom?" I asked, excited to see their reaction.

The men could see that Jesus had apparently followed gangster Matthew into his barrio and joined his homies for a meal.

"So what do you think, would you let Jesus join your gang?" I asked, looking directly at the man I'd just prayed for in his cell and the other gang chief.

They were caught off guard by such a question, but there we all were, deep in their turf being welcomed, Bibles, guitar and all, and nobody was resisting. Big smiles lit up both their faces as we looked at Jesus' reaction to the Pharisees' distain, "Those who are well have no need of a physician, but those who are sick" (Matthew 9:12).

I asked them if they are at all offended to think of themselves as sick and they didn't seem to be at all. I had their attention. Jesus' final word to the religious insiders hit those guys like a spray of spiritual bullets from a drive by: "Go and learn what this means, 'I desire mercy, not sacrifice.' For I have come to call not the righteous but sinners" (Matthew 9"17). Jesus' firm dismissal of the accusing Pharisees "go and learn" and clear preference for sinners as the "called" drew the circle of gang members irresistibly into Jesus' company.

I was delighted that the men agreed to let us lay hands on every one of their bare, heavily-tatted backs as my colleague sang worship songs over them, including: "Jesus, friend of sinners, we love you." I heard from a pastor that the gang leader I had prayed with was amazed at how his "homies" were letting us pray for him and whispered: "It's been a long time since I've felt the Presence of the Holy Spirit in my life and seen the homies at peace. I feel really good."

Two months later, on November 22nd, I spent a day in a bleak French prison in Lyon where suicide was rampant. I was there training French prison chaplains and ministering to inmates. That night I took a train back to Paris to learn the horrific news that the Guatemalan gang leader I'd prayed with who had the hole in his side and three others had been taken in the middle of the night by the police and placed into a prison of 900 inmates that were all violently anti-gang. On the morning of November 22, 2008, rioting inmates killed, decapitated and mutilated the bodies of these four men who we'd laid hands on to bless.

While carrying off these men, authorities also burned all the 150+ inmates possessions, sheets and makeshift shacks they'd built for conjugal visits in a big bonfire, leaving them beaten up, naked and traumatized. Local gang pastors boldly accompanied the shattered families and inmates in the aftermath of this event. They brought over 25 huge bags of clothes collected from churches, deeply touching the gang inmates who are accustomed to being despised and excluded.

Yet anti-gang sentiment is rising in the country and scapegoating continues in full swing. Recently, authorities invaded the prison again and apprehended the other leader and two others, transporting them to another prison. A plot was exposed, showing their killings were being arranged for the anniversary of the previous year's killing of four. This time, high-level advocacy on their behalf before government officials in the United States and Guatemala exposed the plot and led to greater security and visits for these inmates. The gang members inside and outside the prison and their families have been deeply moved by Christian solidarity.

Micro-enterprise & Mission

Gang members, drug-dealers and ex-offenders need opportunities to develop other skills so they can step away from lives of crime and become legally-functioning members of society. Tierra Nueva is working to establish micro-businesses both in Honduras and in the United States to provide skills training, jobs and income to sustain our ministries. We continue to work to help famers improve production and storage of basic grains, bring water to marginal neighborhoods for basic needs and vegetable gardens, increase the quality of coffee and distribution of specialty coffee and establisha water-purification plant to sell bottled water. We import Honduran coffee to the United States, where we train and employ gang members and ex-offenders to roast and market specialty coffee through the Underground Coffee Project. Tierra Nueva runs an organic farm called Jubilee Farm, producing and selling vegetables and flowers as a site for discipleship and training for farm workers and others on the margins. Micro-businesses are increasingly important to provide alternatives for felons, sites for ministry and income for ministries.

Direct confrontation of false images of God through proclamation and holistic responses to people's felt needs, fresh readings of Biblical texts, pastoral accompaniment, advocacy, prophetic ministry and healing prayer are some of the ways that prepare people to meet Jesus as the one who saves them from their sins and transforms their lives. The kindness of God leads to repentance, understood as a change of heart (Rom 2:4). We do everything we can to effectively pluck up, break down, destroy and overthrow the false while also facilitating, ushering in and preparing the way for the revelation of the kind God who has the power to save.

Endnotes

[1] *exousia* Greek, meaning power of choice, liberty of doing as one pleases; power of authority and of right (privilege). Joseph Thayer, *Greek-Engloish Lexicon of the New Testament* (Hendrickson Publishing, 1996).

Chapter 13

A WEAVING OF ANTHROPOLOGICAL INSIGHTS WITH INCARNATIONAL PRACTICE

" *Learning how to deal with cultural differences has always been an important challenge for missionaries. By learning to understand the worldview of other people, we are enabled to communicate the gospel in authentic and relevant ways without imposing our own culture on them. Our model is Jesus, who emptied himself and became like us in order to bring us His good news, not only speaking the message but living it. In the same way, we must learn to incarnate God's eternal truth in the specific, present culture of the people we seek to reach.* "

- Lesley-Anne Leighton

Hūtia te rito o te harakeke

Wrench out the rito (baby) of the lax

Kei hea te kōmako e kō?

Where will the bellbird sing?

Rere ki uta

You fly inland

Rere ki tai

You fly to the sea

Kī mai koe ki au

You ask me

He aha te mea nui o te ao?

What is the greatest thing in the world?

Māku e kī atu

I would reply

He tangata, he tangata, he tangata

It is the people, the people, the people

Maori Proverb from Aotearoa, New Zealand

To the weak I became weak, to win the weak. I have become
all things to all men so that by all possible means I might save
some. I do all this for the sake of the gospel that I may share in
its blessings (1 Cor 9:22-23).

Introduction

I used to think anthropology was associated with the
theory of evolution, which holds that men are descendants of apes,
and that anthropologists were an eccentric breed of people who
had nothing better to do but get ecstatic over discovering bone
fragments and skulls that had been dug up from the ground. I
was also aware that some anthropologists voiced their criticism that
missionaries destroyed culture when people groups changed their
morals, customs and values as a result of their presence.

In recent years, however, I have come to see the value of
anthropology as a discipline for the cross-cultural Christian worker.
Like most social sciences, there is much more to anthropology than
examining bones. Unfortunately, there is some truth to their claim
that missionaries coming from the West have made the mistake of
westernizing converts of other cultures. Sadly, as Whiteman points
out, this pattern of confusing the gospel with one's culture is also
being repeated throughout the non-western world by missionaries
from the south and east.[1]

By now we should have learned from the account in Acts
15:1-35, which tells of just such a situation as this. Judaising
believers (legalists) insisted that in order to come to faith in Christ,
new believers must be circumcised in keeping with Jewish custom.
The outcome of Peter, Barnabus, Paul and James' argument at this
time resulted in the Council of Jerusalem recognizing the Gentiles
as full heirs of salvation and part of the people of God without the
necessity of being circumcised in order to be saved.

As God's people, motivated by the love of Christ,
participating with Him in the nations, we must understand that
the universal nature of the gospel also demands cultural sensitivity.
Love is not rude (1 Cor 13:5). My own premise is that God loves the

world's people; that the Bible speaks to all people and all cultures; and Jesus Christ is the only faithful example of divine love. I also insist on the primacy of the Holy Spirit in mission action as "the living flame of love" throughout the earth.

Who, being in very nature God, did not consider equality with God something to be grasped, but made Himself nothing, taking the very nature of a servant being made in human likeness, And being found in appearance as a man, He humbled Himself and became obedient to death, even death on a cross! (Phil 2:6-8)!

When Jesus was incarnated on earth among the world's people, He emptied Himself of all of Glory's splendor. He came as a vulnerable child and grew among us. With love as His motivation, He entered the human culture of His time in every aspect of human personality, experience, and social relationship to bring His message of love to all humankind. He made His home among us, lived what He preached, and only did what the Father asked Him to do. In so doing, He showed us the "how" and the "who" of mission practice. It's a Christianity of the cross, preferring others. When He ascended to heaven, He was confident of this: that we would carry on where He left off. The call to mission is based in love coming from the Father. As the Father sent Jesus into the world, so Jesus is sending us into the world. He invites us to do what He did, to enter other people's worlds and become incarnated among them. The loving action of laying down our lives to make our home in another culture for the sake of Jesus' call to mission has come to be known as *incarnational missions practice.*

Missionaries who embrace this call will do all they can for their lives to breathe God's message of salvation. They understand that incarnation is not just a matter of living with the people to whom they have been sent, but *how* they live with them. They will not want to run the risk of losing credibility and spoiling the message. Weaving incarnational practice with anthropological insights in their engagement with mission is a tool that can help all missionaries on entering new cultures to bring an incarnational message/life which is not offensive but expressive of divine love.

What is Anthropology?

Anthropology concerns itself with the nature, origin, and destiny of humankind. There are two basic kinds of anthropology, physical and cultural. These can be further subdivided, as detailed by Luzbetak below:

Figure 1
***The Basic Structure of the Science of Anthropology*[2]**

The Study of Human Beings	Orientation Historical or Descriptive	Orientation Scientific
As a biological animal **Physical Anthropology**	Paleoanthropology (the study of early human beings and related species through fossil evidence)	Race
As rational animal **Cultural Anthropology**	Archaeology Linguistics Ethnology	Social Anthropology

1. Physical Anthropology considers man as a biological creature and is further divided into:

a. Human Palaeontology, which discusses the origins and evolution of the human body

b. The study of race, which deals with genetics, measurements and descriptions of bodily characteristics of different peoples; and the grouping of people into types and races

2. Cultural Anthropology describes, analyses and compares the patterns and behaviour of different cultures and is concerned with questions about *why* people are what they are:

a. Archaeology (prehistory) is the study of prehistoric cultures for the light they can throw on later cultural developments.

b. Linguistics is the study of language, which describes, analyses and compares the language of different peoples, the history of these languages and the influence of language on patterns of thought and behavior.

c. Ethnography is the careful, detailed, non-interpretative recording of the material and non-material features of the culture.

d. Ethnology is concerned with living cultures, which takes the raw materials of ethnographic fieldwork and analyses, compares and evaluates it in the light of history to draw out the basic patterns and relationships between various aspects of the culture.

e. Social Anthropology is the comparative study of social systems within a culture such as organization, leadership patterns, family relationships, etc.

f. Applied Anthropology takes the various principles learned from Cultural Anthropology and applies them to problems in fields such as economics, agriculture, politics and religion.

Hiebert illustrates how anthropology seeks to discover the interrelationships between various scientific models of the human being:

Figure 2

The Holistic Nature of Anthropology[3]

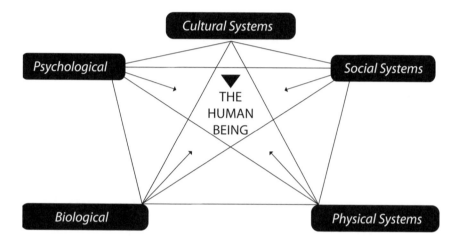

Is Anthropology Important for Missionaries?

Kraft presents the following ten reasons why we should study anthropology for cross-cultural mission:[4]

1. Anthropology attempts to deal with what people actually do and think.

2. Anthropology historically has primarily dealt with non-western peoples.

3. Anthropology has developed the culture concept.

4. Anthropology takes an holistic view of people.

5. Anthropology is a perspective, not simply a subject.

6. Anthropology focuses on communication.

7. Anthropology distinguishes between forms and meanings.

8. Anthropology has developed the concept of worldview.

9. Anthropology has developed the research method most helpful for Christian workers.

10. Anthropology deals with culture change.

We can see from Luzbetak's categorization of anthropology that cultural anthropology in particular has much to do with issues of importance to cross-cultural missions. Further, there are clear relationships between the descriptions of Luzbetak in Figure 1, Heibert's illustration in Figure 2 and the questions raised by Kraft. For instance, a study of Social Anthropology as described by Luzbetak leads us to consider how people relate within various social systems and sub-systems, such as in family relationships, community relationships, leadership relationships, etc. These social systems are then demonstrated by Heibert as being just one aspect of all it means to be human, and need to be viewed in context of their interrelationship with all the other systems which make up human beings. Human beings are indeed complex! If missionaries wish to engage with people in cross-cultural missions in ways that are sensitive and loving, then we must consider the reasons suggested by Kraft for studying anthropology very seriously. If we do not, we run the risk of presenting a gospel that has no relevance because it does not connect with the true personhood of the people in their culture, or worse, causing harm by imposing beliefs of our own culture which are not at home in the culture to which we have been called.

What is Culture?

Culture is a broad term which encompasses the belief systems, world views, symbols, myths, behaviours, attitudes and identities of groups and individuals. While there are so-called "cultural universals" amongst human experience across all cultures, such as natural disasters, wars or terrorism, there are differences amongst the perceptions, attitudes, beliefs and behaviours surrounding those universals. The differences across groups and the shared-ness within them are used to distinguish cultures. Cultures are not static or vacuous. The levels at which cultures can be distinguished are as fluid, over-lapping and changeable as the individuals who co-constitute them. Individuals and groups can therefore identify with multiple cultural identities. Nevertheless, there are culturally-relative ways in which individuals perceive, respond to and behave in relation to events. In the case of catastrophic events for example, culture influences the ways in which people understand, interpret and respond. These cultural responses and attitudes occur at both individual and group/social levels.

Theories and Perspectives on Culture

Hofstede

Significant contributions to an understanding of the effect of culture on thinking and decision making have been made by Hofstede (1980, 1981, 1983, 1998), whose work in allocating a culture-value by assigning cultural dimensions to a particular group of people is widely referenced.[5] Hofstede's work is highly regarded and is relatively simplistic since he identifies only five factors by which one culture is differentiated from another. These are: power distance, which has to do with distribution of power and equality within a society; collectivism vs. individualism, which has to do with the degree to which people are integrated into groups; femininity vs masculinity, which has to do with the gender distribution of roles; uncertainty avoidance, which relates to a society's tolerance for beliefs which are different to their own; and long-term orientation versus short-term orientation, which deals with virtue regardless of truth. Values associated with long-term orientation are thrift and perseverance, while values associated with short-term orientation are respect for tradition, fulfilling social obligations, and protecting one's face.

Hofstede's framework provides a broad understanding of differing cultures, and can help missionaries prepare for some of the differences in values held by their own culture in comparison to the one to which they are going. However, the values he assigns to a particular nation or culture do not take into account the many and various groups represented within a particular culture. For example, it does not allow for multiculturalism or the cultural differences which are displayed and valued by ethnic minorities internationally or for individuals such as Chinese or Greek New Zealanders who may display characteristics of two cultures in their behaviour and decision making.

Straub, Loch, Evaristo, Karahanna and Strite

Other theories, founded in psychology, include Straub's proposal that Social Identity Theory (SIT) is a candidate theory for a positivist model of the role of culture.[6] Whereas Hofstede's definition relies on a national set of cultural indicators to explain behaviour, Straub's theory attempts to explain behaviour at the individual level. It recognises that different layers of culture or sub-cultures of ethnicity, nationality, religion and belief, organisations, urban/rural etc. can interact and mesh in complex ways. Straub *et al* uses the onion as a metaphor. Each layer represents a certain set of values of a particular sub-culture. In different contexts, different layers of values come to the surface, depending on which are personally relevant to a person in that context. Their most important values are closest to the core.

The example is given that in cross-cultural studies in Japan, it is common to assume that all Japanese demonstrate the universal cultural characteristic of collectivism. Yet we know that there will be variation in the strength of this characteristic, and in the case of highly entrepreneurial Japanese, it may not manifest itself at all.[8]

Principles of Straub's theory can be helpful for any cross-cultural missionary because we can already see that having an understanding of a culture, making full use of anthropological insights, can assist us in identifying, participating and connecting with people at a much deeper level. We will encounter the whole complexity of all it is to be human, and through all this, we must be dependent and led by the Holy Spirit as we have the sacred privilege of seeing people restored to their true identity as His image bearers.

For example, in an Asian context, a child who is rejected for being a female in her family, having experienced both physical and emotional abuse may choose to reject the culture of social and community expectations that she believed brought that abuse. By nature of that withdrawal, she may come to identify more with a Western model of individualism, which is not who she really is. By encountering salvation, she is able to realign with her personal and cultural identity and come into her full personhood.

Kearney

According to Kearney, people attempt to understand the world in a way that is consistent with how they see the world.[9] Although their perception is not always considered by others as being accurate, this gives structure to their beliefs. Cobern draws from this anthropological understanding by stating that "a worldview defines the Self. It sets the boundaries of who and what I am. It also defines everything that is not me, including my relationships to the human and non-human environments. It shapes my view of the universe, my conception of time and of space. It influences my norms and values."[10]

Kearney's theoretical model provides an analytical tool for studying worldview at the individual level and for studying subtle worldview variations, without sacrificing the ability to draw broad generalizations about worldview in a society. His model is known as a logico-structural one because it presumes a logical and structural integration of presuppositions. The seven categories he identified to diagnose the worldviews of individuals, can assist us to communicate more effectively and in a culturally-sensitive way as we incarnate ourselves in their world.[11]

These are the kind of questions that this theory allows us to ask in order to help us in this process:

1) Attitude to Other (any person, or thing, that is not self):

- What are the people's attitudes to society, nature and the supernatural (or God)?

- What are their attitudes to authority?

- What is their attitude towards people of various age groups, e.g: youth and the elderly?

- What is their regard for personal loyalty?

- What does "duty" mean for them?

- How formal are their various relationships?

- What are the differing roles of men and women within their society?

2) Attitude to Self:

- How do the people view themselves?

- Do they feel oppressed, disempowered, fearful, timid, unworthy, rejected, self-conscious, or do they feel free within themselves?

- Do they feel connected with their identity?

- How has their upbringing affected the way they see themselves and have they come to know the world?

- How does their understanding of themselves affect their relationships with others?

- Are their relationships with others based on harmony, subordination or dominance?

3) Classification:

- How do the people classify their attitudes of or to themselves, and of other people and the environment?

- What is real for them and what is unreal?

- What is their understanding of the supernatural?

- What is their understanding of God? Are their beliefs pantheistic, monotheistic, animistic, atheistic, agnostic, etc.?

- How does the society view death?

- How does it view marriage and rituals around this?

4) Causality:

- What does the culture understand about cause and effect?

- Are there strong religious or philosophical beliefs that will cause a different attribution of causality?

- Is their thinking based on traditional beliefs, cultural mythology or Western scientific concepts?

- How do they get their knowledge?

- What knowledge is valued in their culture?

5) Relationship:

- How do the various people groups feel about their own place within the culture?

- How do the various people groups within the culture view others: with unity, distrust, fear, suspicion etc.

- What constitutes humour for them?

- What is the distribution of power for the people group when compared with other people groups in the culture?

- What is their understanding of authority?

- How do they solve problems?

- What do they believe about justice?

- What are their moral codes and how are they expressed? For example, concepts of marriage, death and afterlife?

6) Time:

- What is their view on the past, the present, and the future?

- What is their orientation of time? Is it:

  - future-oriented, as exemplified in Western education which focuses on scholastic achievement and personal goal-setting?

  - present-oriented, as exemplified by those living in war zones or under threat of terrorism, for whom the here and now is more real than anything that may happen tomorrow?

 - past-oriented, as exemplified by the Chinese in ancestor worship?

- Is the future for them considered in terms of a few months, a few years, a few decades, or far longer? For instance, short-range planning is preferred by those who have shorter futures.

- How does the culture demonstrate its value of time? For example, do they connect time with money or is building relationships the most important use of time?

- Do they measure time in a linear, cyclical or zigzag way?

- In their culture, does time walk, run or fly?

7) **Space:**

- Do they live in wide open spaces or in small compartments and how does that affect their relationships with self and others? For example, do they accept or resent their living space?

- What is their concept of the environment and their understanding of their responsibility toward it?

- What is their concept of personal space? How is this guided by societal rules? e.g. relationships between men and women in different contexts, body language and acceptable non-verbal behavior?

Missionaries who enter a culture with inquisitiveness and an open heart are positioned to hear and see what God is doing among the people. It alerts them to the vital importance of laying aside their own cultural biases, forms, assumptions and expectations to see God connect people with what He created them to be, in the way that only He can. The story below illustrates how the questions based on Kearney's theory are multi-faceted and overlapping, interrelated and integrated.

Ferdinand, breathless and beaming with excitement, declared to me, "Mama, for the first time, I feel Filipino!" He was enjoying and exuberantly celebrating his new-found identity. For me, this one small statement gloriously punctuated the holiness with which heaven had visited us.

Living among the Filipinos, I was able to observe the form and the sound of their worship, which raised questions about their worldview and their identity. Up until this time, the Western model they had embraced expressed itself in various ways, such as singing in English, dancing to an English beat and form of dance, and wearing Western clothes. By reflecting on the questions that were raised and listening to the Holy Spirit, God opened my heart to vigorously call out their own tribal sounds, their own expressions of identity. It is God's heart to see every tribe, tongue and nation worshipping him in ways that He has created them to be.

Ferdinand, at home in traditional dress, lay on the ground before God; out of his mouth came a haunting, lamenting whistling sound. Like creation groaning, it was a sound that came from the land in a longing and yearning, calling us to worship. In a heavenly concerto it merged with other sounds that began to simultaneously erupt in waves around the room from members of the other twelve tribes present. Quiet, soft pianissimo tones arose among cadenzas of free, rhythmic expressions in a heavenly orchestration of which the Holy Spirit was the conductor. Some danced with wild abandon to the sound of their tribe, completely lost in God, while others beat out the chorus of their awakening with bamboo sticks. It came together in a cacophony of the diverse sounds, rhythms, and expressions of each of the tribes, but we were all one. It was heaven on earth – I have never heard anything as magnificent on earth in all my life.

Hiebert and Meneses

Nida defines culture as: "all learned and shared behavior."[12] This idea is further developed by Hiebert & Meneses as "the more or less integrated system of beliefs, feelings, values and worldview shared by a group of people and communicated by means of their systems of symbols."[13]

System of beliefs: At the core of a culture are shared beliefs about what is real. These beliefs are grouped in categories which help the community understand the world they are in and communicate with one another as a functioning society. An example of different cultural beliefs is presented by Van Dyk of the University of South Africa. He believes that many Western-based AIDS education and prevention programs, relying on their belief that AIDS is a disease, the spread of which can be controlled by education and treated through medicine, have failed in Africa because traditional African perceptions of the causes of illness (including AIDS); traditional perceptions of sexuality; and cultural beliefs influenced by beliefs about ancestors, witches and sorcerers and everyday life have not been taken into account. Other important cultural issues are the belief of some that witchcraft causes AIDS, the importance of sex as a symbol of personal immortality, the value of polygamous marriages, specific cultural beliefs inhibiting the use of condoms (e.g. blockage of the "gift of self", interference with the ripening of the fetus), and the important role of the traditional healer in African communities.[14]

Western cultural knowledge informs us how to do our jobs, drive a car, sail a yacht, use a microwave and how to worship God.[15] In the same manner, other cultures inform the way people behave in ways that are different from the expected norm of the Western culture. For example, Aboriginals from Australia have knowledge which enables them to survive in the desert; Mozambicans have knowledge on how to clean their pots and pans without water by using sand; a man living in the mountain province in the Philippines has knowledge which enables him to find a fish in a deep, fast flowing river and kill it with a spear and keep his clothes dry at the same time by performing the task naked.

Western cultural information can be stored in many different ways, such as in books, newspapers, magazines, documentaries, computers, iPods and billboards. Other cultures may be more inclined to store their information in stories, riddles, chants, songs, proverbs, tribal sayings, dance, genealogy, and other forms of oral tradition that are memorized and passed on to the next generation.[16]

Feelings: Culture also has to do with feelings that people have, their likes and dislikes, such as what they like to eat and wear, and their attitudes and how they are expressed.[17] For example, many Westerners are partial to a cheesy pizza, whereas my Indonesian friend expressively cast it off as "yellow slime." Likewise, many cultures cannot tolerate chillies, whereas it is not unusual for an Indonesian to express their total enjoyment by popping whole chillies into their mouths along with each mouthful of food in a meal.

Values: Every culture has values by which people judge and act out their lives. For a vivid example of differing expressions of the value of gratitude, the Dangombas living North of Ghana do not say thank you to show their appreciation. Instead, they express appreciation in terms of duty. For a Dangomba not to say thank you could be misunderstood as ingratitude in a Western context, just the same it could cause offense for a Westerner to say it, because, it suggests the Dangomba does not come from a respectable family. Respectable families will always do what is expected for the good of the community.[18]

Worldview: Worldviews are the culturally structured assumptions, values, commitments and allegiances that influence the way we see the world around us, and how we respond to those perceptions. It's the perspective from which we view the world. People believe that the world really is the way they see it. In anthropological terms, worldview evaluates cognitive beliefs, judges the emotional expressions of human life and has a moral code by which people assess right and wrong behavior.[19] For instance, it is worse in North America to tell a lie than to hurt someone's feelings. This is not the case in other cultures, where it is more important to encourage people than to upset them.

Intrinsic to that are themes that find expression in many different areas of cultural life. An example of a theme is in the American focus on the individual person as the basis of society.

This is reflected in the importance of individual freedom, self-fulfilment, human rights, and laws granting personal ownership.

Worldviews can also change over time, especially when challenged in a cross-cultural environment. I myself am an example of this, having grown up in an individualistic and task-orientated society, yet having spent thirty-three years in other cultures. As a result, I am aware that most of my thinking and the decisions that come from that, are now based on the "good of the community" and no longer on what is good for any one individual. I recognise there is a tension within me in that I am still passionate to see people and nations enter the fullness of their destinies, however the way this is worked out now is that I place more importance on building transparent, trusting and safe relationships. This reflects a more relational worldview than the task-oriented worldview I had when I first began as a missionary focused on working with all my might to win the lost for Jesus. Clearly, as we enter and participate with other cultures and learn from each other, our lives are enriched through what we receive.

Hofstede's chart comparing group-oriented societies and individual-oriented societies is useful in considering this aspect of worldview.

Figure 3
Group and Individual Worldview Themes[20]

Group Orientated Societies	Individual Orientated Societies
People are born into extended families in which they live their entire lives	Everyone grows up to look after himself/herself and organise nuclear families
Identity is based on birth and the place a person occupies in a group	Identity is based on individual achievements
Children learn to think in terms of "we"	Children learn to think in terms of "I"
Harmony should always be maintained and confrontation avoided	Speaking one's mind is a characteristic of an honest person
Violating the norms leads to a sense of shame and a loss of face for self and group	Violating the norms leads to a sense of guilt and loss of self-respect
Relationships between boss and worker are seen in moral family terms. The boss is responsible for the overall well-being of his worker	Relationships between boss and worker are governed by contracts based on voluntary exchange and mutual advantage
Hiring and promotion must take kinship and friendship into account	Hiring and promotion should be based purely on skills and rules of selection
The relationship is more important than the task.	The task is more important than the relationship.
People should not be fired	People can be readily fired

What is God's view of Culture?

God created culture and He has always shown Himself willing to work with people within their cultural frameworks. Jesus did not come as a generic human being, but incarnated Himself, working within the Palestinian Jewish culture that was shaped by the Roman occupation of the time, all in order to reach the Jews.

God also shows us through Paul's life how He accepted Gentiles without their needing to change their culture to do things in a way that is acceptable to God. John describes in Revelation 7:9 what he saw:

> ...*a great multitude that no one could count, from every nation, tribe, people and language, standing before the throne and in front of the Lamb. They were wearing white robes and were holding palm branches in their hands.*

The Kingdom of God has broken into our cultural lives here and now. God's intent is to demonstrate His glory through the weaving together of all the diverse families for His global purposes. The destiny of the nations is being outworked as we continue to obey Him and flow as one, bringing glory to Jesus (Jn 17:5, 10). The throne room will be a culminating celebration of that glory having been seen over the face of the earth (Hab 2:14).

> *The final goal of God's activity in this present age involves representatives of every culture sharing his rule as royal attendants in his kingdom. Every tribe, language, people group, and nation will be present. Their cultural differences will still be apparent. Indeed, that very diversity will enhance the greatness and glory of Christ. The "glory and honour of the nations" will be brought into the heavenly city as an inherent part of its abiding beauty (Rev 21: 24-26).[21]*

From Biblical studies we well know there is a huge difference between the cultural context of the Bible and contemporary cultures of our time, and in order to communicate the gospel effectively in our day, we need to understand the divine revelation within its cultural and historical setting. Just as importantly, we also need to understand the people we serve in their present day settings to enable us to communicate the gospel effectively with them.[22] If we do not, we are at risk of bringing something that is completely foreign, and not at home within the culture in which we have the privilege of serving. In missions practice today this is considered one of the most critical issues being faced in terms of presentation of the gospel. The challenge now is to advance this from the forum of discussion into practice.

Hiebert and Meneses' perspective on mission is that we should go beyond Christian texts or cultural contextualisation and become incarnational.[23] Contextualisation attempts to communicate the gospel in ways that make sense to people in their cultural context. It is about the gospel penetrating the worldview of a people group at the deepest level and meeting their deepest needs. Critical contextualisation will have the effect of people being able to follow Christ and remain in their culture. We need to incarnate our missions practice in the same way that Jesus lived out His own teaching in a human body and a human life. This is an act that goes far beyond translation of text or contextualisation of practice but one that causes transformation of their lives, their societies, their cultures.

A Weaving of Incarnational Practice with Anthropological Insights

The gospel is to be presented in the context of the infinite variety and complexity of distinct nations. God is God of the nations and as such He is well able to meet particular national and cultural needs and aspirations. Jesus Himself worked with the established customs of others.

The insights gleaned from anthropology, when woven together with incarnational practice and founded on perspectives from within the new culture, position us to more readily understand the 'integrated systems of beliefs, feelings, values and worldviews shared by a group of people and communicated by means of their systems and symbols.[24] Further, it gives us insight, as to how to go about incarnating ourselves in our presentation of the message and life with God to those immersed in other cultures different from our own.

Whiteman, whose cross-cultural research and mission has primarily been in Central Africa and Melanesia, describes seven areas of anthropology that can help us connect the gospel to culture. I am in agreement with his approach and suggest that these points may be taken further than an incarnational connection, to be woven in and through our incarnational practice. In order to highlight this, I have woven his seven points in with my own story of incarnational practice as experienced in my early journey of cross-cultural missions.[25]

At 26 years of age I was commissioned and sent by God from my local church in Aotearoa, New Zealand to Hong Kong and People's Republic of China. Up until that time, my experiences with God and the Christian community, along with my Pentecostal theological training, equipped me to understand the message God wanted me to communicate and the "how to do" of church life, including power evangelism with accompanying signs, leadership and Church planting, but all within the framework of my South Pacific New Zealand context. Initially, I did not have the tool of anthropological insights to draw from to be able to better understand the Chinese culture where I was to serve for the next eleven years, however I did come to live an incarnational model, which is vital for any cross-cultural ministry, not only for being able to be an effective witness, but also for one's personal transformation to take place.

1) Anthropology deals with people's actual behaviour, as well as what they say, how they think, and how they feel. It is a behavioural science, and a dose of realism is good in any ministry.

2) Anthropology seeks to generalize about human behaviour and looks for cross-cultural universals and patterns. This gives us a greater appreciation for distinguishing what is unique to one culture and what is more characteristic of all human beings.

The incarnational model of missionary practice encourages humility because we are placed in a position of dependence on our new culture. We are entering a new culture and we have not yet acquired the knowledge to interpret experience and generate appropriate social behaviour. Eugene Nida further explains:

In the analysis of the patterns of behaviour in any culture, the science of cultural anthropology is concerned primarily with the following questions:

• What makes a culture click? What are the various features (such as food, shelter, transportation, family organisation, religious beliefs, and language) and what are the dynamic drives (e.g. goals, ambitions, value systems and prestige) that provide the spark for human society?

• What makes a particular member of a society act as he/she does? People in any society do not act alike. Why is this? What are the possibilities for diverse behaviour? What is the relationship of the person to the culture? Does he/she have much chance for alternative behaviour (such as in our Western, urban culture), or is the mould rather rigidly fixed and people expected to conform closely to it as in so many primitive cultures? (Primitive as defined by anthropologists in terms of tribal societies)

• What are the factors involved in a culture's stability or change? What are the dynamics of cultural conservation and change? [26]

Even now I cringe as I recall my confidence, the "woman of the hour with the power," landing at Kai Tak airport in Hong Kong, so full of the Holy Spirit, ready to "save all the Chinese people," and have a ministry to the poor, rather than with the poor. It also never occurred to me that God was already in the culture before I came. I thank God that He still worked with and through my sincere heart and am grateful to my host culture for their honouring hospitality, the graciousness they displayed and their patience in accepting and teaching me. The challenge I faced was in recognising that I carried what I call excess ethnocentric baggage. Essentially, I viewed and judged other people's behaviour by my own values and assumptions.

3) Anthropology uses an approach to research called participant observation, which is particularly useful for cross-cultural ministry. It gives us tools for knowing how to discover deeper cultural understanding while living with the people we serve.

Only as I went and served with the poor was God able to give me His heart of love to be able to see as He sees. They became my family. Many times as we prayed and worshiped together I would be overwhelmed as the Holy Spirit moved in love amongst us and the gifts of the Holy Spirit were shared.

Not only was my ethnocentricity challenged in terms of my worldview but I also came to see that my own family culture and upbringing had also shaped me. Having been a first generation New Zealander with parents who had emigrated from the United Kingdom, I did not grow up with the support of an extended family around me. I grew to be a very self-sufficient and independent person. Where God has graciously used this as I have pioneered among the nations, I also understood that the fierce independence within me had to be broken. It has been a process from independence to inter-dependence to self-giving love. Whereas before I would just get on with it, now I recognize more than ever how much we need each other, the body of Christ.

My own culture, which takes pride in privacy, had isolated me from others; we have only to look at the fences around our homes, which seem to be getting higher and higher - not to mentioned the security to keep people out. This was not so with the poor. We are in and out of each other's lives, daily relating to one another, eating together, praying, worshipping, cooking and feeding others who are hungry. I learned to transition from a worldview that honours one another by protecting privacy and isolation to one that honours by inclusion that incarnates among the poor.

As far as my needs were concerned, I soon learned that they had to be defined by local conditions.[27] Put in a position of sharing everything with each other, the power of possessions was broken. I can remember René Padilla once saying that money is a demon and the way to exorcise it is to give it away!

4) Anthropology focuses on the elements in human interaction that relate to communication. It helps us appreciate the need to learn in depth the language of the people and to recognise that most communication is more non-verbal than verbal.

I came to see that the restriction of not being able to speak the Cantonese language at the beginning was a blessing in disguise for me. I was dependent on the local people to teach me, which positioned me as a learner from the start. As part of that learning process, I also came to see how language is the heart of the people.

5) Anthropology deals with people in all dimensions of their existence - socially, culturally, and ecologically. It takes an holistic approach to studying human beings.

John presents in his epistle to "love in truth" which encourages the giving of resources to relieve the needs of others (1 Jn 3:18). This was a distinctive feature of the New Testament Church which took the whole person seriously.

Being initially faced with a hungry man dying on the streets and not being able to speak Cantonese, I could not proclaim steps to peace with God which had been useful in my New Zealand context at that time. So instead I went and got him something to eat and drink, and visited and prayed for his healing and salvation daily. As Mortimer Arias points out, "evangelization can never merely be 'verbal proclamation.' Authentic evangelization will also be 'the incarnation of the gospel' in the lives of Christ's people, Christ's community."[28]

6) Anthropology focuses on how cultures change. Missionaries by definition should be agents of change, but too often the change we introduce is disruptive and counterproductive. We need to understand thoroughly the cultural dynamics of the society in which we serve.

Years later I discovered that ethnocentric belief was not exclusive to Westerners. Through the years I have had the privilege of serving with and training students from the two-thirds world locations and they have related to me their own realisation that they are not supposed to convert people in other tribes to their tribe.

7) Anthropology helps us distinguish between cultural forms and meanings. This is particularly important when we want to communicate Christian meanings in forms that are appropriate for the culture of the receptors of our message.

Although I initially understood my call was one of ministry to the poor, as I began to walk the streets with my friend Heidi, I saw drug addicts and alcoholics living in boxes and the elderly living in cages in dark rooms, and I couldn't walk away. God captured my heart for them. We did not follow the form of hiring a hall for church, but we sat with them and prayed for one another, fed them and worshipped God together on the streets and under motorways, at the poor man's nightclub, outside the Buddhist temple, wherever the people were. I later came to realise that in this, God had given me the privilege of making Jesus at home with them in their own context – on the streets. As I have reflected over the years, I have recognised the impact of this approach was not just that we loved them and fed them and prayed with them, but that they could live their lives in Christ in their own setting. It was not a foreign reality – Jesus was at home with them in their cages and boxes on the streets, not in a building. It was not "Sunday Christianity," but was about Jesus being with them every day in everyday life.

I am thankful for the insights I have since gained through anthropology. They have not only helped me to more fully understand my own journey but have also equipped me to impart the lessons I have learned along the way to students who are embarking on their own journeys to the people of the world. Through a weaving together of an incarnational model and anthropological insights, they will be better equipped to understand and appreciate their own cultural values and assumptions. In laying these aside and learning as many lessons as possible before and as they go, they will be given the best possible advantage of truly serving and presenting the gospel at home within the culture to which God is sending them.

In the process of their discipleship, Hitchen has raised further questions that will need to be asked:

- What will happen to those who receive Christ?

- How will it affect their family?

- What problems will conversion create?

- What are the most realistic ways to solve such problems?[29]

Culture Shock

A reflection on Culture Shock and consideration of some practical ways to deal with its symptoms which I have found useful for myself and have observed in others will be meaningful in this discussion, since it helps prepare missionaries to make the initial adjustment to a new culture more readily and hastens the journey of coming to feel at home. Most importantly, in the context of the weaving of incarnational practice with anthropological insights I also wish to reflect from my own experience on what I consider to be the most effective way to prevent many aspects of culture shock from occurring.

What is Culture Shock?

Oberg defines culture shock as the anxiety that results from losing all our familiar signs and symbols of social relationships.[30] The potential for culture shock happens every time a person moves into a culture that is unfamiliar to them. After the initial honeymoon period of excitement, they can feel quite disoriented and confused, not being able to control the circumstances that surround them. At this time, the intensity of these feelings can even make a person want to return home to their own familiar surroundings.

Some think that culture shock arises from sights of poverty or lack of sanitation, but this is not the case. The same responses are felt by people who come from such cultures to the first world. Rather, it stems from the fact that those in an unfamiliar culture do not yet know the verbal and non-verbal languages or even the simplest rules of social behaviour. It is the shock of realising that what has already been learned is meaningless in this new environment.

To add to the confusion of the changes that are taking place in the newcomer, cultural landmarks that appear familiar may in fact be foreign, because the same behaviour and norms have radically different meanings in different societies. This is short-lived and passes as the person becomes more familiar with the language and cultural cues. In time, they will adjust and learn to become a functioning participant of the new host culture. In this process, one becomes a bicultural person, who has come to grips with the issues of cultural parochialism and relativism.[31]

Symptoms of Culture Shock

Oberg defined six aspects of culture shock as follows.[32] The model he derived from these is still in use today:

1. Strain due to the effort required to make necessary psychological adaptations

2. A sense of loss and feelings of deprivation regarding friends, family, status, career and possessions

3. Being rejected by and/or rejecting members of the new culture

4. Confusion in role, role expectation, values, feelings and self-identity

5. Surprise, anxiety and even disgust and indignation after becoming aware of cultural differences

6. Feelings of impotence due to not being able to cope with a new environment

Luzbetak suggests that the inability to adjust to strange cultural demands may produce the following symptoms:[33]

1. A growing negative and suspicious view of the "strange" people and their ways and values

2. Homesickness, loneliness, boredom, lethargy and tendency to withdraw

3. Rising stress, an overall feeling of dissatisfaction, disgust, irritability and depression

4. Physical illness, especially chronic headaches and hypertension

5. An over-concern about one's health

6. Excessive drinking or some other questionable compensation

Understanding the phenomenon of culture shock can save many missionaries from much heartache. Historically, without having a framework of understanding the source of the culture shock, some have concluded that the depth of the despair and depression they are battling with means they must not have been called to these people after all!

Culture Stress

The next part of the journey is culture stress. This occurs when a person transitions from culture shock, adjusting to the form of the new culture, making it their own. It is associated with settling differences in social roles, language, cultural norms and values, routines of living, ideas about time, anger, etc. This transition can be quite challenging and can take years, but those who persevere will reap the benefits of successfully finding themselves feeling comfortable in two cultures (or more). Taking on many new customs and starting to identify with this new culture as one they share, they can begin to feel more at home and have more of a true sense of belonging.

Helpful Ways to Minimise Culture Stress

Although culture stress cannot be entirely eliminated, from the experience of my own journey I have found a number of ways to minimise stress. The following list also acknowledges Dye's contributions.[34]

1. **Recognition:** Recognise that culture stress is a normal response while making a new home in another culture.

2. **Worship:** Enjoy spending time with Jesus as much as He enjoys spending time with you.

3. **Humour:** Don't take yourself too seriously. Relax, Jesus is the Saviour.

4. **Flexibility:** Recognise that achieving certain things in your new culture may not be as easy to do as in the culture you have come from. Things on your "to do" lists may never be ticked off!

5. **Acceptance:** Accept the people in your new culture. Their way of living is just as valid as yours has been. Accept yourself also. Know who you are in Christ, including understanding the gifts He has given you. Jesus has confidence in you to continue His work in this community.

6. **Friendships:** Develop friendships with the nationals, not as a task, but just to be part of a new family.

7. **Relaxation:** Give yourself permission to take time out. Give yourself special treats like going for walks, reading books, listening to music, painting, riding camels, dancing, etc. Take up a hobby in your community.

8. **Communication:** Enjoy learning the local language. Don't see it as a chore but an opportunity to learn about your new family. Don't be offended when people laugh at your mistakes.

Applying Anthropological Insights Woven with Incarnational Practice to Help Reduce Culture Shock and Stress

Although culture shock is predictable, it is less likely to occur with such intensity when we incarnate and bond with the nationals in their local communities, rather than seeking out like-minded people from a similar culture from which we have come.

Sometimes, because of our own cultural perceptions, we can assume the problem of culture shock and culture stress lies with others and not ourselves. But, by being like a child and growing among them, immersed with them, learning from them, we become socialised all over again into the new culture. We can begin to see what the Father sees and is doing and become able to participate more with Him.

The first couple of weeks in a new country are of critical importance if we want to establish a sense of belonging with the local people. If we do not, you can become isolated, even when living in a community. In that isolation, misunderstandings and trust issues are more likely to occur.

I lacked a sense of belonging in my first four years in Hong Kong. I now understand that occurred because the people I lived with were ex-pats from a similar background to my own, who were living in Hong Kong and serving in the People's Republic of China. But comparing my Hong Kong entry with my time in the Russian Federation, where I lived with the Russian believers from the moment I arrived, there is no comparison. They became my family and they still are, and will be forever.

From the first day it is important to develop meaningful relationships with local people. It is better to plunge in and experience life from the insider's perspective, living with the people, worshipping with them, cooking food together, shopping together, getting water from the well together, using public transport together.[35]

When we belong, deeper levels of trust occur. I did not become homesick or experience other symptoms of culture shock or culture stress because my social needs were fulfilled with the relationships I had within my new Russian community. We would take holidays together, socialize, church-plant, minister with the poor and train disciples together. I can recall hearing them say even in times of conflict, "we know you love us" and it was true. They knew it because I lived with them, through the good and the bad. We built our own community through our relationships and the experiences we shared. Being hungry together as a result of food shortages, we shared what we had with each other. We helped each other financially when rising inflation rates meant many struggled to manage. And when we were cold, which was often, we would share our clothes to keep warm. The reality was that that my Russian family gave me more than I was able to give them.

Living in our own culture we naturally do things in a certain way. We know which way to look for the traffic as we step out on the street, how to get on a bus, how to get needed information, we know how to pay for our groceries at the checkout counter with a credit card and pay our bills. In a new culture, however, the way to do these things seems unpredictable and different. For example, from my perspective, like Americans, the Russians drive on the wrong side of the road. When going to buy food, there may not always be food to buy. It was not a case of what do I feel like eating today but rather, I wonder what there is to eat out there. Such experiences can lead to feelings of disorientation, which lead to culture shock. However, in the first 2-3 weeks it is easier for a newcomer, expecting change, to cope with such unpredictable situations.

My advice to those entering a new culture is to communicate early to the nationals that you are a learner. People will help those who are in need. Having local friendships is essential for feeling at home. When missionaries, already established in a culture group, try to cushion a new incoming missionary out of the goodness of their hearts by protecting them in the ex-pat community, they are doing them a big disservice. Although this is true in most situations, I must add that entering a hostile culture may require a different approach. Overall, however, new missionaries who involve themselves in their new cultural surroundings learn to appreciate them. They become more aware of their own cultural assumptions and of alternate lifestyles, and thus can avoid many of the symptoms of culture shock.

Conclusion

Asking questions raised by anthropologists and discovering

the treasures within the cultures to which we have been called makes a way for the Holy Spirit to truly move. His ongoing presence will result in a glorious transformation within lives, homes and communities. We will have the privilege of witnessing His magnificent work of transformation, as customs, morals and values are yielded to God for Him to change those that need to be changed and enliven those that were dead and buried and through which He expresses His beauty through a particular group or people.

An enormous challenge remains for missionaries from every culture to weave into the tapestry of their own incarnational missionary practice a sense of curiosity for cultural differences, an appreciation for the insights that anthropology can provide, and a determination to pursue cross-cultural understanding. Missionaries who enter a culture with a very inquisitive attitude, filled with the desire to learn the local ways from the local people, recognise we have been given a huge privilege as our hosts allow us to come into their lives and sit across the table from them. Our response to this should be incredible gratitude.

We will not become homesick since our social needs are met by friends who treat us as family members. We will probably get sick and very tired, but will have a community who will lovingly take care of us. Trusted as one of the community, we will no longer be considered as outsiders, but will be included in decision-making. We will be graced with the authority to preach what we ourselves live, therefore being able to call others to join us on the road of discipleship.

Together we will learn to view everything from a Kingdom perspective, loving what God loves and hating what He hates. We will have the privilege of witnessing God's transforming love as people discover their self-worth and dignity in Him. He alone gives meaning, purpose and hope, seen in lovingkindness being expressed through His people towards others in practical ways. In some illiterate communities, we will have the joy of seeing God reveal His heart through visions and dreams, tongues and interpretations. Among the poor we will have the joy of witnessing God giving wisdom, insight, and a voice on how to sustain themselves and their communities. We may then have the honour of being invited to partner with the community, as hearing God's voice for themselves empowers them to speak for themselves.

As sent ones, we are invited on a journey of participation with what God, the living flame of love, is doing in the world among

he tangata,

the people

he tangata,

the people

he tangata...

Endnotes

[1] Darrell L. Whiteman, "Anthropology and Missions: The Incarnational Connection," in *International Journal of Frontier Missions* 21, no. 2, Summer (2004), 82.

[2] Louis J. Luzbetak, *The Church and Cultures: New Perspectives in Missiological Anthropology* (Maryknoll, NY: Orbis Books, 1988), 27.

[3] Paul G. Hiebert, *Cultural Anthropology* (Grand Rapids, MI: Baker Book House, 1976), 24

[4] Charles H. Kraft, *Anthropology for Christian Witness* (Maryknoll, NY: Orbis Books, 1996), 4-13.

[5] Geert Hofstede, *Culture's Consequences: International Differences in Work Related Values* (Newbury Park, CA: Sage, 1980); *Culture and Organizations: Software of the Mind* (London, UK: McGraw Hill, 1981); "Dimensions of National Cultures in Fifty Countries and Three Regions" in *Expications in Cross-Cultural Psychology*, edited by S. Dziurwiec and R.C. Annis J.B. Deregowski (Lisse: Swets & Zeitlinger, 1983); "A Case Study for Comparing Apples and Oranges: International Differences in Values" in *Values and Attitudes Across Nations and Time*, edited by M. Sasaki (Leiden, Netherlands: Brill, 1998).

Examples in which Hofstede's work has been referenced: G. Dafoulas and L. Macaulay, "Investigating Cultural Differences in Virtual Software Teams" in *Electronic Journal on Information Systems in Developing Countries EJISDC* Vol. 7(4) 2001, 1-14; Douglas R.Vogel, Robert M. Davison, Ronnie H. Shroff and Sajda Qureshi, "Sociocultural Learning in Globally Distributed Teams: An Exploratory Study" in *Proceedings of Informing Science Conference* (2001), 527-536; Detmar Straub, Karen Loch, Roberto

Evaristo, Elena Karahanna and Mark Strite, "Toward a Theory-Based Measurement of Culture" in *Journal of Global Information Management* Vol. 10(1) 2002, 13-23; Monika M. Rathod and Shaila M. Miranda, *Telework and Psychological Distance: The Mediating Effects of Culture and Technology in Four Countries* (New Orleans, LA: ACM SIGCPR Conference on Computer Personnel Research, 1999), 268-275; Kursat Cagilitay, "Culture and its Effects on Human-Computer-Interaction" in *Proceedings of World Conference on Educational Multimedia, Hypermedia and Telecommunications*, edited by P. Kommers and G. Richards (Chesapeake, VA: AACE, 1999), 1626.

[6]Detmar Straub, Karen Loch, Roberto Evaristo, Elena Karahanna and Mark Strite, "Toward a Theory-Based Measurement of Culture" in Journal of Global Information Management Vol. 10(1). 2002, 13-23.

Positivism is the theory that knowledge can be acquired only through direct obervation and experimentation, and not through metaphysics or theology.

[7]Geert Hofstede, *Culture's Consequences: International Differences in Work Related Values* (Newbury Park, CA: Sage, 1980); *Culture and Organizations: Software of the Mind* (London, UK: McGraw Hill, 1981).

[8]Detmar Straub, Karen Loch, Roberto Evaristo, Elena Karahanna and Mark Strite, "Toward a Theory-Based Measurement of Culture" in *Journal of Global Information Management* Vol. 10(1). 2002, 20.

[9]Michael Kearney, *World View* (Novato, CA: Chandler and Sharp, 1984).

[10]William W. Cobern, "Distinguishing Science-Related Variations in the Causal Universal of College Students' Worldviews" Paper presented at the Annual Meeting of the National Association for Research in Science Teaching (62nd, San Francisco, CA: March 30 – April 1, 1989), 2.

[11]Michael Kearney, *World View* (Novato, CA: Chandler & Sharp,

1984).

[12]Eugene A. Nida, *Customs and Cultures: Anthropology for Christian Missions* (Pasadena, CA: William Carey Library, 1975), 28.

[13]Paul G. Hiebert and Eloise Hiebert Meneses, *Incarnational Ministry: Planting Churches in Band, Tribal Peasant and Urban Societies* (Grand Rapids, MI: Baker Books, 1995), 37.

[14]Alta C. Van Dyk, "Traditional African Beliefs and Customs: Implications for AIDS Education and Prevention in Africa." *Abstract of a paper presented at the International Conference on AIDS*, 30 June 2000. NLM Gateway: A Service of the US National Institutes of Health, http://gateway.nlm.nih.gov (accessed February 14, 2010).

[15]Paul G. Hiebert and Eloise Hiebert Meneses, Incarnational Ministry: Planting Churches in Band, Tribal Peasant and Urban Societies (Grand Rapids, MI: Baker Books, 1995), 39.

[16]Ibid

[17]Ibid

[18]Example drawn from the "Tamale Institute of Cross-Cultural Studies Newletter" (Tamale, Ghana: September, 1988), 4-5

[19]Paul G. Hiebert, *Transforming Worldviews: An Anthropological Understanding of how People Change* (Grand Rapids, MI: Baker Academic, 2008); Charles H. Kraft, Anthropology for Christian Witness (Maryknoll, NY: Orbis Books, 1996).

[20] Geert H. Hofstede, Gert Jan Hofstede and Michael Minkov *Cultures and Organizations: Software of the Mind: Intercultural Cooperation and its Importance for Survival* (New York: McGraw-Hill, 2010), 113.

[21]John M. Hitchen, "Why Bother About Cultural Differences?" A revision of an article first published in *Reaper*. Vol. 72(3) (June-July 1990), 5.

[22]Paul G. Hiebert, *Cultural Anthropology* (Grand Rapids, MI: Baker

Book House, 1976), xx.

[23]Paul G. Hiebert and Eloise Hiebert Meneses, *Incarnational Ministry: Planting Churches in Band, Tribal Peasant and Urban Societies* (Grand Rapids, MI: Baker Books, 1995), 373.

[24]Paul G. Hiebert and Eloise Hiebert Meneses, *Incarnational Ministry: Planting Churches in Band, Tribal Peasant and Urban Societies* (Grand Rapids, MI: Baker Books, 1995), 37.

[25]Darrell L. Whiteman, "Anthropology and Missions: The Incarnational Connection" in *International Journal of Frontier Missions* Vol. 21(2) Summer (2004), 83.

[26]Eugene A. Nida, *Customs and Cultures: Anthropology for Christian Missions* (Pasadena, CA: William Carey Library, 1975), 27.

[27]Jonathan J. Bonk, *Missions and Money: Affluence as a Western Missionary Problem ... Revisited* (Mary Knoll, NY: Orbis Books, 2007), 173.

[28]Mortimer Arius, "Announcing the Reign of God", 207 in Alan Neely, "Incarnational Mission" in *Evangelical Dictionary of World Missions*, edited by A. Scott Moreau, (Grand Rapids, MI: Baker Books, 2000), 475.

[29]John M. Hitchen, "Anthropology: Friend or Foe?" Paper presented at the Annual Conference of Christian Brethren Missionaries, Papua New Guinea (August 1968), 6

[30]Kalervo Oberg, "Cultural Shock: Adjustments to New Cultural Environments" in *Practical Anthropology* 7 (1960), 177.

[31]Parochialism is the belief that our own 'parish' or local community does things in the only really proper or correct way.

Relativism is the belief that knowledge, truth, and morality exist in relation to culture, society, or historical context, and are not absolute (Oxford University Press: Oxford Dictionary, 2012)

[32]Kalervo Oberg, "Cultural Shock: Adjustments to New Cultural

Environments" in *Practical Anthropology* 7 (1960), 177-182.

Elisabeth Marx, *Breaking Through Culture Shock: What You Need to Succeed in International Business* (London, UK: Nicholas Brealey Publishing, 2001), 5

[33]Louis J. Luzbetak, *The Church and Cultures: New Perspectives in Missiological Anthropology* (Maryknoll, NY: Orbis Books, 1988), 204.

[34]Wayne T. Dye, "Stress-Producing Factors in Cultural Adjustment" in *Missiology* (1974), 61-77.

[35] See Charles H. Kraft, *Anthropology for Christian Witness* (Maryknoll, NY: Orbis Books, 1996), 76-77 for a helpful discussion on etic (understanding a culture as an informed outsider) and emic (understanding a culture as an insider) perspectives.

Chapter 14
ISSUES AND TRENDS IN MISSIONS

" *In order to pursue the goal of world evangelization with maximum effectiveness, it is helpful to learn not only about history but also about current issues affecting the world and the global church today. Globalization, postmodernism, and advances in technology and media are having significant impact on opportunities to spread the gospel. Changing attitudes towards the role of women in ministry, the need for financial accountability, and the use of business as mission are also altering the face of missionary activity. Awareness of these and other trends will allow us to be strategically focused as we join the worldwide church in its Spirit-empowered endeavor to finish the work to which Jesus called us.* "

- Howard Foltz

Why a chapter on a generic theme, "Issues and trends in Missions" in a book on missiology and power? Simply put, although we all want to be like Jesus, something that we tend to overlook is that Jesus Himself was a missionary! A missionary is someone who leaves his home culture and enters a new culture to be used of God in advancing His Kingdom. Jesus left His special placement in heaven and dramatically changed His living conditions. He entered a culture of fallen and depraved mankind and incarnated the love and message of His Father in heaven on earth. After His supernatural ministry on earth, He left His twelve disciples with these final words, "Go into all the world and preach the Gospel to every creature (Mark 16:15). Along with this Great Commission cited in Mark and ultimately in all of the Gospels, Jesus gave His disciples the promise of the Holy Spirit along with a fresh mandate to use this empowering of the Spirit to take His message to the ends of the earth:[1]

But you shall receive power when the Holy Spirit has come upon you; and you shall be witnesses to Me in Jerusalem, and in all Judea and Samaria, and to the end of the earth (Acts 1:8 NASB).

Every believer should have a burning passion to be like Jesus. We are not all called to be missionaries, to leave our home culture and enter another culture as a career missionary, but every Christian should have a passion to reach the lost. All of us should understand that we are owned by God and every breath is given by grace to be used in our being a Great Commission Christian. A Great Commission Christian is a believer who is, first, obeying God's Great Commandment of love:

Teacher, which is the great commandment in the law?" Jesus said to him, "You shall love the LORD your God with all your heart, with all your soul, and with all your mind. This is the first and great commandment. And the second is like it: 'You shall love your neighbor as yourself...(Mt 22:36-39 NASB).

Second, a Great Commission Christian obediently organizes their life around a commitment to be involved in Great Commission activities:

> *Go therefore and make disciples of all the nations, baptizing them in the name of the Father and of the Son and of the Holy Spirit, teaching them to observe all things that I have commanded you; and lo, I am with you always, even to the end of the age. (Mt 28:19-20 NASB)*

This definition of a Great Commission Christian introduces us to our first "issue."

Issue # 1 - Missions R' Us!

It starts with every believer. As Great Commission Christians, the necessary ingredients we must possess are our obedience, our faith and faithfulness, our being filled with the Holy Spirit, our world-changing prayer, and our witness and disciple making. This is what leads us in a fruitful partnership with God to advance His miraculous Kingdom.

A "power word" for Great Commission Christians to understand is "mobilized." It is most often associated with the military and it means "to stand up and be ready for war." Let's consider the explosive potential of Great Commission Christians being mobilized and "ready for war." When we are mobilized and ready for spiritual battle, we incarnate His life, love and message in the world where we live. One of the greatest problems in the church today is the lack of mobilization on the part of individual believers and even local churches. If every Christian becomes a Great Commission Christian and mobilizes for spiritual battle against the powers of darkness, we will see the explosive potential of the world being evangelized.

Since Missions R' Us, Let us think globally

There are 800 million Bible-believing Christians around the world.[2] In *Megashifts*, Jim Rutz calls these believers "core apostolics." Core apostolics are the new saints who are at the heart of the expanding Kingdom of God. The term and the category are both mine, but they're not at all subjective. They stand for a very real and countable movement of more than 800 million switched-on disciples, according to the Joshua Project.[3]

The potential of these "core apostolics" goes even further. There are another 1.37 billion Christians who consider themselves "Christians" simply because they come from a Christian culture.[4] What if a powerful move of God impacted these "cultural Christians" and they became dedicated Great Commission Christians? We would have an awesome global harvest force capable of seeing the Great Comission finished in our generation!

To be like Jesus means that we obey the mission He has given to us, just as Jesus obeyed His mission.

Jesus said to them, 'My food is to do the will of Him who sent Me, and to finish His work. Do you not say, 'There are still four months and then comes the harvest'? Behold, I say to you, lift up your eyes and look at the fields, for they are already white for harvest!'"(Jn 4:34-35 NASB).

We are commissioned to be "finishers" as Jesus was. We should, every day, be nourished and sustained by doing our Father's will. Jesus wants us to "lift up your eyes and look at the fields." He wants us to have a vision for harvest and be gripped with a harvest mentality.

To this end, we must target our resources. If we are to see the Great Commission finished, we must target what are called "unreached people groups." People groups are the ethnic, linguistic and cultural groups that make up the global population of 6.7 billion.[5] Unreached people groups are those where people live without an adequate, resident witness of the Gospel.

The Joshua Project is a strategic research initiative seeking to highlight the ethnic people groups in the world with the least followers of Jesus Christ. Their website identifies 16,352 total people groups in the world and 41% of these people groups, or

6,650 of them, are unreached.[6] A map of the world is not just made up of countries, but also people groups within a country, primarily Muslim, Hindu, Buddhist, Tribal and Non-Religious. The population of these unreached people groups is over 2.7 billion.

You and I would not want to live where they live. The unreached world is made up of towns and villages without churches, and they are the most susceptible to crushing poverty, disease, illiteracy and human rights abuse. Further, over one-half of the unreached people groups are not adopted by any type of missions organization or church; they are "unengaged."

The plight of the unreached is "bad news," but thank God we have some fantastic "good news." With 800 million Bible believing Christians currently ministering on planet earth, plus the exponential growth potential of the latent "cultural Christians," the Church has a bright future ahead. Jim Rutz writes:

> *The growing core of Christianity crosses theological lines and includes [800] million born-again people who are increasing by 8% a year. These "core apostolics" are a powerful mix of Charismatics, Pentecostals, and Evangelicals whose main distinction is that they are in expanding, connected, easily countable networks. The term excludes those groups that are so liberal in theology, so isolated in structure, or so deeply rooted in medieval tradition that they are hardly growing at all.[7]*

What marvelous growth of the global church, eight percent per year! Still, the Western church is often dead-set on "me first" self-centeredness, marginal obedience and stagnant growth. From 1960 on, non-Western evangelicals have been growing at a phenomenal rate, outstripping the growth of the Western church by seven to one. The center of growth in the Church has shifted from the west to the east and from the north to the south. This has dramatically changed the Evangelical landscape. In 100 AD there was only one active believer for every 360 non-believers. This has dramatically changed! Today, there are only 7.3 non-believers for every active believer.[8] This growth, not surprisingly, comes primarily from the non-Western world. They are sending out a new missionary force now; over half of the contemporary missionary force is made up of Asians, Africans, and Latinos. Praise God for the total Western and non-Western global harvest force, for around 180,000 souls are entering God's Kingdom every day!

Yes! Missions R' Us. Every Christian should have a passion to be like Jesus. Our purpose should be like His, "for the Son of Man has come to seek and to save that which was lost" (Lk 19:10). Nothing diverted Him from this task. God help us not to be diverted from being Great Commission Christians. Our task is to personalize the Great Commission. This personalization means:

1) We will earnestly pray for the lost, even for the unreached people groups.

2) As growing disciples, we will learn about the world Jesus died for so we can pray strategically for the lost, even the unreached.

3) We will give to global missions and "live to give, not just live to get."

4) We will help send those who are called to the mission field.

5) We will be willing to go ourselves on short-term missions, and even as a career missionary, if God calls us.

Missions R' Us is part of our self identity. Let's release it!

ISSUE # 2 Home Depot Churches Or Great Commission Churches?

From what you have read so far, certainly you would surmise that I believe every church should be more than a "Home Depot," that is a local home improvement store centered exclusively around one's own home, or church. Let's look at Acts 1:8 (NASB) again:

> *But you shall receive power when the Holy Spirit has come upon you; and you shall be witnesses to Me in Jerusalem, and in all Judea and Samaria, and to the end of the earth.*

Here we see that Jesus Christ has four targets for outreach, and He empowers His people and Church with the Holy Spirit to reach them. The first target is Jerusalem, or people with our own cultural worldview who live in our immediate area. Second, is Judea which again is people with our cultural worldview, but distant from our local area. Third, is Samaria. Samaritans were half Jew and half Greek, so their cultural worldview is somewhat similar to ours, but also somewhat different. Fourth is to the end of the earth, where the culture and worldview is quite diverse from ours.

Let me illustrate this from my own experience. When I was being discipled as a young Christian in my home church of Calvary Temple in Denver, Colorado, those we were targeting in evangelism were of our own culture. To us, this was "Jerusalem," but when we planted a new church across town, this was "Judea." When my wife Pat and I moved to Holland to start the Teen Challenge ministry overseas (we had already pioneered this ministry in Texas), we found the Dutch to be somewhat like us Americans, but they were also quite different. This was a "Samaritan" cultural distance. Later I went to India to help missionaries start the Teen Challenge program and I discovered that the Hindu and Muslim cultures were very different from America or Holland. For me, this was an extreme cultural distance, or "the end of the earth" from the Biblical perspective of Acts 1:8.

In this example, let me emphasize that the distance factor is not miles, but culture. We see that every local church, in obedience to the Acts 1:8 promise and mandate, should have a strategy to reach all of the four strata of Acts 1:8. My home church did. Calvary Temple had an aggressive local evangelism outreach, but also supported missionaries all over the world with a whopping one-third of the church's income going to world missions. This is an Acts 1:8 church!

The definition of a Great Commission Church would incorporate the biblical emphasis and cultural strata of Acts 1:8, but would also include the scriptural dimensions we saw in the definition of a Great Commission Christian. I define a Great

Commission Church as "a local church that is based on Acts 1:8, equipping its people to fully obey the Great Commandment, and has an end vision to fulfill the Great Commission." My conviction is that God desires every local church on this planet be more than a "Home Depot" Jerusalem church, and be possessed with a burning passion for Jesus and the lost, and even unreached people groups. The key to our being Great Commission Christians and building Great Commission Churches is obedience and passion.

Jim Diehl, a Church of the Nazarene general superintendent, made a powerful statement on passion at a Nazarene General Assembly:

> The question before us is this: Is there enough passion in the soul of the church to carry the Gospel to the peoples of this world?
>
> • Our problem is not with our profession but with our passion.
>
> • Our problem is not with our procedures, but with our passion.
>
> • Our problem is not with our policy, but with our passion.
>
> • Our problem is not with our purpose, but with our passion.
>
> • Our problem is not with our programs, but with our passion.
>
> When it is all said and done; "if we lose our passion, we lose our movement.[9]

What Jim Diehl said is a penetrating truth for all of us. We need passion for the Lord and passion for the lost!

I have the joy of being part of a mission team called AIMS, which stands for Accelerating International Mission Strategies. Our vision statement is: "Empowering the Church to take the Gospel where it's never been proclaimed!" Our mission is "to mobilize strategic partners to proclaim the Kingdom of God to the remaining unreached peoples." We serve churches in both the West and non-West to become Great Commission churches, mobilizing them to "adopt" unreached people groups in prayer, outreach and to establish partnerships with nearby national church movements. As these partner churches collaborate together with a focus on unreached peoples, our AIMS training helps the nationals generate a "grass roots" mission movement of their own churches to raise up a prayer initiative, raise funds and send out their own missionaries. The end goal is an indigenous church planting movement in unevangelized, unreached areas. Since 1995, God has given us grace to see over five churches per day planted with this strategy. Praise God – to Him be the glory! We are hungry to see even more fruit.

We have already discussed the need for every Christian to be a Great Commission Christian. Since the church is comprised of these "living stones," individual Great Commission Christians are the building blocks of Great Commission churches. Local churches must be "wired" to generate global missions, so that "the earth will be filled with the knowledge of the glory of the Lord, as the waters cover the sea" (Hab 2:14). This is why our AIMS ministry focuses on helping churches, both in the West and the non-West become mobilized as strategic mission bases. In many cases, though, church renewal must happen first to deal with church malaise: "If renewal does not come to the church, the missions system as we know it is doomed. Continuing on its present path, the system would collapse under its own weight."[10] Renewal can unleash the awesome missions potential of the global church.

Remember - there are currently only 7.3 non-believers for every active believer. Here is another startling fact - with a goal of finishing the Great Commission by reaching all the remaining unreached people groups, we have churches enough. In 100 AD there was only one church per 12 unreached people groups. Now this has been dramatically reversed; there are over 1,000 churches per each unreached people group.[11] What a tremendous potential harvest force!

Several challenging issues face us in finishing the Great Commission. In missions we call this end vision of finishing "closure" or "the completion of the Great Commission in a measurable, observable trajectory by initiating a self-reproducing, indigenous church planting movement in every unreached people group." It is then that "the end will come" as seen in the promise and prophecy of Jesus in Matthew 24:14 (NASB):

> And this gospel of the kingdom will be preached in the entire world as a witness to all the nations (Greek ethne – "people groups"), and then the end will come.

Along with the issues we have discussed, there are several important trends affecting local churches and the entire Great Commission Community today. Author William Gibson wrote: "The future is already here – it's just not evenly distributed."[12] Understanding these trends is important, for as futurist Jay Gary states: "only as we understand the present, can we speculate on the possibilities of the future."[13]

Mission analyst Eric Swanson wrote an excellent article in the Leadership Network – ADVANCE Newsletter citing "Eight Trends That Will Shape the Future of Global Mission."[14] The following list of eight trends is his, but I have added supportive text and four other trends.

1) Mutuality

Globalization is bringing the world together in many ways, and several forces within globalization are positive for missions. Much of the "rugged pioneer" and independent, "go it alone" attitudes are fading. Missions today is from six continents to six continents. As servants of the Lord of Harvest, all nationalities are on a level playing field. Contextualized strategies demand that the indigenous churches take charge wherever possible. The new strategic process starts from the context of the target area, rather than from a board room in the West.

2) Partnering

This builds upon mutuality and seeks multi-cultural collaboration and synergy. The partners all bring their gifting, talents, cultural awareness and resources to the partnership table. This is not only money and personnel. It can also include training, holistic ministry, consultation and specific areas of expertise, such as technology, media, education, business, medicine, health care, agriculture, and the list goes on. Missiology is called "the mother of all theology" and also the "mother of all strategies," so mission partnerships must use every strategic, biblical means to advance God's kingdom. [15]

3) Investing In Leaders

God-called leaders are the foundation stones of building the Church. In many countries where I have taught local church missions and missions mobilization to national pastors, I have heard statements like this: "We've never heard this before" or "We thought missions was for white people." What pure joy it is to see these leaders respond to the biblical mandate and begin mobilizing their churches to reach unreached people groups. This kind of leadership development power shifts leaders into new levels of fruitfulness never experienced before.[16] Similar power shifts can happen when other types of specialized ministries are imparted to national leaders.

4) Combining Good Deeds and Good News

Westerners are shocked to the core of their being when they witness abject poverty in the developing world, particularly for the first time. This can be one of the benefits of short-term mission trips, if the short-termer applies kingdom principles and biblical principles to the poverty problem. The combination of good deeds and good news is called "holistic ministry." Good deeds only is humanitarian ministry and good news only is evangelism. The biblical words in the Hebrew and Greek for "whole" mean "the integrity of completeness, making everything the same color, perfect, undivided."[17] We see that holistic ministry means using every method and resource possible to advance God's kingdom. Evangelizing the poor without a response to their poverty is not completely integrous. Neither is humanitarian work without sharing the Gospel, whenever possible. A vision for advancing the Kingdom means that good deeds and good news are the "same color, undivided and manifest the integrity of completeness." In many cases humanitarian ministry is the "point of the arrow" to enter a resistant culture. Even if the target culture is very resistant, we should be praying that the "arrow" will somehow open the door for the gospel to be shared.

Almost fifty percent of the entire world's people live in poverty, ranging from the needy to those in abject poverty. The World Bank defines abject poverty as someone who lives on less than $375 USD per year; about twenty percent of the world's population (about one billion). The church should be concerned about all of them.[18] Further, 80-85% of the unreached people on planet earth are numbered among the poor. By all means possible, let us make the Kingdom power of God known to the poor and unreached with holistic ministry.

5) Greater Financial Accountability

Technology and international travel are allowing mission agencies and churches to hold their missionaries and national partners to more open accountability and wise stewardship of every dollar. This is an absolute must. I believe that the main factor causing poverty around the world is corruption – in business, international finance, politics and every other societal structure where money flows. Regrettably, it also impacts the Church and its mission cause.

David Barrett and Todd Johnson compile ongoing statistics showing the status of global mission, presence and activities.[19] They calculated that in mid -2007 global ecclestical crime totaled $24 billion and is projected to total $60 billion in 2025.[20] What a shock! This is money stolen, embezzled or misappropriated by the Church, church leaders, mission agencies, humanitarian organizations, missionaries, national leaders, etc. Another shocker! The income of global foreign missions in mid 2007 was $22 billion and is projected to be $60 billion in 2025. Ecclesiastical crime is greater than the giving to global foreign missions.[21]

These statistics are clear indicators that donors to the global missions cause must look for organizations and leaders, Western and non-Western, which adhere to spotless integrity. Mission projects and strategies should bear evidence of sustainability and not require ongoing, outside investment. The dependency of national organizations on Western funding is a negative trend in missions.

6) Business as Mission

This trend has many faces. Some missionaries use business as a front to gain access into a restricted access country. Others start new businesses in foreign countries both to support themselves and create to jobs in the receiving country. Even further, some business/missionaries train nationals in entrepreneurship, how to develop business plans, finance and business administration. These last two methodologies can contribute significantly to the economic development of the local culture and church. Business as mission does not have to be a macro-enterprise. It can be a micro-enterprise like a "store on the curb" or a sewing business in a single home. Some missionaries are adding micro-finance to this strategy. Small loans are made to small national enterprises with the re-payments kept in a fund for more loans. The success of this strategy has been superbly documented in an excellent book by Phil Smith and Eric Thurman entitled *A Billion Bootstraps: Microcredit, Barefoot Banking, and the Business Solution for Ending Poverty.*[22] Two fine sources for training nationals in entrepreneurship and business development are Harvest Field Corners and The Nehemiah Project.[23]

Some applications of business as mission are called tentmaking. Note the following definition and explanation:

> *Tentmaking, in general, refers to the activities of any Christian who, while functioning as a minister, receives little or no pay for his or her church work, and supports him or herself by additional, unrelated work. Specifically, tentmaking can also refer to a method of international Christian evangelism in which missionaries support themselves by working full time in the marketplace with their skills and education, instead of receiving financial support from a church. The term comes from the fact that the apostle Paul supported himself by making tents while living and preaching in Corinth (Acts18:3).*[24]

Even the "father of modern missions," William Carey (1761-1831) was a tentmaker. He was a factory owner and worked as a university professor, using these occupations to incarnate Christ in India and build churches and Christian institutions in that country.

7) Focus

In missions, focus means that the Great Commission community would set its sights like a rifle on a central target. I once met a pastor of a church of about 800-900 worshippers who, although exhibiting significant vision and passion, had a goal for his church to support at least one missionary in every country of the world at $25.00 per month. This was admirable, but inefficient and not strategic. Remember, there are only 7.3 non-believers in the world for every believer and over 1,000 Bible-believing churches for every unreached people group. What if we adopted a people-centered approach instead of country approach? This is what Edward Dayton and David Fraser advocated in their classic mission book, *Planning Strategies for World Evangelization*.[25] The church with an "missionary in every country" vision could harness more strategic energy and concentrate their resources better if they adopted one unreached people group in each of the unreached megaspheres – Muslim, Hindu, Buddhist, Tribal and non-Religious. This approach brings focus and galvanizes our resources in the praying, learning, giving, sending and going "personalizing" of the Great Commission that I discussed earlier. Then, what if ten, maybe even twenty-five churches from a local denomination or fellowship got together and partnered with known and integrous mission agencies and national churches that had different but synergistic objectives (humanitarian, business as missions etc.) and developed a unified plan and vision to initiate an indigenous, self replicating church planting movement in an adopted people group. This model is happening around the world through area partnerships like the Indian Missions Association and people group specific partnerships like one for the Bengali people of India.

Again, globalization helps us here. Modern technology and travel facilitates the communication process of these partnerships. I believe in this strategic process so fervently that four of our AIMS seminars highlight the people-centered approach. One of these seminars is "Final Focus," which is designed to guide local churches in how to adopt unreached people groups and partner with other churches, agencies, and national movements to initiate church planting movements within those peoples.[26]

I love the mountains and have climbed around 50 of the highest mountains in the U.S. and Europe. In my home state of Colorado, there are 54 mountains over 14,000 feet high. How do you successfully summit such targets? One mountain at a time, and for each mountain, one step at a time! The climber or team of climbers must persevere in climbing until they reach the top. Obviously this requires targeting, route finding, training, discipline, and most of all, focus to finish the climb. How will we finish the Great Commission? One unreached people group at a time!

8) Technology

This is one of the mega-forces in the globalization process that has increasing impact on the world day by day. The Church and mission agencies are using technology in creative and powerful ways. There are over 500 million computers currently in use by Christians, with an expected increase to 1.2 billion by 2025.[27] Souls are being saved all over the world, even in unreached people groups, via internet ministry. Add to this television, radio, films like the Jesus Film, and the printed word, and we see a phenomenal harvest being reaped, sometimes without Christians present. Christian broadcasting alone is reaching an audience of over 2.6 billion per month![28] Even so we still need "boots on the ground" whenever possible. Discipling and church planting, even if the new churches are in houses, are best done relationally.

My thanks to Eric Swanson for identifying these eight trends, but for the purpose of this chapter, I need to go further. Here are four more I feel are essential.

9) Globalization

This is a complex trend that is irrevocably shaping the future of missions. Globalization demands a new contextualization of our strategies and methods, while keeping the biblical content of our message the same. What is globalization? Michael Jaffarian speaks to this in an address to mission executives in Atlanta, September 2006:

• Globalization is the fruit of explosive advances in information and communications technology, the rise of the internet, advances in transportation, expansion of literacy and education.

• The internet allows for vast global contribution and access to global information and culture.

• Travel - there is an expanding global community of global culture brokers: people who understand many cultures from extensive, direct experience.[29]

To Jaffarian's definition, I add world migration. These globalization aspects can be positive for missions. There are an increasing number of people in our "global village" who want to learn English, Western business practices, hear international news and buy Western goods and services. Conversely, it seems like most of the items we buy in America are made in China, Indonesia, Honduras, Mexico, etc.

A colleague of mine was talking with several young Chinese men in Starbucks in a major Chinese city. They all came from unreached people groups and had never heard the Gospel, but were computer savvy, knew their favorite rock band from MTV and wanted more access to Western culture. Opportunity plus for the Gospel!

Air travel can take us from any international airport to any major city in the world within 12-24 hours. Most national leaders have internet capabilities or have access to an internet café. Indigenous, national ministries can raise funds from all over the world. This can be positive or negative. World migration has brought the mission field to our Western doorstep, and many of these millions of immigrants are from unreached areas. God has a purpose in globalization. Richard Tiplady in *One World or Many: The Impact of Globalization on Mission* states:

> *Globalization impacts every part of human life, including our cultural and religious existences. Since we are whole human beings embedded in communities, globalization has an effect on every aspect of our lives.*[30]

We need to be certain that we throw positive elements into the "stew" that advances God's end goal, His Kingdom established on earth. "We are not just a stick floating in the torrent. We are a hand throwing ingredients into the stew."[31]

10) Changing Mission Structures and Relationships

Church, Mission Agency, Training Institution, National Church: the list above defines four essential mission structures. Each one assumes they can work independently, but in the changing world of globalization and post modernism, can they work together in role identity and biblical unity without tripping over one another?

We have explained globalization, but what is postmodernism? This is a world of pervasive cynicism, distrust of authority, unbridled consumerism, media and advertising distractions, plurality and multiple options, and it can lead into self-centeredness. Daniel Yankelovich, a sociologist, wrote in *New Rules*: "By concentrating day and night on your feelings, potentials, needs, wants and desires and by learning to assert them more freely, you do not become a freer, more spontaneous, more creative self; you become a narrower, more self-centered, more isolated one. You do not grow, you shrink."[32] We must understand the core of the postmodern worldview because it impacts the structures and relationships of the entire Great Commission community. The older Boomers grew up in a "modern" world, but culture has shifted and the Busters and Gen Y folk have known only postmodernism.

How can the equippers in the church, mission agencies and training institutions challenge and activate this kind of generation to work toegther according to God's purposes? Clearly, we must encourage a renewal of the minds by the Word and the Spirit. This is a discipling issue. This generation needs a God-centered focus, a vision of His end goals, and passion for suffering humanity.

Globalization and postmodernism go hand in glove. Howard Synder in *Earth Currents* believes that the shift from modernism to postmodernism is "an inseparable part of the emerging global culture."[33] Postmodernism and globalization are probably the most aggressive of all of today's cultural currents.

Getting the postmodern generation to work with God's purposes is one thing, but another reality is the changing attitude of local churches toward mission agencies and training institutions. Can these three work together? One pastor said: "The local church doesn't need to be told what to do, but it needs to be helped by the missions agencies to do what she wants to do." [34] This kind of pastoral expression is common. Could postmodern attitudes affect some pastors as well? Many churches are establishing their own type of missions agency and training programs within their own church. This can be quite positive, if these churches do not reject the agencies and training institutions for the wrong reasons. A new appreciation of the role of all four of the mission structures needs to be established, so together a missions awakening can happen in this global, postmodern generation, and we work together according to the music of God's revealed purposes.

The equippers in the Great Commission Community need to ward off the negative implications of postmodernism and engage the current culture with the transforming power of the Word and the work of the Holy Spirit. All four identified structures of mission must model biblical unity and "stand on the shoulders" of one another to release all the gifting of all the Body of Christ. We dare not forget the vital role of the national church. They are integral in evangelizing the unreached, for they can go where no Westerner can go. They need our prayers and partnership. Many developing world missionaries go to precarious places. David Barrett has said that being a developing world missionary is the most dangerous job in the Church. About 175,000 Christians are martyred every year, most of them from the non-Western world.[35]

11) God Has Found A Few Good Men and Women – He Wants More!

In 1997, Jay Gary gave an address to the World Future Society entitled, "Ten Global Trends in Religion."[36] He was projecting into the 21st century when he identified one of these trends as "an increase of women in pastoral roles." This has already been a historic reality in missions, and it's increasing.

Loren Cunningham talks about a man who heard from God that He was about to raise up a harvest force that would be key to finish the Great Commission. As this man considered the statement, he thought, "Maybe the Chinese…Maybe some other people." The Lord finally said, "Women."[37] What a shock, for many people, even today, would consider this outrageous!

The early missionaries of the 18th century were primarily single men, but one of the female early pioneers was Ann Judson, wife of Adoniram Judson. She went to Burma with her husband, one of the first wives allowed, she fervently believed that her missionary calling was as valid as her husband's; her life proved this true. She founded schools for women and children and became an expert at translating the Bible and other Christian literature into the Burmese language. She paved the way for the acceptance of missionary wives doing their own ministries.[38]

Hudson Taylor's China ministry actively recruited women for ministry. In 1878, Hudson Taylor made a widely criticized move allowing single women, and later married women, to join his mission team in China. Taylor discovered that the only way to reach Chinese women was through other women. Women that had been barred for decades from active participation in ministry are now streaming out of the West to China and other countries.[39]

British Dr. Helen Rosevere was influenced by these brave women. After hearing the Gospel in college Helen committed her life to the Lord and discovered a deep longing to go to Africa to share Christ. "If Christ be God and died for me, then no sacrifice can be too great for me to make for Him," was her motto. In 1953, she arrived in the Congo to share the Gospel and train nationals in medicine. Her work was often discounted because she was single. After many internal struggles, she realized that serving God as a single woman was His plan for her life. By 1960, her work was bearing fruit, but political instability threatened the country. Many missionaries left, but Helen stayed. Eventually she was taken captive by the rebels who repeatedly abused and raped her. It was during this time that the Lord used her to minister His unconditional love to other Christian women who suffered the same fate. After her release, she returned to England for a time of recovery, but went back to Congo in a few months to continue her ministry until 1973. God not only changed many through Helen's life, but He transformed her life in the process.[40]

Another young woman from England, Jackie Pullinger, also took bold steps of faith to reach the world. In 1966, at 22 years of age, Jackie searched for a missions agency to send her to fulfill her calling as a missionary. Finding none, she used her own money and bought a one-way ticket to Hong Kong. She ended up in the Walled City, home to drug triads, drug addicts, prostitutes and criminals. Jackie began to simply tell these desperate people that Jesus loved them. She started a youth club where young men were transformed by Jesus. Then she started a rehabilitation center to disciple them. Eventually even the triad bosses began to support and protect her ministry. Now, more than 45 years later, Jackie still ministers in Hong Kong. Her rehabilitation center is one of the largest and most successful such ministries in the world. She says, "I went up to a man and said, 'Jesus loves you,' but I realized that it didn't mean anything unless I did it."[41]

Another woman with a powerful influence in missions today is American Heidi Baker. She and her husband, Rolland, have been missionaries for almost 30 years. As a teenager, Heidi experienced a powerful vision of Jesus calling her to be a missionary to Africa. Part of the Baker's original ministry was working in Hong Kong with Jackie Pullinger, but the Lord led them to Mozambique, one of the world's poorest countries. Their calling was to minister to the poorest of the poor. Heidi says, "The Beatitudes are God's recipe for revival. They are a portrait and description of Jesus. When we walk as Jesus walked, we will be blessed." They are experiencing revival in Mozambique and now oversee over 5000 churches that have been planted through their ministry.[42]

A further example is the "Back to Jerusalem" movement in China. Our AIMS team has trained hundreds of Chinese house church Christians who are raising up a missionary force to reach all the 452 unreached people groups of China, and then evangelize all along the Silk Road back to Jerusalem. A Chinese leader told me, "The 19th century was for British missions, and the 20th century for American missions, but the 21st century is for Chinese missions." Remarkably, about half of their missionaries are women!

12) Earthquakes and Volcanic Eruptions

This statement describes the burgeoning Pentecostal/Charismatic movement. This book is based on this trend. It seems like the Holy Spirit has His own tectonic plates and the powerful friction of these plates is producing a Pentecostal/Charismatic movement that is growing faster than the global population rate. There are now well over 603,000,000 believers in the group.[43] Yes, it's an earthquake and volcanic eruption both, and it is impacting the globe.

From this group flows the biblical emphasis on signs, wonders, miracles, healings and the other supernatural manifestations of the Holy Spirit. In world evangelization, this demonstrates the power of Christ along with proclaiming the truth about Christ. This combination of power and truth is the real hope of finishing the Great Commission. That's what this book is about – devour, incarnate and demonstrate power and truth through your life! I encourage you to be a Spirit-filled Great Commission Christian and help your church be a Great Commission Church. Let's be Finishers for God's glory!

Endnotes

1 Patrick Johnstone, Operation World (Gabriel Resources 21st Century Edition, 2001).

The evangelistic challenge in Mark 16:15.

The discipling/church planting challenge in Matthew 28:18-20.

The teaching challenge of Luke 24.

The missions challenge of John 20:21.

The global challenge of Acts 1:8.

2 Joshua Project: www.joshuaproject.net

3 James Rutz, Megashifts, (Colorado Springs, CO: Empowerment Press), p14.

4 Mission Frontiers, September-October 2009, p.30.

5 Joshua Project website.

6 Ibid.

7 James Rutz, op. cit. p. 15.

8 Mission Frontiers, op.cit. p. 30.

9 Jim Diehl, cited in http://home.snu.edu.

10 Paul McKaughan, Dellana O'Brien, William O'Brien, Choosing a Future for U.S. Mission, (Monrovia CA: MARC 1989), p. 4.

11 Mission Frontiers, op. cit. p. 32.

12 Eric Swanson, "Eight Trends that Will Shape the Future of Global Missions," 2010 www.pursuantgroup.com/ leadnet/advance/feb10s2a.htm.

[13] Jay Gary, "Ten Global Trends in Religions," http://www.wnrf.org/cms/tentrends.html.

[14] Ibid.

[15] McKaughan, O'Brien and O'Brien, *Choosing a Future for U.S. Missions* (Marc, 1998).

[16] The AIMS model of training national pastors in missions is called, "Equipping for the Harvest." For information in being part of this equipping ministry, even being trained how to do it yourself, contact AIMS at: www.aims.org

[17] Harris, Archer and Waltke, *Theological WordBook of the Old Testament* (Moody Publishers, 1980).

Also

W.E. Vine and Merrill F. Unger, *Vine's Complete Expository Dictionary of Old and New Testament Words* (Thomas Nelson, 1996).

Also

Geoffrey W. Bromiley, *Theological Dictionary of the New Testament* (Grand Rapids: Williams B. Eerdmans Publishing Company).

[18] Choosing a Future for U.S. Missions, op.cit. p. 21.

[19] David Barrett, George Kurian and Todd John, *The World Christian Encyclopedia* (New York: Oxford University Press, 2001).

David Barrett and Todd Johnson, World Christian Trends A.D. 30-2200 (Pasadena, CA: William carey Library Publishers, 2003).

[20] Todd Johnson, Status of Global Mission 2007: An Annual Update," *Lausanne World Pulse*, www.lausanneworldpulse.com/research.php/627/?pg=all.

[21] Ibid.

[22] Phil Smith and Eric Thurman, *A Billion Bootstraps: Microcredit, Barefoot Banking and the Business Solution for Ending Poverty* (New York: McGraw-Hill, 2007).

[23] *Harvest Field Corners*, http://hfci.org.

The Nehemiah Project International Ministries, http://www.nehemiahproject.org.

[24] "Tentmaking," *Wikipedia*, http://en.wikipedia.org/wiki/tentmaking

[25] Edward R. Dayton and David A. Fraser, *Planning Strategies for World Evangelization* (Grand Rapids: WM. B. Eerdmans Publishing Co, 1990).

[26] For information on the AIMS seminars, manuals, and consulting services see www.aims.org.

[27] Todd Johnson, Status of Global Mission 2007: An Annual Update," *Lausanne World Pulse*, www.lausanneworldpulse.com/research.php/627/?pg=all.

[28] ibid.

[29] Michael Jaffarian, michaeldawnd@earthlink.net.

[30] Richard Tiplady, *One World or Many?: The Impact of Globalisation on Mission* (Pasadena, CA: William Carey Library Publishers, 2003).

[31] Michael Jaffarian, op. cit.

[32] Jim Raymo, *Refections on Missionary Malaise*," EMQ, October 1997, pp. 442-6.

[33] Howard Synder, *Earth Currents: The Struggle for the World's Soul* (Nashville, TN: Abingdon Press, 1995).

[34] Choosing a Future for U.S. Missions, op. cit. p. 27.

[35] Todd Johnson, Status of Global Mission 2007: An Annual Update," *Lausanne World Pulse*, www.lausanneworldpulse.com/research.php/627/?pg=all.

[36] Jay Gary, op. cit.

[37] Loren Cunningham, "Releasing Women in Ministry," *YWAM*, www.ywampodcast.org.

[38] Dana L. Robert, "The Mother of Modern Mission," *Christian History*, www.christianitytoday.com/ch/2006/issue90/7.22.html.

[39] P. Lane Williams, "Christians in China," *Los Angels Chinese Learning Center*, http://chinese-school.netfirms.com/Christians-in-China.html.

[40] Rebecca Hickman, "Helen Roseveare," *The Traveling Team*, www.thetravelingteam.org/node/118.

[41] Howard Ingham, "Jackie Pullinger," *rejesus*, www.rejesus.co.uk/site/module/jackiepullinger/.

[42] Rolland Baker, *Iris Ministries*, www.irismin.org.

[43] Todd Johnson, Status of Global Mission 2007: An Annual Update," *Lausanne World Pulse*, www.lausanneworldpulse.com/research.php/627/?pg=all.

Chapter 15
DEVELOPMENT AID AS POWER EVANGELISM: THE MIEZE MODEL

" *The supernatural power of God enables, empowers, and accelerates ministry fruitfulness because it reveals God as He really is and compellingly demonstrates His goodness and love.* "

- Don Kantel

Sociologist Donald Miller notes that "a number of social theorists writing at the turn of the [nineteenth] century in Germany and France thought that religion would disappear by the end of the twentieth century."[1] And it's true that by the 1970s and 80s evangelism in the West had become hard work among the established traditional denominations, as the programmatic approach to church growth failed utterly. Over the same period, however, some conservative evangelical groups and a vast new renewal movement grew spectacularly, both in the West and, especially, in the developing nations of Asia, South America, and Africa. These churches and movements focused on the necessity of personal salvation and the fastest-growing among them were also committed to the active lordship of the Holy Spirit over Jesus' church and seeing His lordship demonstrated through supernatural signs, wonders, and miracles.

This renewal element embraces the worldwide Pentecostal movement, described by Peter Wagner as the "first wave" of the Holy Spirit. It also encompasses the amorphous charismatic movement, which missiometrician David Barrett cited as the leading edge of church growth entering the twenty-first century. Included in the latter are charismatic streams within mainline denominations - Wagner's "second wave" of the Holy Spirit in the twentieth century, as well as the exploding "third wave"[2] of postdenominational or "new paradigm"[3] churches (sometimes also called "neocharismatics," of which Barrett has identified at least 18,810 separate groups).[4] Taken together, this Pentecostal/Charismatic movement numbers some 700,000,000 globally (or 10% of the world's population) and is projected to reach 961,000,000 by 2025 (or more than 12% of the global population).[5] These numbers are all the more remarkable in light of the fact that Pentecostal/Charismatic Christians were almost nonexistent in 1900, constituting perhaps only one-fifth of one per cent of the world's population at the time (roughly 2,000,000 people).

All these movements are distinguished from mainline Christendom by their reliance upon the Person and gifts of the Spirit for victorious Christian living and fruitful ministry, and many of them also actively seek and experience supernatural signs and wonders which markedly accelerate their ministry fruitfulness. As noted in his chapter, Randy Clark reported that he had been approached in 2003 by an evangelical, non-charismatic missionary who had been delegated to contact him by a gathering of all the evangelical missionaries from the Sinai Peninsula. As the missionaries had been talking together, they made what was described as "a shocking discovery." Reflecting on their ministry experience in that region, which ranged from two to twenty-two years in length, they discovered not one of them had ever seen a Muslim accept Jesus Christ who hadn't first seen a healing, a miracle or had an angelic visitation. When they realized that, they said to one another, "What we've been doing isn't working. We must have the power of God."

There are countless possible strategies for evangelism and church growth; and one of the ministries of the Holy Spirit is to lead us to adopt the most fruitful strategy for any given situation or set of circumstances. In our contemporary world - where many minds and many countries are closed to the gospel - one of the most timely and effective strategies is an adaptation of the simple but profound biblical principle of a cup of cold water given in Jesus' name. As Jesus said in John 4:13-14, a cup of water by itself can only temporarily satisfy thirst: people will become thirsty again. But a cup of water in Jesus' name can be transformational! In many underdeveloped countries of the world today, Christian economic and social development workers, and programs offered in Jesus' name, can be a wedge into the cultural and spiritual darkness which have kept people in poverty and bondage. Development programs inspired by the Holy Spirit and offered unconditionally as tangible expressions of the love of God have the power to defeat strongholds and bring God's Kingdom and its goodness flooding into the lives and circumstances of families, communities, and regions.

Iris Ministries, under the leadership of Rolland and Heidi Baker, began working in remote northern Mozambique in 2002. The region was predominantly Muslim, with Catholics constituting a small minority - a hold-over from nearly 500 years of Portuguese colonial rule. The Portuguese era ended in 1975 following the war of independence and nearly 20 years of brutal civil war ensued, leaving the country in social and economic ruin. The chaos and bloodshed left over a million Mozambicans dead and left Mozambique statistically the poorest nation in the world by 1992. The Marxist Frelimo faction, which emerged victorious from the civil war and formed the first popularly elected government in 1994 under a new constitution, systematically set out to eliminate all religion from the land (a policy that was only abandoned some years later as generous offers of financial aid from the United States, Canada and countries of the European Union were tied to explicit expectations of continuing extension of democratic freedoms).

Pemba is the capital city of Cabo Delgado, northern-most province of Mozambique. With a population of 150,000, Pemba is the fourth largest city in the nation. But even in 2011, ninety percent of Mozambique's twenty-one million inhabitants still live in small towns and even smaller, often remote, villages. Over half the total population lacks access to safe, potable water. Few outside the cities have electricity. Illiteracy is rife; school attendance is very low; unemployment stands at a staggering 85%; and the statistical life-expectancy is a shocking 36.7 years in northern Cabo Delgado - only 42 nationally.

When we know the odds are overwhelmingly stacked against us, it should help disabuse us of any thought that ministry advancement or success depends on our own efforts or abilities. That was certainly the case when Iris Ministries began its work in northern Mozambique and, in particular, when I began working in the village of Mieze. Heidi and Rolland Baker concentrated their initial evangelistic efforts in Cabo Delgado Province within the city of Pemba. After planting a few small churches in Pemba, Iris held its first evangelistic outreach outside the city in the rural village of Mieze (pronounced Mee-AY-zee), a village of 20,000 in 2004. As usual, Iris had first secured the permission of the village chief to present the JESUS Film, but the crowd that gathered in Mieze was so hostile that the team had to pack up quickly and literally flee for their lives. All was not lost though and Iris did manage to establish a small church in Mieze under the leadership of Pastor Joao Juma. By 2006, that tenuous start had grown to a vibrant church of about 125 regular worshipers.

In 2005, my wife Elizabeth and I left our home on Prince Edward Island in eastern Canada to join the Bakers and Iris in their new work in Pemba. A short time later, our home church in Prince Edward Island decided to visit Iris for its first-ever missions trip. They also decided they would like to focus their visit on a village setting and try to leave behind a tangible blessing that would continue to make a difference long after their team had returned to Canada. The village decided upon was Mieze and the project was the construction of a playground for village children.

The team's visit was a watershed for both the village and the Prince Edward Island church. Neither has been the same since. The playground was such a big hit that the Mieze primary school called after a few days to ask if it could be closed during school hours because so many children were skipping school to play there.

My encounter with the people of Mieze - especially with the children - had left me very broken. I hadn't been confronted by that depth of poverty on such a wide scale before. A UN survey of child suffering a few years ago ranked Mozambique fourth worst in the world; the only three nations whose children suffered more were experiencing protracted war or civil unrest. I realized, for example, that most people in Mieze only had food of any kind once a day and many went days with no food. They all had bloated bellies filled with intestinal worms, so whatever limited nutrition they did receive had to be shared with the parasites. There was only the most limited access to potable water, and because it took most of a day for women to walk to a water source and then return with a heavy 20-liter container of water on their head, no one was drinking enough water to stay healthy. As a result, children's skin was dry and cracked like alligator skin due to chronic dehydration; healthy babies frequently died from dehydration after only a short episode of simple diarrhea. Villagers were also tormented by skin mites, called scabies, and scratching the itchy, fiery bites with dirty hands inevitably resulted in infected sores. There was also a large and growing number of orphans and extremely vulnerable children in Mieze due to the ravages of HIV/AIDS. Moreover, most villagers regularly got malaria and many died, particularly the elderly and very young. The people of Mieze - especially the 10,000 or more children under 15 - were typically dirty, smelly and dressed in tattered rags for clothing, with the youngest and poorest naked or nearly so.

Mieze and Mozambique are only part of the much broader picture of global poverty in the twenty-first century. In a world of general affluence and abundance, the gap between the rich and poor is widening at an alarming rate. The comforting "trickle-down" theory that the poor benefit automatically and inevitably from the advancement of the rich has proved statistically untenable. Serious reflection on the real plight of the world's poor paints a grim picture of widespread injustice, suffering, deprivation and dehumanization on a scale unimaginable even two generations ago. Oxford economist Paul Collier, writing about the problem of global poverty, notes that the last three decades of the twentieth century were a period of unprecedented economic growth in the world. Despite this, a billion people in the fifty poorest nations (including most countries in Africa) not only failed to advance economically during this period, they actually experienced absolute economic decline, such that "by the turn of the millennium they were therefore poorer than they had been in 1970."[6]

Any illusion one might have entertained about how advanced the world is today is put to rest by the voices of the poor themselves describing their life and conditions - or by the impassioned reason of radical Christians calling the church to rise in prophetic condemnation of injustice and in defence of the defenceless in this world.

Author Jayakumar Christian compiled an index of power relationships which play out between the powerless poor and the economic, social, and political elites that use and abuse them for their own gain. The powerlessness and vulnerability which characterizes the poor manifests itself in their utter hopelessness: "Hopelessness [among the poor] prevents meaningful action in the present...and without a 'minimum of hope, we cannot so much as start the struggle'...this hopelessness perpetuates powerlessness, and powerlessness in turn perpetuates hopelessness."[7] A study of poverty in South Africa published in 2001 further observes that "poverty is not simply inadequate income; rather it is a condition of being which can be described as crushing, dehumanizing...the poor are those who have come to doubt the inherent value of their humanity, those who have been systematically broken in every aspect of their being."[8]

My own work among poor village children and families in Mieze and elsewhere more than confirms these observations. Hopelessness is the most telling characteristic of the extremely poor and vulnerable, followed inevitably by passivity. Prior to any intervention on our part, they know only suffering and misery: chronic hunger and thirst, sickness, nakedness, violence, abuse, the inability to provide for themselves or for their own children and family, no possibility of attending school, miserably primitive and inadequate shelter, utter boredom, early and sudden death - with absolutely no prospect of anything ever changing for the better. If they have ever allowed themselves to hope in the past, they have typically seen those hopes dashed every time. So they have learned to protect themselves from such disappointment by never hoping again. Their faces do not reflect pain or hunger; in fact, their faces do not reflect anything vital. They are expressionless, dehumanized, sitting in the dust as life passes them by. People created in the image of God, who have been reduced by extreme and protracted poverty to this level of dehumanization, are simply no longer able to help themselves. Outside intervention is essential to restore their humanity and create a glimmer of hope.

When my wife and I were serving with Iris in the south of Mozambique in 2002, we happened to discover that there was a large refugee camp located on a remote, abandoned military base some distance away. By agreement with other African nations, Mozambique had accepted several hundred refugees dislocated by conflict in Rwanda and other countries. The refugees had been transported involuntarily to this isolated encampment with the expectation this was only a temporary arrangement. Three years later they were still there, with no prospect of change or improvement. The government made one monthly food delivery which was barely adequate for two weeks, and the people had no money or other resources whatsoever. So they just sat there starving, with no medical care, unable to communicate with surviving family or friends, in utter boredom, despair and hopelessness.

When we learned of their existence, we took truckloads of people and food and made our way to their encampment. We spoke with them in English and French, worshipped together and distributed food from ragged tent to ragged tent. When we left, we said we'd return the following week.

When we returned, we were enthusiastically welcomed as we approached. The encampment had been cleaned up and people had obviously put on whatever "best" clothing they had left. They had also done an inventory of residents to guide the food distribution so that each family would receive a portion appropriate to their number of family members. The worship and singing was noticeably more enthusiastic and much of it was led by the refugees themselves this time.

When we returned the following week, it was clear that some leaders were emerging from among the people and we realized for the first time that there were a number of professionals among the refugees. Several teachers had fixed up a dilapidated building and begun teaching classes to the children. Two doctors had opened a tiny infirmary and begun treating patients; they requested some basic medicines and a stethoscope to improve what they could offer. A child care center had been set up by some mothers so that others were freed to do other useful things for the community. They also began holding regular worship times throughout the week.

The lesson was immediately clear. The oppression of their poverty and helplessness had robbed these people of their essential humanity, and it required compassionate intervention from outside to "set the prisoners free" - spiritually even more than materially. What we see on the surface may suggest that poverty of such an extreme nature is material and economic, but it is also fundamentally spiritual in nature and origin. And this becomes undeniably evident when the result of such poverty is deep oppression, hopelessness and despair. People cease to believe their lives have any value or that their very existence matters to anyone one way or the other.

The Bible says God is love (agape), and that Satan is the complete opposite. The power of God's Kingdom is the power of God's love (1 Cor 4:20). Kingdom love is transformational, it is revolutionary, it signals the very presence of God as loving Father, redeeming Son, and sanctifying and empowering Spirit. However, the present world order in which more than 30,000 children die every day from preventable causes, in which the wealthiest 225 individuals are richer than the poorest three billion, and in which more than a billion are chronically hungry and malnourished, is nothing less than a sinful perversion of God's good creation. The UN Development Program's Human Development Index, for example, shows such vast disparities as a statistical life expectancy in Mozambique of less than half Japan's 82.7 years or a Gross Domestic Product in Mozambique of $802 (adjusted for purchasing power parity to the US dollar) which is less than one percent of Liechtenstein's $85,382!

Economic and human development programs drawn up by committees and ratified by nations can do some good in alleviating immediate suffering, but we need to recognize the implications of saying that poverty is a spiritual problem as much as a material one. Satanic principalities and powers are able to wreak such devastating suffering in parts of the world where God has not historically been acknowledged and where deep sins have been committed (such as slavery and human sacrifice) and not spiritually atoned for. However, when God's love is released into such a region and when Christians come in humility and love to serve the poor and bind up the broken-hearted, the pall of spiritual darkness begins to lift. The darkness of evil must flee as the brilliant light of the supernatural power of God's love breaks in. The terrible hopelessness on the faces of the poor begins to change to hopefulness. Those in authority begin to respect the poor. Poor children begin to dream of a brighter future, and the sovereign rule and reign of God—the Kingdom of God—begins to bring territory under the goodness of God's realm.

The mission of the church is to reflect the mind and heart of God in the world. Good works done in Jesus' name are a compelling witness to the reality of God's love and God's love is the "power" which demonstrates the reality of His Kingdom to a spiritually bankrupt and needy world. Ronald Sider observes that Jesus' "extensive engagement with the poor and disadvantaged contrasted sharply with the style of His contemporaries."[9] The message of Jesus' words and life could not be more pointed, and the Bible makes it abundantly clear that God is for the poor.

I began working in Mieze in the latter part of 2006. I believed that God was calling me to begin serving that village in Jesus' name and that He alone would be responsible for the outcome - provided, of course, that He alone also received all the credit! Since the human needs all around me were so overwhelming, had I not had that assurance I think would have been catatonic within a few days. We had also received strong prophetic words from three different and credible sources painting a huge picture of God's plans and purposes for Mieze. Each person independently said essentially the same thing at salient points, even using identical imagery and words. To be honest, because the prophetic picture was so startlingly different from the immediate reality, I scarcely took the first speaker seriously. When nearly the same prophetic words were offered by two others within a matter of weeks, however, God had my attention.

What followed certainly didn't begin as a clear and grand vision. Rather, it was a matter of responding in my weakness out of obedience to God to try to meet pressing human needs with the compassion of Jesus for the poor and suffering. I believe authentic vision is often, if not usually, like that. If God had downloaded His full plan and purposes for Mieze, my head would have exploded. Instead, he basically pointed to my right foot and told me to put it in front of my left foot. Then He directed me to put my left foot in front of my right foot. I went forward by baby steps, attempting to meet the real and immediate needs of real people in Jesus' name as I confronted them.

I began by driving out to Mieze several times a week, sitting on the tailgate of my pickup with a cardboard box of simple medical supplies, offering whatever help I could to those who quickly lined up when they saw me arrive. Whether it was an aspirin, a bandage, scabies lotion, or worm medicine, each one received my care, my love, and prayer in Jesus' name. Sometimes it meant driving people to the provincial hospital in Pemba or to our own clinic at the Iris Base for further help. Typically, the back of my truck quickly filled with kids who just wanted to be around where something good was happening. Relationships were formed, and Sunday church attendance started to increase noticeably.

In time, missionary colleagues and visitors with a medical background joined in - and then took responsibility for - what I came to dignify as our "medical outreaches." Conservatively, at least 14,000 village people have received a touch of Jesus' love through these medical outreaches up to the time of writing in mid-2011. There have been many miraculous healings, like the man who came complaining of pain in his hip. When two visiting nurses examined him, it became obvious that one leg was a couple of inches shorter than the other. In fear and trembling they laid hands on him and began to pray in Jesus' name and then watched in wonder as Jesus caused his short leg to grow to the same length as his other one and he could walk without pain. There is also, always, the element of spiritual warfare. Babies sometimes arrive with fevers and headaches that can't be traced to obvious natural causes. Then we find the baby has been taken to the local witch doctor and is wearing some kind of fetish. When we explain the problem and ask the mother's permission to remove the fetish, we see babies' condition instantly restored to normal.

The scabies problem was widespread among the poor in Mieze and elsewhere. Our nurse-physician at the Pemba Base at the time told me she had tried valiantly to make headway in bringing relief to village people, but she had finally given up because people would put the same unwashed clothing back on and sleep on the same worn grass mat and quickly become reinfested. However, at Mieze I was finding that one application of scabicide almost always got rid of the problem permanently and never did it require more than two applications. After a couple of years, it seemed that scabies had disappeared entirely from the village - they are no longer to be found on people there. There's simply no natural explanation for this. To God be the glory!

In June 2011, we held an Iris regional conference at Mieze and at least 3,500 people gathered for the three days, many sleeping on the ground overnight. Randy Clark spoke on healing one evening and then began ministering healing in Jesus' name to the huge crowd. An eight-month-old baby was brought to Randy for prayer. She had been born without pupils in her eyes and was totally blind. Randy prayed for awhile, then passed the baby to some students to continue praying. Then Heidi Baker began to pray for little Albertina, who by then had closed her eyes. Heidi held her facing her mother and told her mother to call her name. Little Albertina opened her eyes; she had big beautiful brown pupils in both eyes and could see her mother for the first time!

It has been the practise for several years that when someone in the village becomes so sick and weak that he or she is expected to die, relatives and friends often bring the dying person to the Mieze church building and lay the person on a grass mat near the front of the church. All day long, people will go in and pray for the sick person. And very frequently the "dying" person is able to get up and return home, healed in Jesus' name.

These days, many poor people travel to our medical outreaches at Mieze from distant villages. The small amount of money it costs them to travel on the crowded "chapas" (minibuses) is a huge sacrifice for people with almost no money at all and they often drive past one or more government-run rural health centers to get to our clinic. When we ask why they have gone to the trouble and expense of coming to Mieze the answer is always the same: they've heard about the miracles and that's why they've come!

Access to potable water was a pressing challenge when we began our Mieze work. Iris Ministries is drilling wells in many rural villages, but because of Mieze's proximity to the Indian Ocean, every attempt to drill a well in Mieze has resulted in brackish water unfit for drinking. However, the water main carrying the water supply for the city of Pemba from its source passes right through Mieze. We secured permission from the water utility to tie into their system and ran 800 meters of underground pipe to provide water from two simple garden taps located in front of the Mieze church. Now women come all day long to get water for their families and to socialize. People of all ages in that part of the village are now drinking enough water to stay healthy; the dry, cracked skin condition formerly caused by chronic dehydration has disappeared completely and there is a marked improvement in people's health and well-being in general.

Early in 2007, I began talking to Mieze Pastor Joao Juma about the possibility of building accommodation for orphans and vulnerable children in the village. A few weeks later during the medical outreach, Pastor Juma showed me five little girls and asked if they could be considered for admission to the orphan village when it was ready. The girls were sisters ranging in age from 10 to 1-year-old twins. Pastor Juma explained that the girls' mother had died during the birth of the twins a year earlier. Their father had cared for his five daughters but he, too, had died. Then their grandmother had taken care of the girls, but she also had die - all within one year. The girls were being cared for by two very poor village women, but they were all so poor they were severely malnourished and the twins were close to death. I said we had to begin feeding these children immediately, so with the financial support of Iris Ministries Canada we began providing food, powdered formula and medical care for these children. Even two weeks later when a visiting pediatrician saw the twins, she didn't think they were going to survive. Today the twins are healthy, robust 5-year-olds, still living with one of the village women but being cared for financially by our Mieze Project. The three older girls are residents in the children's village which we opened later that year. A year ago, during a time of testimonies in the Mieze church, the village woman went forward with one of the twin girls and publicly thanked God and the church for their intervention and support for the two girls, without which, she said, the twins would certainly have died.

From that beginning, a village feeding program evolved for orphans and vulnerable children in Mieze and surrounding communities. We currently provide full nutrition for over 250 children, many of whom could not survive without our support. We also provide powdered formula for babies whose mothers cannot supply breast milk. At any given time, we have about thirty babies in this program; and most of these babies would have died without our help.

Somewhere along the way, I began to realize we were not simply acting in response to unconnected needs, but rather that God was sovereignly unfolding a wonderful vision for compassionate ministry that was making Jesus widely known and respected. We now refer to this vision as the "Mieze Model for Village Transformation" and it is chronicled at www.harvestinafrica. com.

As we were preparing to build some accommodation for village orphans and vulnerable children, I was given $15,000 by a foundation in California. I thought we could probably build a couple of simple bamboo, mud, and grass structures for some children with that sum. Almost immediately the Lord spoke clearly to me and said, "Build for the future, not for the past." I recognized that what I had in mind certainly didn't reflect the future and that God was confirming His Jeremiah 29:11 promise for these children - that He had a plan for their lives, to give them hope and a future.

So we began to plan and build permanent concrete buildings with high airy ceilings, electricity, and running water. And as the building progressed, the funds were always provided as needed.

It was amazing to be present as the children began to arrive in small groups over several days in November 2007. These were truly the least of the least: extremely poor and most without any immediate living family members. Very few had had any previous opportunity to go to school. They arrived with all their earthly possessions, which in most cases consisted of nothing more than the worn clothes they were wearing. Not one had a toy or a teddy bear or anything of the sort. They were shown to their shared room and to their own bed. Not one of them had ever slept on a bed or a mattress before. None had ever had three meals in a single day before. They had never flipped a switch and had lights come on or turned a tap and had water come out. Most had absolutely no idea what a toilet was for or how to use it and almost none of these kids had ever even see themselves in a mirror before. They all spent a lot of time in the first few weeks in front of the mirrors in their rooms getting used to what they looked like. One of the biggest novelties was the shower rooms. We discovered the kids were showering five or six times a day for the sheer joy of feeling clean water washing over their bodies.

Christmas was just a few weeks away and we quickly realized these kids had never heard the "Christmas Story," even though many had already given their lives to Jesus. They were filled with wonder hearing about the angelic annunciation to Mary and the birth of the Lord of Glory in a humble stable and asked to hear the story over and over again. Elizabeth and I prepared individual gift bags for the children for Christmas Day and were humbled to realize that none of these kids had ever received a gift of any kind before and none had ever before had a piece of clothing that was new.

We named the new children's village the "Village of Love," and that turned out to be prophetic as it continues to be saturated with the love of the Father. Many visitors remark on the palpable love they experience in the very atmosphere, as well as in the children themselves. In fact, a couple of years ago a child psychiatrist from the UK was visiting Iris and spent half a day at Mieze. After a few hours of observing and interacting with the children she came to me in tears. She knew enough about the background of deprivation, neglect, abuse, and suffering these kids had come from to know what to expect. Instead, she found happy, well-adjusted, loving children who were playing together, sharing with one another and eagerly enjoying the affection of complete strangers who were visiting their center. She said what she was seeing in these beautiful children went against everything her professional training had taught her. The supernatural love of God can reverse the effects of the devil's worst and has the power to utterly transform from the inside out.

In His goodness, God has supernaturally multiplied food on at least four occasions in Mieze. On the first occasion, in January 2007, I had taken a team of medical personnel to Mieze to assist with our medical outreach. Our makeshift "clinic" was a slightly shaded area alongside the original Iris church building. As usual, dozens of adults and seventy or more children gathered, many seeking medical attention, others socializing and the children playing on the recently constructed playground equipment.

After a couple of hours in the heat and dust, I gave Pastor Juma some money to send an older boy to the market to buy some cookies and juice powder as a rare treat for these impoverished and malnourished children. When the drink was prepared, Juma instructed the children in their Makua tongue to form two lines to receive their cookies and then to proceed toward the playground to receive a cup of juice. He began to pray in exuberant thanksgiving for this gift, and the children joined in loudly and enthusiastically.

The two bags of cookies had been dumped into a clear plastic bag and Pastor Juma was about to begin distributing them. He asked me whether we should give two or three cookies to each child. I looked at the bag and then at the two long lines and imagined how disappointing it would be if the cookies ran out before the children at the end had received any. "Two," I said. Juma nodded in agreement.

I was only a few feet away, observing the various medical stations, answering questions and watching the kids scamper happily toward the playground clutching their two cookies. Then I noticed the bag of cookies was still very full. Juma noticed my look, raised his hands in a gesture of surprise and began giving three cookies to each child. A few minutes later, I looked again: the bag was still full and we both began to grin. Our God was doing something marvelous before our very eyes! The kids who had quietly taken their place at the back of the line and waited their turn were rewarded with handfuls of cookies. Still the bag was full. Juma gave more cookies to every child in sight and then went around to the several dozen adults and gave them large handfuls of cookies. And when we couldn't find anyone else to give cookies to, Juma held up the bag which was still as full as at the beginning. We both praised God for His miraculous provision and love!

A second occasion in April of the same year was similar to the first. I went to Mieze to do repairs on the children's playground and gave Pastor Juma some money to buy some cookies and juice for a treat for the children. The cookies were in one clear plastic bag about the size of a small plastic grocery store bag. The drink was in three plastic wash basins about five inches deep. This time, the children were seated in neat rows inside the tiny church building, and when everything was ready, there was extended prayer of gratitude to God by Pastor Juma and all the children for this unexpected blessing.

Again, Pastor Juma asked me how many cookies I thought he should give to each child. I sized up the situation and said, "Three." As he distributed the cookies to each child, I counted the children: 45. Other helpers were following, distributing plastic cups of the juice to the kids who already had their cookies. I thought there would be some cookies left over for a second round, but I had my doubts about the juice. When all the kids had received their cookies, Juma held up the bag to me - and it was clearly as full as when he began! We both started shouting "Hallelujah!" and I motioned Juma back to the first row to start again. This time he was giving four or five or more cookies to each kid. Their cheeks were bulging with cookies and they were stuffing them into all their pockets. I also noticed that at least another 15 kids came in during this time and all 60 or so received another four or five cookies. That's well over 350 cookies in total and at the end, the cookie bag was still as full as at the beginning!

The juice supply also multiplied. The helpers gave a cup to each of the original 45 kids, and then they too went back to the first row and started over. The second time, 60 kids received a cup of juice and all three basins still had lots of juice when they were finished! Pastor Juma led the children in nearly an hour of spontaneous, joyful worship and praise.

I had already spent considerable time reflecting on the January miracle during a few weeks when Elizabeth and I were back in Canada for a break and I wondered what it all signified (besides the extravagant goodness and love of God!). Why children's cookies when there is so much suffering all around? In fact, one of the first things I learned when I returned from Canada was that Pastor Juma's only son, two-year-old Moises, had died two weeks earlier. I immediately went out to Mieze and Juma and I wept together. He explained that he had had to choose to reject bitterness and embrace joy in the face of this devastating loss.

As I witnessed the outpouring of praise by Pastor Juma and the children in response to this further miracle, I began to understand. I noticed that several of the songs were being led by young children. I recognized many of the children as coming from Muslim families and they were singing and worshiping with such joy. Juma called on two 9-year-old girls to pray and they prayed with a maturity, intimacy and fervour that made me think I was the child. I think what the Lord showed me through these miracles is that if revival is to come it will be through the poor - especially through poor children like these precious children at Mieze. That's why God is allowing them to experience His presence and power breaking through the suffering of their daily reality. When revival comes through "the least of these," God alone will get the glory.

The third occasion took place a month later and had the most witnesses who actually realized what was taking place as it was happening.[10] I guess it's only natural to question the supernatural. Sometimes we doubt ourselves, wondering if we really saw or experienced what we thought we did. Sometimes we doubt our sources. Maybe the reports were exaggerated, wishful thinking or based on coincidence or misinformation. But the truth is that we often actually doubt God Himself. Our Western mindset has convinced us that we live in a natural, cause-and-effect universe and that the supernatural isn't real, that true miracles not only don't happen, they can't happen. This anti-supernatural mindset is what the Bible calls unbelief. It was enough to prevent Jesus from doing many miracles in Nazareth and it's enough to limit the Spirit of God's activity in the Western world today.

In Africa, there is a different prevailing mindset. Of course, the objective reality doesn't differ from one culture to another, but cultural and religious beliefs do vary widely. Hundreds of millions of people in sub-Saharan Africa believe that reality is basically spiritual and that spirits control or influence the natural realm. The problem is that the spiritual powers most Africans traditionally believe in are evil, deceptive, tormenting and demonic. Millions of Africans live in superstition and fear and most have never been introduced to their loving heavenly Father and the Lord Jesus Christ who died and rose again to release us from bondage to evil and death.

In his landmark study, *Christianizing the Roman Empire*, Yale professor and secular historian Ramsay MacMullen concluded that the two most convincing evidences for the veracity of the Christian message in the first centuries after Christ were the love and care the young Church demonstrated for those in need - and the abundant accounts of supernatural miracles![11] Interestingly, during the early stages of the Reformation in the sixteenth century, the Catholic Church challenged the credibility of the Reformers' message, not so much on doctrinal or ecclesiastical grounds, but by saying, "Show us your miracles." Despite the irony of the situation, their own history had taught clearly that God can be expected to authenticate His word and His work by supernatural signs and miracles.

When we tell Africans about Jesus and God's love for them, the only question they really need answered is which spiritual reality is more powerful - which should they give their life to? It is very like the situation Elijah faced when confronted by the prophets of Baal. This is God's battle, as it clearly was in Elijah's case also, and only God can answer the ultimate question in a person's heart. One of the reasons there is such an abundant spiritual harvest taking place in Africa today is that God is regularly confirming His word and His witness by supernatural signs and wonders, just as in the Book of Acts (cf. Jn 1:50).

In our own work in Africa over the years, the Lord has confirmed His word and His reality with signs and miracles on a regular basis. Our experience is that these moments when "heaven invades earth" are more "normal" when we are breaking new ground for the gospel. As the church becomes established in an area, these kinds of dramatic demonstrations of the supernatural seem to become somewhat less frequent, though they never cease (thankfully!) and we continue to pray in faith for the impossible! This is likely because God uses the miraculous as a dramatic demonstration of His reality to call people out of spiritual darkness. Once converted, the journey to maturity has more to do with personal spiritual discipline and building our relationship of faith and love with God. We are meant to walk more by faith and less by sight, whereas the realm of the miraculous is more in the realm of experience, of sight.

In the annals of Iris Ministries, there were many instances of the dead being raised in the early years - more than fifty, in fact. There have been dramatic healings numbering in the many hundreds, including blind eyes being opened, deaf hearing, dumb speaking, and many forms of lameness and deformity being supernaturally healed. These wonderful divine interventions continue to occur with some regularity, though in general, they seem to be more prevalent when we are taking new territory for the Lord. I have witnessed a few of these miracles at close enough hand that I have absolutely no doubt about what I saw. I was two feet from a blind man and watched his milky pupils change to a solid colour - he could suddenly see clearly. I've watched the indescribable excitement in young village children when one of their friends who had been totally deaf from birth could suddenly hear and repeat sounds and words. I've held a boy's badly broken forearm and watched the arm straighten and be completely healed as I prayed. Of course, there have been thousands of testimonies of headaches and pains in legs, stomachs and backs healed in response to believing prayer. We thank God for every such instance, but admittedly these are more difficult to verify objectively. The same is true of women and couples who receive prayer to conceive. We have had the joy of dedicating a number of babies who have come in seeming response to such prayer, but it's next to impossible to prove conclusively that these are supernaturally aided conceptions.

For all who believe God does supernaturally heal and perform other similar miracles today, the most challenging theological and pastoral question, then, is why God heals or intervenes in the natural order sometimes, but not all the time. At one level, of course, this is an unanswerable question. The finite cannot comprehend the infinite. We can only know about God what God reveals about Himself, and God doesn't happen to have included an extensive primer on healing and miracles in the Bible. The Bible certainly testifies to the reality of healing and other miracles, but it mostly does so anecdotally, so we are still left with our questions. Of course, when we are praying for miracles - especially for healing - we are usually motivated by a strong emotional desire to see someone or something get better. We are gripped by an immediate need, and that understandably shapes our perspective and drives our prayers. But God's perspective is much broader; in fact, it's universal and eternal. The immediate and temporal good we are praying for may be eclipsed in God's perspective by a higher and eternal good.

Moreover - and this is a perspective specifically expressed in at least a few biblical accounts - the higher purpose attributed to healings and other supernatural interventions is often (and perhaps always)primarily more to do with God's revelatory purposes than with meeting man's immediate needs. For example, in Exodus 6:6-7, the Lord says, "I will bring you out from under the yoke of the Egyptians. I will free you from being slaves to them...Then you will know that I am the Lord your God..." The Lord is not saying, "I will free you so you will no longer be in bondage to the Egyptians" - He's saying, "I will free you so you will know I am the Lord your God." Similarly in John 9:2-3 we read, "'Rabbi, who sinned, this man or his parents, that he was born blind?' 'Neither this man nor his parents sinned,' said Jesus, 'but this happened so that the work of God might be displayed in his life.'" In other words, this man is about to be healed of his blindness not so that he will be able to see but so that his healing will stand as a testimony to God and His deeds. And in John 10:38, Jesus says, "...believe the miracles, that you may know and understand that the Father is in me..."

A further important theological reflection in talking about healing is to consider the relationship of healing prayer and miracles to the Kingdom of God. The Kingdom is a realm and it is the realm of complete and perfect submission to the sovereign rule and reign of God. God's Kingdom is perfect by definition, because it is God's Kingdom. In heaven, the Kingdom is both perfect and complete, but on earth, while it is perfect by definition, it is not yet complete. There is still much opposition to God's Kingdom and much of what has volition is not in willing submission to God's rule and reign. In God's future, perfect and complete Kingdom there will be no opposition, no sickness or death, no injustice, no suffering - indeed, neither male nor female. But that doesn't describe our present earthly reality, does it? That's why Jesus taught us to pray in the Kingdom, that it might increasingly be "on earth, as it is in heaven."

Moreover, since God is eternal He exists in a realm that stands outside of time. He created time as a construct to measure the passage of linear events in human history. We experience life in this linear fashion and we use time to mark the chronological relationship of events, including the passage of our own physical life from birth to death. But at the consummation of all things, time will be no more. The redeemed of the Lord will have passed fully from time into eternity, and there will no longer be a consciousness of the passing of what we now call time. The point of this is to say that because God exists outside of the boundaries of space and time, He sees everything as existing in the eternal present. As difficult as this is to begin to grasp, that means that God sees everything taking place simultaneously, without reference to time-related categories of past, present, and future. At this moment, God can see Rome burning nineteen hundred years ago and the future birth of my great, great grandchildren. This may help us understand how God can know the end from the beginning without violating free will.

In God's future everything will be perfect. In my heavenly bodily existence, I will be perfect - whatever exactly that may mean. But the important point is that God sees that already: God sees me that way already. So when I ask for prayer to restore my fifty percent hearing loss, I'm really asking God to reach forward to the perfect and complete "me" that He has in view in His future Kingdom and apply that aspect of eternity and Kingdom completeness to my deficient or suffering condition in my present earthly being: "On earth, as it is in heaven!" So prayer for healing is Kingdom prayer, but we have to remember in framing such petitions what was said above: the higher purpose attributed to healings and other supernatural interventions is often - and perhaps always - primarily more to do with God's revelatory purposes than with meeting man's immediate needs. We are always free to ask; but to ask anything in Jesus' name is to ask what is in accordance with God's self-revelatory purpose first and foremost. I think that's why in Iris Ministries we see the most miracles occurring in the places where God is least known.

When we experienced the two occasions when food was supernaturally multiplied for the poor Mieze children, I wrote enthusiastically about these remarkable events to our own friends and supporters, one of whom was John Arnott, the recognized leader of the Toronto Blessing Renewal. As it happened, John's daughter Vicki (whom I didn't know at the time) was organizing a large group to visit Iris Ministries at our base in Pemba, Mozambique. After reading my account of the multiplication of food for children, John put Vicki in touch with me by email. I remember Vicki asking if I thought God might do it again at Mieze during their visit. My response was simply to encourage her to spend half a day there with her team to meet the children and to organize games and activities for them.

As a result, on a Saturday morning in May 2007, I took Vicki Arnott and her group out to Mieze for a visit. They had been playing games with the kids for a couple of hours when it occurred to Vicki to ask me when the kids would be going home for lunch. I explained that these kids were so poor many would only have one meal of boiled rice a day or perhaps every other day. Vicki began to weep and asked if we could at least provide some kind of a snack for the kids if she gave me some money. She specifically mentioned a bottle of Coke and something to eat for each one. So we sent several teenagers to the local market with the money I was given. I had done a quick head count and estimated there were about 100 kids present. The instructions to our shoppers were to get five cases of Cokes (120 bottles), at least 100 buns and as much fruit as possible with whatever money was left.

When the teenagers returned with their purchases on their heads, we gathered the children in the church building for their surprise treat. There were 120 bottles of Coke, 110 plain buns, and what looked like about 60 bananas. But when all the children crowded into the little church building and sat down, it suddenly seemed like God had supernaturally multiplied the kids this time! There were well over 200 of them. During a time of lively worship led by Pastor Juma, my mind was racing to figure out what to do. I decided we could pair the kids up and give one bottle of Coke to each two kids. That worked well and we had three bottles left over. We had 234 kids! I then asked the visiting team to break the buns in half and give a half to each child. I knew that would still leave us short a few, but I figured it would more or less work out. The visitors fanned out among the crowd of kids with their armloads of buns, giving a half to each waiting child. Pastor Juma and I watched from the front and our jaws began to drop as we realized the visitors had worked their way through most of the crowd and still seemed to be holding as many buns in their arms as when they started! They got all the way to the back of the building and turned around to face us. All 234 children had received some bread when there shouldn't actually have been quite enough to go around; all the visiting team still had armloads of buns. So we signalled them to work their way from the back up to the front again giving out more buns, as long as the supply continued. Again, every child received more bread, and the team members all still had their arms full of buns when they reached the front. What an awesome God we serve!

Then Pastor Juma announced that the children could leave by the small side door and each would receive a banana as they left. My heart sank at those words because there were only 60-70 bananas in the basket at most, not even enough for a third of the kids. Nonetheless, Pastor Juma began enthusiastically handing the bananas to the children one by one, and he was quickly joined by a few of the visitors. Then he stepped back and watched with me as the visitors continued to give out the bananas. We watched 80 kids go by...100 kids...125 kids...God was doing it again! 150 kids...200 kids...230 kids. We jumped into each other's arms for joy as we watched Vicki Arnott pick up the last banana and hand it to the last child to go out the door! Exactly 234 bananas, one for each child! Vicki later said that she thought she had seen it all during the heyday of the Toronto Renewal, but she'd never experienced anything like that!

The next day, my wife and I visited the Mieze church for the Sunday service. Four hours of energetic worship with 350 African brothers and sisters in a building built for 100-125 is an experience to remember! I likened it to a spiritual sauna. We especially watched the offering with fascination. A few people brought some small coins, but most brought fruit or vegetables because they had no money at all. There were even three live chickens added to the mountain of produce. Then Pastor Juma announced that the entire offering would be given to the Iris Pemba Base as a love-gift from the Mieze church. What grace and generosity from people who live in such poverty and are always in need themselves! Is this why God chose to perform such a remarkable miracle in this forgotten and out-of-the-way place?! I spoke about what had happened there the day before, and not surprisingly, the church was noticeably even more packed with children than usual. The people shouted their praises. He had not forgotten them! The children were the most enthusiastic of all and we commissioned about 200 of them, who had experienced God's supernatural provision, to be witnesses and evangelists to all their friends and neighbours throughout their village.

The Mieze church has continued to grow in response to many, many demonstrations of the love of God for His precious people there. In 2009, we built a simple but wonderful new church and community building many times larger than its predecessor. We also began a new children's evangelistic program on Saturday mornings which regularly draws as many as 500 children from nominally Muslim families. All these kids now know the Lord and many have had angelic and heavenly visions. We've also held several workshops to teach at least 40 other local pastors how to organize similar children's programs in their local churches and they have returned for subsequent workshops reporting that thousands of village children have received the Lord! We learned that a Muslim father in Mieze had recently gathered his ten children and three wives outside their mud and bamboo hut and given his children permission to become as involved in the life of the church as they wanted because he'd been watching closely for several weeks and he'd seen nothing but good coming from it!

These precious Mozambican children - many of whom have only worn rags for clothes and had never been to school before our project began - now live in a relationship of faith and trust in God that often challenges and encourages me. They place no limitations on their faith in God because of what they have experienced. They know He can do anything and everything He does is good! The superstition and hopelessness of the past is gone and they now live in the lively expectancy of God's Jeremiah 29:11 promise of "hope and a future" for their lives! And, because these children are "the least of the least" in the world's eyes, only Jesus will receive the glory for what He has done and continues to do in Mieze and the surrounding district!

Most recently, during a three-day Iris conference at Mieze in June 2011 attended by over 3,500 people, 1,500 buns were delivered each morning for distribution for breakfast to those sleeping on the ground overnight. But on the Sunday morning, to everyone's surprise 2,500 people lined up to receive bread and hot tea. Pastor Juma simply said, "We've done our best to provide for the people. Jesus has to do the rest!" Then he and his leaders began to pray as the buns were handed out. Every one of the 2,500 received bread!

The local church in Mieze has grown quickly in response to God's many supernatural acts of love and in 2010 we dedicated the new church and community center building, which can accommodate over 1,000. This in itself would have seemed unimaginable only six years earlier when the hostility of the crowd watching the JESUS Film caused our evangelistic team to run for their lives. But over 3,000 packed into the building for the official opening service in June 2010 - including fifty community leaders and at least a thousand children. The district chief - wearing his Muslim robe and cap - had asked to speak on behalf of the local leaders and he took the occasion to read through a lengthy list of specific things we had done through this project over the previous four years - each sentence began with the words, "And we thank you for..." We thought we had been working away largely unnoticed over that time, but the community leaders had been taking careful note and took the first public occasion to acknowledge and thank us for releasing so much good into their communities. In fact, Pastor Juma has recently told me it is being reported to him regularly that the conversation among villagers in the local market in Mieze is all about the love they are seeing expressed through the work of the church and our Mieze Project.

We have prayed that the devilish spirit of poverty and the equally devilish orphan spirit would be broken and banished from the entire village of Mieze by the presence and power of God's good Spirit. We have clearly been witnessing a measurable improvement in general prosperity, a significant reduction in infant and child mortality, a marked improvement in general health and an obvious new joy released into the whole village in response to the blessing of God in their midst. Today, the 700 people who normally attend Sunday worship come dressed in a colourful array of African fabrics. The children all have some good clothes to wear for such special occasions. Everyone is healthy, clean and happy. All 360 children in the church of school age are enrolled in school with our financial support and with the encouragement and support of the entire church. In fact, each child has been called forward by name to the applause of the whole church to receive backpacks, school supplies, uniforms and prayer. The whole village culture has shifted measurably and those who may not be participating directly yet are still very aware of the difference and -like the Muslim father who gave his children permission to get involved in the life of the church - they know that the difference is very good! The name of Jesus is now widely honoured and respected and people speak openly of their faith and personal experience of God's goodness. This is just a small beginning and Mieze is only one village, but I believe Mieze to be a prophetic picture of how God means to release the power of His Kingdom love to raise up the poor and prepare them to take their appointed place at His banquet - today, as well as in the life of the world to come. Development aid in Jesus' name is transformational love in action. It is the supernatural power of God's Kingdom focused on meeting the real needs of ordinary people in Jesus' name. And where God's Kingdom is breaking in, the Holy Spirit can be expected to bring other miracles, signs and wonders as well to demonstrate His reality and His glory. In the developing world today, Christians have an unprecedented opportunity for making Jesus known through deeds of extravagant, Spirit-dependent love. In the village of Mieze this has been the only strategy we needed to employ to see such dramatic transformational changes come to pass in just a short period of time.

At the outset of this book, Randy Clark asks if the power of God makes a difference in the work of ministry and mission. From our experience in Mieze described above - and in the work of Iris Ministries in Mozambique in general - our only possible answer is resoundingly YES, the power of God makes all the difference!

Endnotes

1 Donald E. Miller, *Reinventing American Protestantism: Christianity in the New Millennium* (Berkeley: University of California Press, 1997), 3.

2 This terminology was first coined by missiologist Peter Wagner. See C. Peter Wagner, *The Third Wave of the Holy Spirit: Encountering the Power of Signs and Wonders Today* (Ann Arbor: Servant Publications, 1988).

3 Ibid., 1.

4 Stanley M. Burgess and Eduard M. van der Mass, eds., *The New International Dictionary of Pentecostal and Charismatic Movements* (Grand Rapids: Zondervan Publishing House, 2002), xviii-xxi.

5 David B. Barrett and Todd M. Johnson, "Global Statistics," *The New International Dictionary of Pentecostal and Charismatic Movements*, 287.

6 Paul Collier, *The Bottom Billion: Why the Poorest Countries Are Failing and What Can Be Done About It* (New York: Oxford University Press, 2007), 9.

7 Jayakumar Christian, *God of the Empty-Handed: Poverty, Power and the Kingdom of God* (Federal Way, WA: World Vision International, 1999), 138.

8 Molefe Tsele, "Christianity, Poverty and Wealth in the 21st Century," *Association of Protestant Development Agencies in Europe* (APPRODEV), 2001, 5.

9 Ronald J. Sider, *Rich Christians in an Age of Hunger: Moving from Affluence to Generosity* (Dallas: Word Publishing, 1997), 48.

10 This story is recounted by Donald R. Kantel, "God's Work God's Way" *Modern-Day Miracles* (Shippensburg, PA: Destiny Image Publishers, 2011), 89-96.

11 Ramsay MacMullen, *Christianizing the Roman Empire (A.D. 100-400)* (New Haven: Yale University Press, 1984).

ABOUT THE AUTHORS

RANDY CLARK

Randy Clark, now a noted international speaker, is a doctoral candidate at United Theological Seminary, received his M.Div from Southern Baptist Theological Seminary. His bachelor's degree was in Religious Studies from Oakland City University. He was called to the ministry in 1970. He pastored churches in the General Baptist, United Church of Christ, American Baptist denominations, and planted two Vineyard churches. He was on the Council of the Vineyard during its earliest few years of existence. He is the founder of the Apostolic Network of Global Awakening and part of the six networks that make up the Revival Alliance. He was used of God to birth the revival that broke out in Toronto Canada in January 1994 that continued six nights a week for over twelve years. He is best known for the gift on his life for activating and imparting gifts of the Holy Spirit. The late John Wimber was the first to recognize this grace on Randy's life. John heard the audible voice of God tell him twice that Randy would one day travel the world laying hands on pastors and leaders to activate and impart to them gifts of the Spirit. Randy also continues to demonstrate the Lord's power to heal the sick with great tenacity. While having been used to launch several famous ministers into the new level of their anointing by laying hands on them and prophesying to them, the focus of his ministry is on the average person in the congregation, encouraging them that they too can be used of God in the gifts of the Spirit. His message is simple: "God wants to use you." Randy is the author of four books, *There Is More, Lighting Fires, God Can Use Little Ole Me*, and *The Baptism in the Holy Spirit*. He has co-authored two books with Bill Johnson: *Essential Guide to Healing* and *Healing Unplugged*. He compiled and contributed to five books, *The Ministry Team Training Manual*; *Power, Holiness, and Evangelism*; *Changed in a Moment*; *Entertaining Angels* and *Supernatural Missions*. He was the general editor of four workbooks based primarily upon his teachings, *School of Healing and Impartation: Kingdom Foundation*; *School of Healing and Impartation: Empowered*; *School of Healing and Impartation: Healing – Medical and Spiritual Perspectives*; and *School of Healing and Impartation: Anthology*. Randy has written ten booklets, *Awed By His Grace/Come Out of the Bunkhouse*; *The Biblical Basis For Healing*; *Evangelism Unleashed*; *Learning to Minister in the Anointing of the Holy Spirit/How to Have a Healing Ministry in Your Church*; *Words of Knowledge*; *Open Heaven*; *Thrill of Victory/Agony of Defeat*; *Pressing In/Spend and Be Spent*; *The Healing River and its Contributing Streams*; and *Falling Under the Power*.

Leif Hetland

In 1995, while serving as pastor of First Baptist Church in Sandnes, Norway, the Holy Spirit transformed a dried out, burned out, hard working Baptist pastor into a passionate lover filled with the Holy Spirit and compassion for God's world. God used Randy Clark to facilitate this transformation in Leif's life. Randy approached Leif and had a prophetic word for him that later changed the direction of his life. The word was, "I don't know you but I can see over your life that you are like a bulldozer. God is calling you to prepare the way in unchartered territory. You are a forerunner and you are here to prepare the preparers for the coming of the Son of man". He shared that Leif was an apostle with a calling to prepare nations who had never yet heard the Gospel of The Kingdom. A father, an author and a businessman, Leif is the founder and president of Global Mission Awareness and Leif Hetland Ministries. More than anything else, though, Leif is a lover of God.

Bill Jackson

Bill Jackson obtained his B.A. from Wheaton College and his M.Div. from Gordon-Conwell Theological Seminary. He is currently working on his D.Miss. at Fuller Theological Seminary. Also an author of two books - *The Radical Quest for the Radical Middle: A History of the Vineyard* and *NothinsGonnaStopIt! The Storyline of the Bible* - he planted two Vineyard churches and has taught in numerous schools. In addition to being a church elder, Bill travels, speaks and writes for Radical Middle Ministries. He specializes in delivering his NothinsGonnaStopIt! seminar, which traces the biblical storyline in seven hours and is currently raising up teachers who will help him take the biblical storyline around the world. Bill and his wife, Betsy, live in Corona, California and have three grown children, Luc, Megan, and John.

Peter Prosser

Dr. Peter Prosser was born in England and was converted after immigrating to Canada as a young man. He has served as a pastor in French-speaking Quebec and a missionary to numerous nations. He has conducted training seminars in 25 countries across Africa and Asia for missionaries, pastors, and lay people, earning his B.Th., M.A., and Ph.D. from the University of Montreal.

Dr. Prosser was a full time professor of Church History and Christian Doctrine at Regent University in Virginia, USA from 1983 - 2006. He has also taught courses at universities and seminaries around the world. He has now returned to Quebec to enjoy partial retirement, continuing to teach part time at Regent. He and his wife, Elfriede, have been married for forty years, and they have two daughters.

Clifton Clarke

Bishop Dr. Clifton Clarke was born in the United Kingdom to Caribbean parents. He is an Ordained Bishop in the Church of God (Cleveland TN) and studied Theology at the University of Nottingham (B.A), University of Derby (M.A) and the University of Birmingham (PhD). After teaching theology at the University of Nottingham and pastoring in the UK for many years, he and his family answered the call of God to move to West Africa (Ghana) in 1997 to work as missionaries.

Dr. Clarke has seen thousands of people come to Christ, hundreds of leaders raised up, numerous churches planted, demons cast out, and the Devil defeated through the power of God. He also played an instrumental role in building the Church of God's first african university in Ghana: the Pan African Christian University.

After spending ten years living and working in western Africa he felt the leading of the Lord to move to the United States. Today Dr. Clarke is the Professor of Missions and World Christianity at Regent University in Virginia Beach. He is a highly sought after speaker who has traveled widely, including Russia, Saudi Arabia, Europe, Africa, Caribbean and the United States. His burden is to see a global move of the power of the Holy Spirit. He is married to Reverend Marcia Clarke and they have two children, Joel and Jessica.

Rolland and Heidi Baker

Rolland and Heidi Baker are the founding directors of Iris Ministries, which began in 1980. They arrived in Mozambique in 1995 after ministering for twelve years in Asia and three years in the UK. They began to pour out their lives and hearts among the street children in Mozambique. Iris now oversees fifteen bases and has planted thousands of churches, mostly on the African continent. The ministry has literally exploded in Mozambique and the surrounding countries, where over ten thousand children are cared for every day. Ministry teams travel to remote areas via four wheel drive and four-ton trucks, bush planes and boats. The Lord has graced this work by pouring out His healing and miraculous power in village after village. The deaf hear, the blind see and the poor hear the good news. Iris Ministries includes eight bible colleges, medical clinics, bush outreaches, church based orphan care, children's villages, primary schools, cottage industries, widow's programs, well drilling projects, missionary training schools, village feeding programs, houses for the disabled and more.

Heidi earned her BA and MA degrees at Vanguard University and her PhD in systematic theology from King's College London. She has co-authored three books: *There is*

Always Enough, Expecting Miracles and *Compelled by Love*. When not in Pemba, Mozambique, Heidi and Rolland travel around the world, speaking at conferences. Heidi is passionate about calling people into a radical place of intimacy with the Lord Jesus and on to their destinies in Him.

Rolland also earned his BA and MA degrees at Vanguard University and did his PhD work at King's College in London. He is a third-generation missionary born and raised in China and Taiwan. He was greatly influenced by his grandfather, H.A. Baker, who wrote "Visions Beyond the Veil," an account of the extended visions of heaven and hell that children received in his remote orphanage in southwest China two generations ago. Today, Rolland and Heidi cry out for a continuation of the visitation of God experienced by the children of H.A. Baker's orphanage in China long ago.

D.J.

DJ is a long-term missionary living in the Arab Muslim World. He and his family have ministered throughout the Middle East and have lived in six different Arab countries. They are involved in power evangelistic outreaches, discipleship and Church planting. They are committed to training and equipping believers to release God's Kingdom in supernatural ways. They maintain a website devoted exclusively to chronicling miraculous testimonies in the Middle East. Their blog can be found at: joel2generation. blogspot.com.

Jonathan Bernis

Jonathan Bernis has worked on the forefront of world evangelism since 1984, taking the good news of Israel's Messiah to the far reaches of the earth. He serves as President of Jewish Voice Ministries International (JVMI), where the mission is two-fold: proclaiming the Gospel to the Jews and to the Nations (Romans 1:16), and equipping the Church by providing education about the Hebraic Roots of Christianity and how to share Messiah with the Jewish people.

Jonathan's weekly television program, "Jewish Voice with Jonathan Bernis," airs throughout the U.S., Canada, Europe and Asia. In addition, JVMI proclaims the good news through print media and large-scale international Festivals of Jewish Music & Dance in Eastern Europe, India, Africa and South America, and humanitarian/medical outreaches to the Lost Tribes of the House of Israel in places like Ethiopia and India - the poorest Jewish communities on earth. A sought-after conference speaker, Jonathan also teaches at seminars and in local congregations worldwide. He is a passionate supporter of Israel and a prominent leader in the Messianic movement for over 25 years.

Jonathan Bernis earned a degree in Jewish Studies (secular) from the University of Buffalo, going on to study Archeology & Jewish History in Israel. He attended Yeshiva through the Union of Messianic Jewish Congregations (UMJC) and the International Association of Messianic Jewish Congregations (IAMCS), the two ordaining national organizations in the United States. He has been formally ordained with the IAMCS since 1985.

Jonathan and Elisangela Bernis are the parents of a daughter, Liel, and reside in Phoenix, Arizona.

Bob Ekblad

Bob Ekblad, is executive director of Tierra Nueva and the People's Seminary in Burlington, Washington. A minister in the Presbyterian Church (USA), he holds a PhD in Old Testament and is known internationally for his courses and workshops on reading the Bible. He is also the author of *A New Christian Manifesto* and *Reading the Bible with the Damned*. His passion is to see leaders recruited, equipped and empowered by the Holy Spirit to minister to society's least. He teaches courses in Biblical studies in missions at Regent College in Vancouver, BC, Mars Hill Graduate School, Seattle and Westminster Theological Centre in the UK and leads workshops around the world on jail/prison ministry and missions. Bob and his wife Gracie minister at Tierra Nueva and at their home-based retreat center New Earth Refuge (www.bobekblad.com). They have three children.

Lesley-Anne Leighton

Lesley-Anne Leighton holds a Bachelor of Ministries and Master of Theological Studies (Tyndale Graduate School of Theology, Aotearoa, New Zealand) and is continuing her post-graduate studies through Oxford Centre for Mission Studies (Oxford, United Kingdom). She is ordained with Iris Ministries.

Coupling her extensive missionary experience of over thirty-three years with her educational background, she marries sound theology with practicality and teaches missions with great effectiveness. Most importantly, Lesley-Anne imparts all that she has received from the Lord without holding back, allowing her ceiling to be the floor on which future missionaries will be launched.

She set up Diadem International in 1994, initially as a humanitarian charity providing medicine for hospitals and Bibles for Christians in the Russian Federation. It has since grown to encompass other ministries such as local church planting, a leadership discipleship school, missions practice programs and ministry with the poor. In February 2005, Lesley-Anne founded and established Holy Given International School of Missions with the purpose of training a new generation of missionaries. Schools continue to be established in international locations. She also speaks extensively in conferences and churches, ministering with marketplace missionaries and university students all over the world.

Howard Foltz

Dr. Howard Foltz has been active in ministry since 1963 when he pioneered the Teen Challenge program in Dallas/ Fort Worth. He began the first Teen Challenge overseas and expanded the ministry's overseas programs into 27 countries. In 1985, Dr. Foltz became Professor of Global Evangelization at Regent University in Virginia Beach. He has helped to train hundreds of pastors and missionaries in local church missions, strategies to reach unreached people groups and inter-cultural ministry. He is now Professor Emeritus at Regent University.

Dr. Foltz also founded AIMS (Accelerating International Missions Strategies with the purpose of challenging and mobilizing churches to take the Gospel where it has never been proclaimed before. Under Dr. Foltz's leadership, AIMS has trained more than 132,500 church leaders and businessmen worldwide to engage in cross-cultural ministry among the world's least reached people groups. Through their efforts, an estimated 30 million people have heard the

Gospel, most for the first time, and approximately 31,000 new churches have been planted and over 2.1 million souls have come to Christ.

Dr Foltz received a B.S. in Missions from Southwestern University, an M.A. in Cross-Cultural Communications from Assemblies of God Graduate School, and a D.Min. in Missiology from Denver Seminary. He has published four books - *Triumph: Missions Renewal for the Local Church, Healthy Churches in a Sick World, For Such a Time as This: Power Shifts in Missions* and *Paradigm Lost: Recovering God's Plan for Spiritual Harvest.* He has also written magazine articles about missions. Dr. Foltz has two grown sons and lives in Colorado Springs with his wife and missions companion of 48 years.

Donald Kantel

Born in Toronto, Don's formal education includes a B.A. in Political Science from Toronto's York University, B.Th. and M.Div. degrees from the University of Toronto, and a Doctor of Ministry in Leadership and Renewal from Regent University in Virginia Beach. He has previously published articles and book chapters, and his first full-length book is currently being published.

From 1971-2001, Don served as founding President and Professor at St. Stephen's University, a Christian university in New Brunswick, Canada. He has been a fulltime missionary with Iris Ministries in Mozambique, Africa since 2005. In July 2010, Don was the subject of an article in Christianity Today featuring some of his recent development work in the village of Mieze in northern Mozambique.

Don is affectionately known as "Papa Don" to hundreds of Mozambican children whose lives have been dramatically changed by their encounters with the Father's love. These children place no limits on their understanding and expectations of God because of the many supernatural signs, wonders, and miracles that God has been pouring out in their midst.

Don and his wife Elizabeth have been married since 1967. They have a grown son, Tim, and three young grandchildren. Don and Elizabeth's Canadian home is in Summerside, Prince Edward Island. Their ministry website describing their work with Iris Ministries at Mieze can be found at: www. harvestinafrica.com.

OTHER BOOKS BY RANDY CLARK

Essential Guide to Healing

Healing Unplugged

Entertaining Angels

There is More

Power, Holiness and Evangelism

Lighting Fires

Changed in a Moment

TRAINING MANUALS AVAILABLE

Ministry Team Training Manual

Kingdom Foundations Workbook

Empowered Workbook

CORE MESSAGE SERIES

Words of Knowledge

Biblical Basis of Healing

Baptism in the Holy Spirit

Open Heaven

Pressing In/Spend and Be Spent

The Thrill of Victory/The Agony of Defeat

Awed By His Grace/Out of the Bunkhouse

In "There Is More," Randy lays a solid biblical foundation for a theology of impartation as well as taking a historical look at impartation and visitation of the Lord in the Church. This is combined with many personal testimonies of people who have received an impartation throughout the world and what the lasting fruit has been in their lives. You are taken on journey throughout the world to see for yourself the lasting fruit that is taking place in the harvest field - particularly in Mozambique. This release of power is not only about phenomena of the Holy Spirit, it is about its ultimate effect on evangelism and missions. Your heart will be stirred for more as you read this book.

"This is the book that Randy Clark was born to write."
- Bill Johnson

Each year of ministry has taken international speakers Bill Johnson and Randy Clark on a journey into a deeper relationship with the Father and a fresh understanding of healing. Their experiences have played a pivotal role in shaping not only their own lives, but also the lives of those they come in contact with and minister to every day.

Join these two spiritual fathers in a conversation about their journey into the healing ministry. Listen as they discuss the highs and lows of a life led in service to the Kingdom and how each mountaintop experience and every desert season impacted who they became and how they walked out their calling as Apostles and spiritual fathers. Be challenged by each testimony as they share advice and wisdom gained through years of hands-on experience on the mission field and be encouraged that you too can walk out this journey with God.

International Ministry Trips

Global Awakening travels across the globe, ministering to the nations. God has given us great favor for these trips and the resulting testimonies are remarkable All of our trips offer a unique opportunity for believers of every level of experience to take part in ministry teams, aiding in praying for the sick, interceding for the nations and so much more. Global Awakening Ministry Teams have traveled to places like Brazil, Africa, South Pacific, Europe, India, Mexico, Cuba and other regions.

Join us as part of the ministry team!

imt.globalawakening.com

With an emphasis on offering an educational experience often overlooked in traditional seminaries, the Christian Healing Certification Program presents a practical, theologically grounded option for anyone looking to expand their ministry training. CHCP offers three primary areas of study – Healing, Deliverance and Soul Care. Classes will build from the ground up, introducing students to the experiences and advice of ministry leaders already operating under a strong anointing for healing or gifting in deliverance. For more information, see our website at;

healingcertification.com

VISION

To release followers of Christ into their specific destiny and calling, in order to live out the Great Commission.

STRUCTURE

Global School of Supernatural Ministry is a one or two year ministry school with an emphasis on impartation and equipping students for a life of walking in the supernatural. Classes start each September and end the following May. Courses are offered on-site at the Apostolic Resource Center in Mechanicsburg, PA. Upon completion of each program year a Certificate of Completion is awarded. Students seeking additional educational training may do so while attending GSSM through the Wagner Leadership Institute.

COMMUNITY

The GSSM student body is diverse in age, culture, ministry experience, and educational accomplishments. From high school graduates to professionals to retirees - the students come together seeking more of God. Supernatural power, passion and honor are key values of GSSM and are reflected in our worship, outreach and personal relationships.

For more information - or to enroll in classes - contact us at
**1-866-AWAKENING or apply online at
gssm.globalawakening.com**

globalawakening

For a schedule of upcoming events and
conferences, or to purchase other products from
Global Awakening, please visit our website at:

globalawakening.com